BY THE EDITORS OF CONSUMER GUIDE®

The Cook's Store

How To Buy And Use Gourmet Gadgets

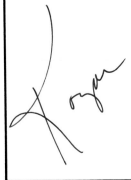

A Fireside Book Published by Simon and Schuster

1

CONTENTS

Copyright © 1978 by Publications International, Ltd.
All rights reserved
This book may not be reproduced or quoted in whole or in part by mimeograph or any other printed means or for presentation on radio or television without written permission from:

Louis Weber, President
Publications International, Ltd.
3841 West Oakton Street
Skokie, Illinois 60076

Permission is never granted for commercial purposes

Manufactured in the United States of America
1 2 3 4 5 6 7 8 9 10

A Fireside Book
Published by Simon and Schuster
A Division of Gulf + Western Corporation
New York, New York 10020

LIBRARY OF CONGRESS CATALOGING IN PUBLICATION DATA

Main entry under title:
The Cook's store.
    (A Fireside book)
    Includes index.
    1. Kitchen utensils — Catalogs. 2. Cookery.
I. Consumer guide.
TX658.C66   382'.45'68382   78-15464
ISBN 0-671-24589-9
ISBN 0-671-24590-2 pbk.

CONTENTS

Cover Design: Frank E. Peiler

Color Photography: Mel Winer

Acknowledgments: The Editors of CONSUMER GUIDE® would like to thank Linda Carter, Judy Vance, Nancy Immel and the many others who contributed their expertise to the product selection, techniques and recipe development. Our thanks also go to The Cook's Mart, Chicago, Illinois, for allowing us to use their kitchen for photography; and to both The Cook's Mart and The Complete Cook Inc., Glenview,

Illinois, for permitting us to use some of their products for photography and for their aid in obtaining prices and sources of supply.

The Editors of CONSUMER GUIDE® have made every effort to ensure the accuracy of the approximate retail prices given in this publication. Please note that prices may vary from coast to coast within the United States. Additionally, many of the items covered are imported products and their prices could change with the fluctuation in the value of the American dollar.

WELCOME TO THE COOK'S STORE

The Cook's Store is a fabulously photographed account of the fun you can have with unusual kitchen equipment, specialized utensils and high-quality cookware. It's an international shopping tour and a series of cooking lessons with step-by-step illustrations. It's a guide to the vast and often mysterious assortment of gadgets you're likely to encounter in cookware shops and gourmet departments.

Although *The Cook's Store* is stocked and organized like a cookware shop, it is not meant to be a sales catalogue; we are not trying to sell the items in this book. The purposes of *The Cook's Store* are to bring to your attention the utensils that can simplify food preparation, to show you how to use the equipment and to analyze the merits of various gadgets. There are some pieces of equipment that actually make a task more complex than it need be; if so, we tell you. If we had problems making something work, we describe the problem and tell you our solution. If the gadget is not as simple to use as the manufacturer advertises, we say so. If a tool requires assembly know-how, we explain. If you can achieve the same results without investing in a special gadget, we're the first to admit it.

Compiling *The Cook's Store* was an extraordinary adventure for us. And we loved every minute of it. In selecting the items to be featured, we deliberately sought those sold without instructions or even identification. We made a beeline for equipment that comes with instructions in foreign languages only. It took some practice before we could master many pieces of equipment, but we mostly found the effort justified by delicious and attractive results. Every implement was tested and retested repeatedly.

We developed recipes to go with much of the cookware, both as part of our testing procedures and to provide you with tantalizing examples of what is, after all, the ultimate purpose of this guide. You don't need a *cordon bleu* certificate to prepare these recipes; they are all straightforward and simply written. You may find yourself lingering over the color illustrations of such delights as our rich Chocolate Cheesecake, the satin-smooth Raspberry Mousse or the crisp succulent Duckling à L' Orange — and then rushing out to the kitchen to assauge your appetite.

While cooking is becoming ever more popular as a leisure-time activity, many people are only slowly growing aware of the amazing quantity and variety of cookware available. The array is dazzling — and can be intimidating. Even experienced epicureans with well-equipped kitchens have been known to wander quizzically down the jammed aisles of a gourmet cookware shop, stopping to exclaim from time to time, "Look at this little gadget! What on earth is it for?"

Less experienced cooks have been known simply to slip out the door, too overwhelmed by it all to attempt to unravel the mysteries.

It seems like there is a gadget for every conceivable task. *The Cook's Store* previews the exotic and the obscure, as well as the generally useful, so that when you walk into a cookware shop you'll not only recognize the items stocked but also know whether you need or want them. And when you bring a cherished gadget, pot, pan or implement home, you can refer to *The Cook's Store* for explicit use and care directions, as well as recipes that will surely keep the items from gathering dust on the shelf.

The equipment we chose to test and include ranges from inexpensive kitchen "toys" to lifetime-investment cookware. There are also inexpensive, serious tools and luxury-priced "toys." But, then, one cook's "toy" is another's necessity. Whether you view an item as essential or frivolous depends on your culinary frame of reference and such factors as how much you cook, what kinds of food you prepare most often, and whether you do much baking or home canning. A gadget that French-cuts green beans, for example, will rank either as a necessity or a waste of money depending on your taste in beans. You could find black steel pans invaluable or worthless, depending on whether you bake or buy bread. Similarly, if you're especially fond of

WELCOME TO THE COOK'S STORE

Mexican food, you should invest in a tortilla press and a Mexican griddle; if not, these items would only clutter your shelves. We did discover in testing such items, however, that knowing how to use them sparked our imaginations. Every tool suggested ways we could expand our cooking repertoire, and we found ourselves proudly accomplishing tasks we had never before dreamed of attempting. We truly hope that learning about such things as pastry cutters and fish molds, fire pots and clam shuckers will lead you to share the excitement we felt when we produced flaky puff-pastry shells and fluffy mousses, an Oriental feast and a succulent fresh chowder.

We used two separate sets of criteria in selecting equipment for *The Cook's Store*. On the one hand, we wanted to stock items that need explanation — those that are unusual, hard to use or quite specialized. But in the cases of pots and pans and knives, we chose a comparative selection of high-quality items, because these are investments that every cook should make and that should provide lasting satisfaction. We have not tried to be all-encompassing. You won't find an eggbeater among our "Great Inventions," not because this isn't a handy item but because we assume you're acquainted with it; you will find a discussion of how to beat eggs with a balloon whisk in a copper bowl. You won't find a cheap frying pan in our "Cooktop Collection," but you will discover the comparative merits of copper and stainless steel as well as those of various manufacturers' products.

When you're shopping in a cookware store, you'll find that some utensils are identified by manufacturer, but others are not. Some items are merely stamped with the name of the country in which they were made. We have tried to mention the manufacturer where appropriate. For instance, no one but Mouli makes a Mouli grater; the words "Mouli Grater" are clearly embossed on the gadget and the grater is identified thus in *The Cook's Store*. But items like melon ballers, French vegetable peelers, whisks and wooden utensils are often just jumbled in a bin or arranged haphazardly on a rack. What we say about them extends to all gadgets of the same type. In the back of the book, you will find a source index that lists the equipment in each chapter. The source index includes the name of either the manufacturer or one importer/distributor of the product. In some cases there may be other importers or manufacturers of similar equipment, but space limits us to one entry per item.

Each of the fifteen chapters in *The Cook's Store* is devoted to a separate aspect of cooking. We begin with "Great Inventions," which focuses on utensils used in general food preparation. These range from whisks, sieves and strainers to salad spinners and kitchen scales. In "Cutlery Classics," the next chapter, we examine a stock of knives. "The Blade Boutique" features cutters other than knives — everything from cherry pitters to food processors. Of all the gadgets in this chapter, we're especially fond of the little Krisk bean slicer and the grand French mandoline. The bean slicer specializes in French-cut green beans; the mandoline cuts everything from julienne strips to waffled potatoes.

In the "Cooktop Collection," you'll find a variety of pots and pans. But remember when you're shopping that nowadays old-fashioned pots and pans are called "cookware." It sounds classier — which well befits the fancy prices of the best-quality lines. Our most exciting discovery in this chapter is the Firmalon line of specially-treated aluminum cookware. We found these heavy-gauge, non-reactive pans to be superb. Of course, we coveted many other beautifully-designed pots as well — especially the silver-lined copper. Even if we wouldn't indulge our own kitchens with these terrifically efficient pans, we would consider them perfect gifts for cooks who own everything else.

In the next three chapters, we explore oven equipment from the standpoint of various techniques for pastry making, bread baking and meat cookery. Those of you who love to bake bread, pies, tarts and other goodies may find these sections hard to read — you'll want one of everything. The recipes are fantastic. Watch out for the half-cylinder Rehrücken cake, draped in a satiny chocolate glaze. And the delicious cocktail pumpernickel loaf baked in a pain de mie. And a juicy cherry tart and a buttery pound cake — the list goes on and on.

From "Pick of the Catch" through "Something's Brewing," you'll find a stock of limited-purpose contrivances. "Pick of the Catch" includes aids for preparing seafood, such as fish scalers, shrimp deveiners, clam knives and fish poachers. The wonderful assortment of molds in "Molded Art" is designed to shape everything from a steamed pudding to a chicken mousse, from ice cream to sparkling ice sculptures. If you long for homemade sausage or fresh cream, greaseless gravy or squirtless lemons, you'll discover the right tools in "Palate Teasers." Espresso makers, coffee pots and tea paraphernalia comprise the fascinations of "Something's Brewing."

In our last four chapters, we take a cook's tour of the equipment that will help you capture the essence of cuisines from around the world. The secret of perfect puff pastry can be found in the "French Gallery." Fabulous homemade pasta will tempt you to join the "Italian Fiesta." For wok cookery, turn to the "Oriental Market." And for couscous, tortillas and Scandinavian pastries, join us as we travel "Once Around the World."

We welcome you to *The Cook's Store* and invite you to browse to your heart's content. We are quite excited about all the discoveries we have made, both as shoppers and as cooks, and we hope you will benefit from them as we have — by using them like keys to unlock the myriad fascinations and pleasure of all kinds of cooking.

GREAT INVENTIONS

"Theoretically," claims Julia Child, "a good cook should be able to perform under any circumstances, but cooking is much easier, pleasanter, and more efficient if you have the right tools." We couldn't agree more.

Some of these right tools are so simple and quickly become such reliable helpers that, once they've been acquired, you wonder how you ever managed without them — a good strong whisk, a conical sieve, or an egg separator, for example. And the more you cook, the more such tools you discover. Every time you try a new recipe you may realize there are one or two little items missing from your *batterie de cuisine*. This section is loaded with such little gadgets.

For openers, there is a crockful of appealing wooden utensils. Some you may never have seen before — and probably could live a long time without. You'll not only be charmed by them, however, but you'll also find that their limited utility is matched by small price tags. It may not matter that you already own a blender, a mixer and a food processor. There's still every reason to reach for a primitive wood swizzle blender for a single milk shake. And no reason not to own an adorable honey dipper — even just for the pleasure of admiring its simple efficiency.

Some implements so simplify certain crucial cooking steps that just owning them can expand your repertoire of standard fare. Consider, for instance, a raspberry mousse, that pink cloudlike dessert whipped up from a smooth, seed-free raspberry puree. Once you strike up a working acquaintance with a tamis (wooden drum sieve) designed both to puree and strain berries (and a legion of other foods) simultaneously, the confection is rather easily and quickly prepared.

The raison d'être for any piece of cooking equipment is to produce finished dishes that taste as food ought to taste — glorious with flavor. Those who have forgotten the delicate, fresh flavor and smooth, fluffy texture of simple homemade mashed potatoes (the kind our grandmothers took for granted) would do well to try a potato ricer. Cooked, peeled potatoes passed through a ricer before whipping result in perfect, lumpless mashed potatoes every time. And from there it's one short culinary step to making puffed golden deep-fried Potato Puffs, from the same riced potatoes. A rotary ricer, a slightly more complicated member of the same machine family, may easily entice you to make real Italian Marinara — a heavenly pasta sauce.

The same basic principle of home preparation makes a world of difference in a host of ingredients. Whole spices crushed or powdered in a mortar and pestle are a flavor world apart from their pre-ground commercial counterparts. And the difference between packaged pre-grated nutmeg that has been languishing on a grocer's shelf and the indescribable fragrance of freshly grated nutmeg is yours to savor with the aid of a nutmeg grater. If you assign a chunk of Romano or parmesan cheese its own grater, you'll experience the cheese as you never can when it's purchased in a shaker.

Much of the preparation equipment in this section brings out the best by enhancing the natural texture of food. Just-washed salad greens are inevitably limp and soggy, and a ream of paper towels can't restore them to natural crispness the way a salad spinner can. An egg was never laid with the white part standing in airy peaks — but you can change all that with a balloon whisk and a copper bowl. Altering the identity of a piece of meat can help your budget and palate at the same time. Tough cuts can be tenderized with a steel-pronged roller; dry cuts flattened with a meat pounder into thin discs or rectangles to appear at the table as succulent veal scallopini, wienerschnitzel or Beef Rouladen.

The food preparation tools introduced in this section serve to expand a cook's repertoire. They encourage cooking for its own sake by simplifying and demystifying many procedures and shortening others — all of which builds culinary skill. These implements that produce beautiful food tend to be aesthetically pleasing in and of themselves, featuring the special charm of functional design. Many of these inventions are small and dime-store inexpensive; all are mechanical. So why do we call them "great?" Because of the showmanship they bring out in us!

GREAT INVENTIONS

Wooden Utensils

There are several practical reasons for the appeal of wooden utensils: They are softer than metal; so they won't scratch or damage cookware. Wooden utensils don't get hot; because wood is a poor conductor of heat, you don't have to worry about burning your fingers while stirring your next chocolate custard. In addition, wooden utensils won't discolor delicate sauces the way some metallic ones will, nor will they leave any metallic taste behind in your lemon soufflé.

There are hundreds of wooden utensils available in all shapes and sizes: spoons, spatulas, ladles, mashers, strainers, scoops and forks. Most are made out of beechwood, maple, olivewood, boxwood or pine. Pine spoons tend to be the cheapest and poorest made; the denser woods, like boxwood or olivewood, make better utensils.

Left to right: Pinewood strainer, swizzle blender, honey dipper, tasting spoon, potato masher, olive scoop, olivewood spatula, champignon.

Olivewood Spatula

A favorite in our collection, the beautifully grained olivewood spatula has fairly large slots. The 12-inch implement serves some draining chores, such as lifting pan-fried fish fillets out of the skillet; it's also a handy stirrer/scraper for heavy sauces. Avoid wood spatulas with narrow slots as food particles get stuck in them and they are very difficult to clean.
Approximate Retail Price: $2

Tasting Spoon

Both the spoon and handle are scooped out in the Swedish tasting spoon. So if you want to taste your spaghetti sauce for its final seasoning, you can scoop a little sauce into the spoon and let it run down the length of the hollowed handle into your mouth. The spoon has two advantages: You don't have to keep washing it because the end you are tasting never goes into the sauce, and you do not burn your tongue because the sauce is cooled as it runs the length of the handle.
Approximate Retail Price: $2

Honey Dipper

Looking like a miniature beehive on a candy stick, this Italian-made delight is a honey dipper. Just dip the 6-inch beechwood dipper in a jar of honey and rotate it around a little; the honey stays in the hollowed out grooves instead of dripping all over the counter.
Approximate Retail Price: $1

Swizzle Blender

The swizzle blender originally was designed for mixing chocolate drinks. You could use the 10-inch swizzle for making milkshakes and for light mixing chores. Place the swizzle blender in a tall glass or other vessel. Hold the handle loosely between your palms and rub them together; the head that rings the handle and the floating head will spin at different speeds and in different directions. The Spanish-made swizzle blender is clearly the forerunner of our hand-held, rotary egg beater — and great fun.
Approximate Retail Price: $1.50

Potato Masher

A great looking weapon, the old-fashioned potato masher is made of unfinished wood. This 13-inch masher is of good quality and durable enough to handle any mashing or smashing chore, but it will not produce extra-fluffy, lump-free mashed potatoes. You might wield its old-fashioned weight to mash rutabaga and potatoes together for an interesting dish.
Approximate Retail Price: $2

Pinewood Strainer

The Portuguese pine spoon is an example of good quality pine; it is nicely finished and satiny smooth. It has a 10-inch-long handle and a broad 3-inch bowl with seven small drainage holes. It is a good tool to use for draining spoonfuls of vegetables or for scooping up clamcakes out of hot fat.
Approximate Retail Price: $2

Champignon (Wooden Pestle)

It's called a champignon, which means mushroom, because it looks like a mushroom. A most practical utensil, it is used to force foods through a strainer or sieve. Its rounded contours nicely accommodate the rounded shapes of some strainers and sieves, but it won't fit into a pointy chinois.
Approximate Retail Price: $2.50

Olive Scoop

You can scoop olives from barrels or cans with a perforated 14-inch natural wood olive scoop. Brine or juice drains through holes as you scoop. But you don't have to have a barrel of olives handy: This utensil can simplify other draining chores — and add a note of élan to a crockful of wooden tools.
Approximate Retail Price: $6

Whisks

We use whisks for a variety of tasks: beating air into ingredients, such as egg whites; stirring sauces and gravies till smooth; and mixing light-consistency foods, such as egg batters.

You will need different whisks for different chores. No matter the size, always consider the comfort and feel of the whisk in your hand. Examine the wires — are they firm enough or flexible enough for the job at hand? Whisks range in size from minute (5 inches) to gigantic (15 inches), and prices range from dime-store cheap to gourmet-shop expensive.

Left to right:
Swedish Visp, natural wood whisk, Danish whisk, small flat-bottom whisk, large flat-bottom whisk, spoon whisk, bar whisk, stainless-steel whisk, short whisk, dough whisk, balloon whisk (top).

Swedish Visp

The bunch of twigs wired together is a Swedish Visp, the forerunner of the modern stainless-steel whisk. The Swedish Visp will not win an award as the easiest item to clean, though it certainly is the most rustic. We recommend the Visp as kitchen decoration, not as a practical item.
Approximate Retail Price: $2.50

Natural Wood Whisk

Another charming Scandinavian import, the natural wood whisk has a beechwood handle and the whisk "wires" are curved twigs. A decorative, rustic item, the 10-inch whisk is not all that durable and should be used only for lighter mixing chores or for display.
Approximate Retail Price: $2

Danish Whisk

The Danish whisk is about the same size as the stainless-steel one, though quite different in design. It has a lighter, natural wood handle and only five heavy thick wires, which makes it suitable for heavier chores, such as a thick Crème Pâtissière.
Approximate Retail Price: $3.75

Flat-Bottom Whisk

The lumps in our gravy disappeared like magic when we used this 10-inch Danish flat-bottom whisk. It is a perfect example of design beautifully adapted to function. The whisk end itself has four stainless-steel wire loops securely fastened into a nicely contoured, natural wood handle. The angle of the whisk on the handle is sloped so that the whisk will rest flat on the bottom of the pan and can fit into hard-to-reach corners. You can hang it up by the hook in the handle.
Approximate Retail Price: $4

Spoon Whisk

The flat-bottom spoon-shaped whisk measures about 8 inches in length. It is excellent for stirring small quantities in small saucepans, bowls or glasses. Try it for smoothing out a melted chocolate mixture.
Approximate Retail Price: $3.95

GREAT INVENTIONS

Large Flat-Bottom Whisk

This flat-bottomed whisk measures 12 inches in length, making it better than the shorter version for reaching into the depths of a larger simmering pot of sauce or stew. The horseshoe-shaped whisk has a wire coiled around it and the rounded contours allow it easy access into pan edges. A hook in its polished natural wood handle makes this a handy tool for hanging.
Approximate Retail Price: $3.75

Bar Whisk

Give this little 6-inch stainless-steel whisk a home at your bar and it will reward you with smooth Bloody Mary's and satin Manhattans. It outclasses plastic stirrers and will mate well with your bar knife for cocktail-hour conviviality.
Approximate Retail Price: $1.25

Balloon Whisk and Copper Bowl

The pièce de résistance of whisks! This stainless-steel, balloon whisk measures about 14½ inches in length and it's almost 5 inches at its widest circumference. It holds 12 loosely coiled wires designed to incorporate the maximum amount of air into egg whites. **To Use:** For those of you who resist the temptations of machines and like to do things by hand, here are instructions for beating egg whites:

1. Start with a clean, dry balloon whisk and a clean, dry rounded bowl 9 to 10 inches in diameter and 5 to 6 inches deep. Unlined copper is best because the copper's acidity reacts with the egg whites to keep them stiff. Stainless-steel is next best, but you will have to add ¼ teaspoon cream of tartar for every 4 egg whites.

2. Place egg whites in the bowl and add a pinch of salt. Start beating in a vertical, circular motion. Go slowly at first, about 2 strokes per second, using lower arm and wrist muscles, until whites begin to get foamy. (If not using a copper bowl, add cream of tartar now.)

3. Increase speed, about 4 strokes per second, beating as much air as possible into the whites, turning the bowl as you do so. Try to keep the whole mass of egg whites in continual motion.

4. Start testing as soon as whites seem to be stiff. Whites should still have a satiny sheen and peaks should be stiff enough to hold their shape when the whisk is lifted. Egg whites beaten by hand increase in volume by sevenfold, as opposed to 5 or 6 times by mixer.

Hints for egg whites:

- For maximum volume when beaten, eggs should be at room temperature. If eggs are cold, place them in a bowl of warm water for a few minutes.
- Make sure there are no traces of egg yolk in the whites. Yolk is a fatty substance that will keep the whites from stiffening.

Approximate Retail Price: $15 (whisk); $20 (bowl)

Start beating egg whites with a vertical, circular motion.

Keep the mass of whites in motion as you increase speed.

Whites should have a satiny sheen and hold a firm peak.

Dough Whisk

We like to gaze at the dough whisk hanging on the wall. It is made out of a heavy tinned-steel wire beautifully coiled into an abstract design and set into a 10-inch natural wood handle. The construction makes it good for mixing bread dough in the early stage when the dough is still fairly loose. But, frankly, a heavy-duty mixer is easier on the arms than the handsome whisk.
Approximate Retail Price: $5

Stainless-Steel Whisk

Two features distinguish the stainless-steel whisk: a heavy-weight, durable handle and steel wires that are more flexible than those on other heavy-duty whisks. It is very comfortable in the hand. The handle of the 14-inch whisk is completely sealed; so it's easy to clean and doesn't catch and hold food particles. The superior flexibility is due to the 10 fine wires.
Approximate Retail Price: $6.95

Short Whisk

The Japanese-made stainless-steel short whisk is only 8 inches long, but it is one of the most powerful whisks. The thick handle gives it strength for stirring. There are only five thick wires held together by one central wire, which loops around them all as a reinforcement. It is definitely recommended for heavy-duty mixing and blending.
Approximate Retail Price: $5.95

Egg Separators

Remember Katherine Hepburn desperately trying to separate eggs in one of the final scenes of *Woman of the Year?* An egg separator simplifies a nerve-racking chore and virtually eliminates all human error, though it is nowhere near the fun of separating eggs through your fingertips. Separators come in an interesting variety of shapes and sizes; they're made out of stainless steel, bright yellow plastic, glazed ceramic and speckled pottery. They are all variations on the same design. **To Use:** Place an egg separator over a small bowl. (Some separators fit right over the edge of a cup.) Break an egg into the egg separator and gently tip the separator to allow the egg white to slither through the horizontal slots. Transfer the egg yolk to another container and repeat procedure.
Approximate Retail Price: $3 (pottery); $2 (plastic); $2 (ceramic)

Three similar egg separators.

Metric Measuring Spoons

We're featuring some Swedish-made, plastic measuring spoons to demonstrate that there is nothing scary about metric measuring. They look just like customary measuring spoons. The embossed markings read 1 ml, 5 ml, 15 ml and 1 dl (mi means milliliter, one-thousandth of a liter; di means deciliter, one-tenth of a liter). The largest measurer has a ½-dl marking inside. **To Use:** You do not need to figure out what 1 ml equals in customary measurements. When a recipe calls for 1 ml salt, just use the little spoon marked 1 ml. Taking out a set of customary measuring spoons and comparing the amounts they hold with the metric amounts will give you more practical knowledge than calculations will. In general, the metric measurers are 5 percent larger than the customary ones.
Approximate Retail Price: $3

International Measurer

Grams, ounces, milliliters, American cups and English cups, pints and gills are all indicated on a 5¼-inch high plastic measuring beaker. Made in Germany by Efi, this measurer has a silver-painted, removable plastic base. We wish it had a handle. Ordinary baking ingredients — salt, sugar, flour, semolina, raisins, cocoa, rice and oat flakes — can be measured by weight or by volume. We checked out rice, salt, flour and sugar and found this measurer in approximate agreement with the other scales we tested. The painted markings and the silver base won't take much scrubbing, but this measurer certainly is adequate for anyone who only occasionally uses European or British recipes. **To Use:** If you are faced with a recipe calling for 100 grams of sugar, for example, find the heading "sugar" on the measurer, locate the mark nearest 100 grams on the line below "sugar" and fill the beaker to that point. Be sure your eye doesn't move over to "salt" — the markings are close together.
Approximate Retail Price: $2.50

Metric measuring spoons and weight/volume beaker.

GREAT INVENTIONS

Wall Scale

A wall scale can be hung at any convenient height; a countertop scale sits on a counter and you'll have to bend over to read the weight. The compact Eva wall scale is a triumph of modern Danish design. The round weighing pan neatly closes up over the scale's face. The scale is 8½ inches in diameter; the removable pan sticks out about 10 inches from the wall when in use. The weighing pan comes in stainless steel or assorted colors of plastic. The scale registers up to 6 pounds 10 ounces or 3 kilograms; it works on the pendulum principle, without springs. As the food pulls the pan downward, the weight registers on one of the two arcs of numbers. Small amounts of weight, up to 2 pounds 3 ounces, 1000 grams divided into quarter ounce or 10-gram units, are indicated by a large hand pointing to the outer arc. Anything heavier is registered by a smaller hand pointing to the inner arc. **To Use:** Attach the mounting template and upper screw according to the direction booklet — don't try to hang the scale on a single hook — it won't register properly. Remove the locking pin on the back before hanging the scale. Lower the weighing pan. Add the desired amount of food;

The Eva wall scale folds up when not in use. The Cuisinart and Terraillon countertop scales each have two sizes of trays. All measure both pounds and grams.

then slip the pan out of its loop to empty it. The weighing pan is not dishwasher proof.
Approximate Retail Price: $26.50

Countertop Kitchen Scales

Terraillon and Cuisinart both offer small, rectangular kitchen scales. These countertop scales work on the spring balance principle: Press down on the spring and the weight registers on the dial face. They both are 7 inches high, 6½ inches wide and 4½ inches deep. Except for the dial face, they are designed similarly. The dial that registers pounds and grams is easier to read on the Cuisinart because pounds and grams are shown in separate windows. The Terraillon has one large round face with grams on the outer perimeter and pounds on the inner circle; the closely spaced white lines on black background are hard to distinguish. Neither the orange-colored Terraillon nor the beige and orange Cuisinart is as easy to read as the Eva wall scale. The snug-fitting tops on both countertop scales double as containers for the food being weighed. A larger tray (measuring 11 inches by 7 inches) can be used for bulkier foods. The Terraillon registers up to 10 pounds or 5000 grams; the Cuisinart registers up to 6½ pounds or 3000 grams. **To Use:** Invert the cover or set the larger tray in place. Adjust the dial to read 0 by turning the handle on the side. You have to adjust the dial to compensate for the weight of the tray. Set the food to be weighed in the center of the container or distribute it evenly in the container for the most accurate reading.
Approximate Retail Price: $22 (Terraillon); $27.50 (Cuisinart)

Rotor Salad Spinner

What this salad dryer lacks in versatility it makes up for in performance. The beautifully crafted Swiss Rotor salad spinner is made of an unbreakable plastic in basic white to suit any kitchen decor. It is easy to clean and a joy to use, eliminating the most time-consuming aspect of salad making: the necessarily thorough drying of the fruits and vegetables — watercress, lettuce, spinach, parsley, grapes and strawberries, just to name a few. The salad spinner's only disadvantage is that it does not collapse and is a bulky thing to store: It measures 9½ inches in diameter and 5½ inches deep. You could use it as a storage bin for onions or potatoes, but don't keep greens in it in the refrigerator. **To**

Use: Wash the greens and place them in the removable basket. Hold the spinner by the handle with your left hand and pull the ring firmly with your right hand until the belt has unwound. Follow the return motion of the belt, restraining the ring just as it approaches the spinner. (Don't just let go, or the belt could break.) Repeat the procedure several times. Centrifugal force, that phenomenon we all learned about in seventh grade science class, pulls all drops of water from the leaves to the wall of the spinner, where they are drained off into the bottom. The hole for the belt is near the bottom, so be careful not to tilt the spinner when it collects water. After the greens have been spun dry, you can roll them in several layers of paper towel or a clean dishtowel, put them in plastic bags, and store in the refrigerator for 12 to 24 hours. They will stay crisp.

Approximate Retail Price: $15

When you pull the belt on the Rotor salad spinner, basket spins greens dry.

Triumph Salad Spinner

This salad spinner from France also works by centrifugal force. Made of polypropylene, the 10-inch-wide, 6-inch-high spinner has an orange basket inside the white container, and an orange lid. Instead of pulling a belt, you rotate the handle on the lid to turn the basket — a simple, effective way to dry greens. **To Use:** Place washed greens in the spinner basket and replace the lid. Hold the spinner firmly and give the handle on the lid several turns. Water will accumulate in the bottom. Greens are now ready for serving or for storing in the refrigerator.

Approximate Retail Price: $14

When you turn the handle on its lid, the Triumph salad spinner removes water from greens.

Spinach Salad

Salad Dressing

- 1 clove garlic, minced
- ¼ cup wine vinegar
- 2 tablespoons white wine
- 2 teaspoons soy sauce
- 1 teaspoon Worcestershire sauce
- 1 teaspoon sugar
- 1 teaspoon dry mustard
- ½ teaspoon curry powder
- ½ teaspoon salt
- ¼ teaspoon pepper
- ⅔ cup vegetable oil

Salad

- 1 pound fresh spinach
- ½ pound bacon
- ¼ pound mushrooms, sliced
- 2 hard-cooked eggs, chopped

1. In a cruet or jar with lid, mix all ingredients for salad dressing and shake until slightly thickened and thoroughly blended.
2. For the salad, wash and trim spinach. Spin dry in a salad spinner.
3. Cook bacon until crisp; drain well on paper towels.
4. Place spinach in a large salad bowl. Add the sliced mushrooms and toss gently with salad dressing.
5. Top salad with chopped hard-cooked egg and crumbled bacon.

Makes 4 to 6 servings

GREAT INVENTIONS

Wire Salad Basket

A multipurpose wire basket is a welcome item out of the past. It can be used as a salad dryer, vegetable washer, steamer, deep-fry basket, bottle sterilizer, colander, or even as a hanging planter. How many kitchen items can be put to such a variety of uses? Crafted out of heavy-duty tinned steel, the Mouli salad basket is 8½ inches in diameter and about 5½ inches deep. The basket is collapsible, folding flat for easy storage. It also has a locking device that holds the handles rigid to form a base; so it can be used as a colander or as a stand for fruits and vegetables. **To Use:** When using as a salad dryer, wash the greens and put them in the basket; then go out in the backyard or any place that doesn't mind a little sprinkling. Grasp the handles and whirl the basket in the air. Marvelous exercise! Technique varies: Some prefer the straight-arm, single-circle twirl; others like a more creative motion with figure eights and over-the-head passes to change hands. A wire basket's efficiency depends on how long and how vigorously you spin it.
Approximate Retail Price: $5

Mouli basket can be used as a colander or a salad spinner.

Strainer-Skimmer

A sleek-looking, Italian-made utensil bridges the gap between a strainer and a skimmer. Beautifully fashioned with a fine, stainless-steel mesh basket, this strainer-skimmer would be helpful in skimming stock or soup in its early stages of cooking. Or use it for lightweight straining tasks, like lifting small shrimp from boiling water. The stainless-steel handle is securely welded to the rim, making it the "top-of-the-line" of skimmers. **To Use:** When skimming foam, dip the skimmer into the liquid and push the foam to the edge of the pot to skim out. For straining, place basket under food and lift up.
Approximate Retail Price: $10

Use a long-handled stainless-steel skimmer with a fine mesh basket for both straining and skimming.

Skimmer

Concentric wire circles, reinforced by spoke-like wires, make this tinned-steel skimmer a simple and sturdy utensil. Like most skimmers, it has a fairly shallow scoop. The wide-set wires on this model allow for maximum drainage, making it good for retrieving large items from a deep-fat fryer. Overall, it measures 16 inches in length and has a large scoop, 5 inches in diameter. The long handle keeps you away from the bubbling fat. **To Use:** Just dip the skimmer into the pot and lift to extract whatever you're cooking.
Approximate Retail Price: $3.95

Skimmer with wide-set wires is good for lifting deep-filled foods like Potato Puffs from hot oil.

Pot-Edge Strainer

Draining food can be a tricky business. How many times have you tried to strain vegetables by tilting the pot over the sink with the lid propped ajar — only to lose peas or carrots down the drain? You could haul out the colander, but it seems faster to do the old lid trick, even if you scald a hand and lose a pea or two, right? The pot-edge strainer solved the problem for us. Shaped like a machete, the 14-inch pot-edge strainer fits nicely over pots up to 10 inches in diameter. It has a stainless-steel straining edge with a lip to secure it to the edge of the pot. Made in Hong Kong, the strainer is riveted to a bright red plastic handle with a hole on the end, making it another gadget to add to your hanging collection. **To Use:** Hold the strainer on the edge of the pot. Tilt pot to drain off liquid. *Approximate Retail Price: $1.50*

Pot-edge strainer eliminates need for colander; it fits over pots up to 10 inches in diameter.

Tamis or Wooden Drum Sieve

A raspberry mousse studded with raspberry seeds defies elegance.

For seedless mousses, and other smoothly strained foods, you must use a fine-mesh strainer like this drum sieve. A lightweight sieve, compared, say, to a heavy-duty rotary ricer, its natural wood frame is 9 inches in diameter and 4 inches deep. This tamis can sift dry ingredients, smooth out lumpy sauces or custards, or sieve fruit purees. Unfortunately, the mesh is hard to clean and the wood stains hopelessly. **To Use:** Rest the tamis on top of a bowl so that the mesh surface is up and the wood rim fits into or outside of the bowl. Scrape or press food through the mesh with a rubber dough scraper, a wooden spoon or a rounded champignon. *Approximate Retail Price: $10*

Use tamis to puree and strain raspberries for Raspberry Mousse. The sieve's wide rim fits into or over a bowl and you rub food through the flat mesh surface. Some sieves come with a wood pestle to force the food through the mesh, but many cooks prefer to use a stiff rubber scraper.

GREAT INVENTIONS

Raspberry Mousse

**4 packages (10 ounces each)
    frozen raspberries,
    thawed**
1½ packages unflavored gelatin
4 eggs, separated
½ cup sugar
**2 to 4 tablespoons raspberry or
    orange liqueur**
1½ cups heavy cream, divided
**¼ teaspoon cream of tartar
    (optional)**
Pinch of salt

1. Drain raspberries, reserving syrup.
2. Force raspberries through a tamis or strainer. You should have 1 cup puree. Reserve.
3. Soften gelatin in ½ cup of the raspberry syrup. Set remaining syrup aside. Heat gelatin mixture over a very low heat, stirring constantly until gelatin is dissolved.
4. Using a mixer, beat egg yolks until creamy. Slowly add sugar and beat until thick and lemon colored. Add raspberry puree and mix.
5. With mixer on low, add gelatin in a slow stream.   Add liqueur and beat together.
6. Whip 1 cup of the cream until slightly thickened. Fold it into raspberry mixture.
7. With a wire whisk and copper bowl, or mixer, beat egg whites until frothy. Add cream of tartar (if not using copper bowl) and salt.   Beat just until firm peaks form. Gently fold the whites into raspberry mixture.
8. Carefully spoon raspberry mixture into a 1½-quart soufflé dish and chill for several hours until firm.
9. When ready to serve, whip remaining ½ cup cream until stiff. Spread over top of soufflé. Decorate with fresh raspberries, if in season. Leftover raspberry syrup can be used as a sauce to spoon over individual servings.

Makes 8 servings

Fine-Mesh Chinois

A French chinois sounds like something that belongs in your boudoir, but it functions brilliantly in the kitchen. The name means "Chinese" and, supposedly, these sieves look like coolies' hats. The chinois shown has a tinned-steel mesh so fine that it could be used for straining consommé or jelly, duplicating the function of a cheesecloth bag. You also can buy a chinois with a coarser mesh or with large perforations. This chinois, sturdily constructed of stainless steel, measures 7 inches in diameter and 7 inches deep. The hook on its rim holds it on the edge of a pan or bowl. **To Use:** Place the chinois over a bowl or pot and pour the food to be strained into the conical sieve. For the clearest liquid, just let it drip — do not force food through the sieve. All solids will be trapped in the tip of the cone and liquid will drain through the sides.
Approximate Retail Price: $25

Chinois hooks securely to edge of pot for straining or pureeing.

Quick and Easy Vegetable Stock

3 carrots (½ pound)
2 medium onions
4 green onions
2 leeks (½ pound)
2 ribs celery
3 tablespoons butter
10 cups cold water
Small bouquet garni (2 sprigs parsley, small bay leaf, ⅛ teaspoon thyme tied in cheesecloth)

1. Peel and slice all vegetables.
2. In a large pot or stockpot sauté the vegetables in the butter until soft.
3. Cover with the water, bring slowly to a boil, skim well with a fine-mesh skimmer and add the bouquet garni.
4. Simmer for 2 hours or until liquid is reduced to 8 cups.
5. Strain stock through a fine mesh conical strainer or chinois. (Or if using a not-so-fine strainer, line it with cheesecloth.)
6. Store in refrigerator or freeze.

Makes about 2 quarts

Strain stock through fine-mesh chinois for clear broth.

Rotary Ricer with Stand

If you ever helped your grandmother make applesauce, pear butter or fresh tomato sauce, you may be familiar with this implement. A cross between a potato ricer and a chinois, the rotary ricer is used for pureeing and ricing tasks. It is made out of tin-plated steel and comes complete with its own stand and a hardwood, tapered pestle to push the food through the holes in the conical-shaped sieve. Standing 9 inches high, the ricer measures about 7 inches across the top. It's not an easy item to store. The sieve snaps out of the stand for easy cleaning. The rotary ricer could be used for straining and pureeing peas for a delicious pea soup or to create the silky smoothness of a delectable Marinara Sauce. **To Use:** Place rotary ricer in a large bowl or pot. Place food to be pureed or riced in the conical sieve and rotate the pestle around the edge of the sieve, forcing food out through the perforations. Lined with cheesecloth, this ricer makes a good tool for fine straining too.

Approximate Retail Price: $7

Rotary ricer comes with a pestle.

Marinara Sauce

¼ cup olive oil
2 cups chopped onions
1 cup chopped carrots
1 cup chopped celery
2 cloves garlic, peeled
2 (28 ounces each) cans Italian plum tomatoes or 4 pounds fresh tomatoes
28 ounces heavy tomato puree
1½ teaspoons salt, divided
¾ teaspoons pepper, divided
4 tablespoons butter
1 teaspoon oregano
1 teaspoon basil
Pinch of thyme
Pinch of rosemary

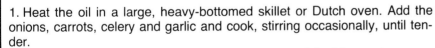

1. Heat the oil in a large, heavy-bottomed skillet or Dutch oven. Add the onions, carrots, celery and garlic and cook, stirring occasionally, until tender.
2. Cut the tomatoes into pieces. Add tomatoes and liquid, tomato puree, 1 teaspoon of the salt, and ½ teaspoon of the pepper to the vegetable mixture. Simmer for 15 minutes.
3. Put mixture through a sieve or rotary ricer, extracting as much of the solids as possible.
4. Return mixture to pot. Add the remaining salt and pepper, the butter, oregano, basil, thyme and rosemary.
5. Simmer partially covered for 30 minutes. *Makes about 2½ quarts*
Note: This sauce freezes well.

Use rotary ricer to make a smooth Marinara Sauce, rich with tomatoes and herbs.

GREAT INVENTIONS

Swedish Potato Ricer

"Stop playing with your food!" Who doesn't remember both the admonition and the great temptation, as a child, to construct a mashed potato fortress with windows oozing melted butter? Mashed potatoes probably are one of the all-time favorite foods. Everybody, from kids to grandparents, is a gourmand when it comes to judging the fluffiness, the texture and flavor of mashed potatoes. No lumps are allowed! A favorite way to produce lump-free mashed potatoes has been with a potato ricer. The Swedish model has a V-shaped, tinned-steel sieve that rices potatoes with slightly less effort than potato ricers shaped like flour sifters. The pusher is also tinned steel and the frame is enameled steel. The entire gadget is about 11 inches long. The orange plastic Italian ricer is not quite as sturdy, but still does a good job. Of course, you can use it to rice or puree other foods besides white potatoes — sweet potatoes, chestnuts, carrots or cauliflower, to suggest a few. **To Use:** Open the handles and place the potato (or whatever) in the ricer. Holding the ricer over a bowl, bring the two handles together to force the food out through the small perforations and into the waiting bowl. *Approximate Retail Price: $7 (Swedish ricer); $5 (Italian ricer)*

Use a ricer for fluffy potatoes.

Potato Puffs

3 large potatoes (1 pound)
1 cup warm pâté à chou
½ cup grated Swiss or
    Parmesan cheese
    Salt and pepper to taste
3 quarts vegetable oil for deep
    frying

Pâté à chou

½ cup milk
 3 tablespoons butter, cut into
    pieces
½ teaspoon salt

Pinch of pepper
Pinch of nutmeg
½ cup flour
2 eggs

1. Peel and quarter potatoes. Boil in salted water until tender. Drain, let dry a few minutes and put through a potato ricer. You should have 2 cups.
2. Make pâté à chou: In a saucepan, bring the milk to a boil with the butter, salt, pepper and nutmeg and boil slowly until butter has melted. Remove from heat and add flour all at once. Stir vigorously with a wooden spoon until the mixture forms into a ball and pulls away from the side of the pan. Add the eggs one at a time, beating well after each addition. Beat until mixture is well-blended, shiny and smooth. (This step can be done in a mixer.)
3. Add the riced potatoes and grated cheese to the pâté à chou. Mix together until thoroughly blended. Taste and season with more salt and pepper, if necessary.
4. Heat oil to about 350°F. Using a teaspoon, drop the batter into the hot oil and brown. Drain on paper towels and serve. *Makes 8 servings*

Tasty Variations: Any of the following can be mixed into the mixture along with the cheese:
   3 to 4 tablespoons fresh herbs, such as parsley or chives
   ¼ to ½ cup minced cooked ham or bacon
   ¼ to ½ cup sautéed mushrooms or onions

Riced potatoes, shredded cheese and pâté à chou are combined in exquisitely light Potato Puffs.

Food Mills

In the days of yore, the Dark Ages before the enlightened era of blenders and food processors, cooks actually pureed food by hand. Old-fashioned food mills were the chefs' only mechanical accomplices. But these were, and still are, excellent for making applesauce, creamed soups, vegetable purees and baby food. Food mills also perform some straining chores, including separating skins and seeds from purees without the mess of most strainers. The sturdy, stainless-steel Mouli food mill and plastic Italian Supernova mill both come with three interchangeable discs: a fine grate for a perfectly smooth puree suitable for Vichyssoise; a medium grate to produce a thicker apricot sauce for a tart; and a coarse grate for an even thicker, fresh tomato sauce. The Mouli mill has a 1-quart capacity; it is also available in 2- and 3-quart sizes. Three collapsible, rubber-padded legs support the mill over a plate, or fit securely over bowls up to 8 inches in diameter (the larger mills fit large containers).

The 1-quart Supernova mill has short legs attached to the top to steady it on a bowl. Both mills work well. **To Use:** Place the appropriate disc in the bottom of the container in a dome-like position. Insert the handle attached to the rotary blade into the opening in the center of the disc; snap the bar into place to secure it. Put the food in the mill and turn the handle. The food will be forced under the curved blade and through the perforated disc. Reverse the blade if any food gets stuck. The harder the vegetable, the more difficult it is to grind. Mouli mills are dishwasher safe.

Approximate Retail Price: $13 (1-quart Mouli); $9 (1-quart Supernova)

The Supernova food mill is plastic; the Mouli mill is made of stainless steel.

Watercress Soup

4 tablespoons butter, divided	3 large potatoes (1 pound), sliced	Pinch of thyme
1 large leek (½ pound), sliced	5 cups chicken stock	¼ teaspoon pepper
2 bunches watercress		1 cup heavy cream

1. In a large pot, heat 2 tablespoons of the butter. Gently sauté the leek and watercress until wilted, stirring frequently.
2. Add the potatoes, chicken stock, thyme and pepper. Bring to a boil, cover and simmer until vegetables are tender, about 30 minutes.
3. Strain the soup. Return stock to the pot and put solids through the finest blade of a food mill. Add the puree back to the stock and mix or whisk them together. Strain again, if desired.
4. Add the cream and reheat. Taste for seasoning (salt may need to be added, depending upon stock used).
5. Stir in the remaining 2 tablespoons butter, bit by bit, just before serving.

Makes 6 to 8 servings

Note: This soup is also delicious chilled. To serve cold, omit the butter enrichment in step 5. Top each bowl with a little shredded apple and garnish with a watercress sprig.

Puree soup vegetables.

GREAT INVENTIONS

Mouli Julienne

At night, when all humans have gone to bed, the Mouli Julienne turns into a miniature space station — you can tell that by looking at it. During the day it is a manual food processor. The Mouli Julienne has a strong plastic frame and five removable steel discs: a slicer and four shredders of various sizes. The largest shredder cuts thick strips of meats, cheese and vegetables. The finest shredder makes very thin, thread-like shreds of parmesan cheese, or, if used on almonds, a beautiful almond powder for an almond torte. Though it duplicates many of the functions of a hand-held grater, the Mouli Ju-lienne is easier, safer and faster to use. The entire gadget comes apart for cleaning. Three legs with little rubber feet keep it securely positioned. Due to the placement of the legs, it is hard to set the grater over a plate or bowl, so just put it on your counter with a piece of waxed paper under the cutting disc. **To Use:** Insert the appropriate disc in the slots on the underside of the food receptacle. Place the handle in the center to line up with the disc. Food has to be cut to fit the receptacle — a bother. Put the prepared food in the receptacle and bring the cover down over the food. Hold the cover down and turn the crank to shred or slice. When slicing, trim the food so it has a flat top and bottom to produce more uniform slices. Also, fill up the food receptacle to maximize the amount of food being processed at one time. If you want to use it as a space station, you're on your own.
Approximate Retail Price: $8.50

Mouli Julienne with discs.

Mouli Rotary Grater

You'll never grate your knuckles or nails with the little Mouli grater, and every particle of food gets grated. Its 2-inch-square food container has to be reloaded frequently, though, if you are grating any quantity of food. Model MG1 comes with a fine grating attachment only. Model MG3 has additional coarse-shredding and slicing attachments. The 7-inch-long, tinned-steel grater has a plastic handle. **To Use:** Place the drum with the crank in either the right or left side, depending on

Assemble and fill grater.

whether you are right- or left-handed. Place food in the food container. Bring cover down over food. Tilt the grater slightly as you turn

Turn handle and tilt grater.

the handle so the food falls out of the drum. Firmer pressure on the cover handle yields a coarser grate.
Approximate Retail Price: $3 (MG1)

Hard Cheese Graters

Some people love the smell of freshly ground coffee. We adore the aroma of freshly grated parmesan and Romano. By comparison, packaged grated cheese is sawdust. Two superior stainless-steel cheese graters come from Italy. The round grater is 2½ inches deep and 7½ inches in diameter and holds up to 6 cups of grated cheese. When the grater top is removed the cheese is in a handy container, ready to be sprinkled on your favorite pasta dish. The collapsible grater is about 8 inches long, 4 inches wide and 4 inches tall when the grater is set at a 45-degree angle in its ridged tray. The tray collects the cheese and the grater folds up for storage. **To Use:** Obviously, anything could be grated on these heavy-duty graters. Invest in a stiff-bristled brush to help you clean out the little holes.
Approximate Retail Price: $5.95 (round grater); $2.50 (collapsible grater)

Graters handle hard cheese.

Nutmeg Graters

Freshly grated nutmeg can turn an ordinary béchamel into an exceptional sauce. Both graters shown have storage compartments for whole nutmegs in the top. The old-fashioned, tinned-steel nutmeg grater has a curved grating surface. The modern plastic and stainless-steel grater from West Germany has a flat grating surface. They both are about 6 inches long and 2 inches wide. **To Use:** Grate whole nutmeg and use in creamed dishes and sauces, eggs, vegetables and fruit desserts.
Approximate Retail Price: $2 (old-fashioned and modern grater)

Grate whole nutmeg on curved or flat-surface grater.

Nutmeg grinder mills the whole spice to an aromatic powder.

Nutmeg Grinder

It looks just like a peppermill, but it's a nutmeg grinder. One of the first things you should do if you buy one is label it so your family and guests won't get the two confused. (If you want to thoroughly confuse them, have two peppermills, one for black peppercorns and one for white peppercorns, a salt mill for rock salt and a nutmeg grinder!) This lovely polished maple nutmeg grinder fits quite comfortably in your hand and a turn of the handle produces a nutmeg powder. An advantage of this 4½-inch-high grater is that it does not have to be refilled at each use — it is always loaded and ready for action. **To Use:** Turn plate on the bottom of the grinder in clockwise direction and remove it. Put the whole nutmeg in the center and push it down, exerting a downward pressure on the handle, until the nutmeg is in grinder. Replace the cap and gently turn the handle.
Approximate Retail Price: $9.95

Mortar and Pestle

Some of the world's largest mortars can be found in Yosemite Valley — gigantic, flat-topped boulders dimpled with holes. The holes were made by Indians grinding acorns on the rock surface, generation after generation. Monolithic mortars for communal grinding are out of fashion, and it is hard to find a really good acorn mash recipe, but small mortars and pestles still have a place in the modern kitchen: Freshly pulverized herbs, spices and nutmeats simply have more flavor than preground ones. Mortars for grinding and pounding come in a variety of materials and sizes. The larger, more expensive ones made out of marble are used for pounding or pureeing seafood; smaller marble mortars can be used for garlic and other potent-smelling foods, since marble will not absorb odors. Less expensive small mortars made out of porcelain or wood are good for grinding herbs and spices and pounding nuts. The business end of the pestle is usually made out of the same substance as the mortar. The pestle should fit your hand comfortably and also be the right size for the mortar. Prices reflect material and size: Large, marble mortars can cost more than a Cuisinart. We have selected a small porcelain mortar and pestle to show here. It is made in England and has a bowl 4¼ inches in diameter. The porcelain pounding end of the pestle is attached to a smoothly polished 5-inch wooden handle. **To Use:** If you are using a large mortar and pestle to puree a fish mixture, crush the fish with an up-and-down pounding motion. If you are grinding herbs, spices or nutmeats in a small pestle, crush them with a rotary motion, pressing them around the sides of the mortar.
Approximate Retail Price: $10.95

Mortar and pestle grinds spice.

GREAT INVENTIONS

Meat Pounders

Pounding meat is great therapy for pent-up aggression, but don't take it all out on the poor scallopine! You have to exercise control when pounding veal for paupiettes, beef for rouladen or chicken breasts for chicken suprêmes. A meat pounder should be heavy and durable enough to smooth out meat in a forceful, deliberate manner. Pounders are not used to tenderize meat; they eliminate the grain and flatten the meat. A tenderizer, on the other hand, breaks down the muscle fibers. We have selected three representative meat pounders.

The heavy, 11½-inch steel-plated pounder comes from Italy. It can subdue any cut of meat. The design places the handle on a different plane than the head, so your fingers will not slip and be turned into scallopine. This pounder has a hole in the handle for hanging on the wall.

The smaller pounder with the stainless-steel disc on a short plastic handle is a favorite of ours. Its less wieldy design allows more control in pounding.

The 15-inch wooden stick that looks like it would make a fine baseball bat for a three-year-old is a chicken pounder. It is very nicely weighted and smooths out chicken breasts without tearing the meat.

To Use: Meat to be pounded should start no thicker than ½ inch. The basic "pounding" motion isn't pounding at all — it is more like ironing. Smooth the meat by "pounding" down and out from the center of the meat to the edges, following the grain. Be careful not to tear or crush the fibers. For the best results, keep the pounder moving across the meat. Sometimes wetting the pounder with cold water helps it slide without making holes in the meat.

Approximate Retail Price: $18 (Italian pounder); $6 (short-handled pounder); $5.50 (chicken pounder)

Meat and poultry pounders.

Beef Rouladen

2½ pounds thin-sliced round
    steak
4 tablespoons butter, divided
1 medium onion, chopped
½ pound ground veal
½ cup fresh rye bread crumbs
¼ cup chopped parsley
2 tablespoons capers
¼ teaspoon marjoram
¼ teaspoon salt
¼ teaspoon pepper
2 to 3 tablespoons Dijon-style
    mustard
2 dill pickles, cut lengthwise
    into 8 slices
7 or 8 slices bacon, cut in half
    Flour for dredging
1 cup beef stock
½ cup dry red wine
½ cup tomato puree
½ cup sour cream (optional)

1. Pound beef with a meat pounder to about ¼-inch thick and trim meat into rectangles about 3 by 5 inches. You should get 12 to 15 pieces, with some leftover scraps.
2. Heat 2 tablespoons of the butter in a skillet and sauté onion until tender. Add veal and cook until no longer pink.
3. In a bowl, combine onion-veal mixture with bread crumbs, parsley, capers, marjoram, salt and pepper. Blend well.
4. Spread each beef slice with a little mustard. Place a heaping tablespoon of filling and 1 piece of pickle in the center and roll. Wrap a piece of bacon around the roll and tie with a string. Dredge in flour. (Leftover filling can be added to sauce.)
5. Heat the remaining 2 tablespoons butter in a large heavy skillet or Dutch oven. Brown the rouladen.
6. Combine beef stock, wine, tomato puree and any leftover filling and add to pan. Cook, covered, for about 1½ hours or until meat is tender.
7. Remove rouladen to a warm platter and discard thread. Skim fat from gravy.
8. If desired, blend in sour cream and simmer, stirring, for 5 minutes. Pour gravy over rouladen. Serve with Spaetzle (see Index). *Makes 6 to 8 servings*

"Pounding" motion is like ironing; slide pounder from center.

Chicken Suprêmes with Shallot-Butter Filling

Filling
  3 tablespoons chopped
    shallots
10 tablespoons butter, softened
  4 chicken livers, cut into pieces
½ cup dry bread crumbs
  2 tablespoons chopped parsley
  2 tablespoons cognac
¼ teaspoon tarragon
¼ teaspoon salt
⅛ teaspoon pepper

Suprêmes
  8 suprêmes (skinless and
    boneless chicken breast
    halves)
  1 cup flour, approximately
  2 eggs
  1 tablespoon water
½ teaspoon salt
¼ teaspoon pepper
  3 cups fresh white bread
    crumbs
    Vegetable oil

1. Cook shallots in 2 tablespoons butter for 3 minutes. Add chicken livers and cook until no longer pink.
2. Cream remaining butter and add liver-shallot mixture, bread crumbs, parsley, cognac, tarragon, salt, and pepper; mix until thoroughly combined. Refrigerate mixture until firm.
3. Meanwhile, prepare suprêmes: Lay chicken breast between two sheets of wax paper. Gently pound the meat with a poultry pounder to flatten and enlarge it. Move the pounder up and down and across the meat, being careful not to tear it, until the meat is about ⅛ inch thick and almost double in width. Repeat procedure until all suprêmes are prepared.
4. Remove firm butter mixture from the refrigerator and divide it into eight equal pieces. Shape each piece into a 3-inch long stick about ½-inch square.
5. Place shaped stick of flavored butter in center of suprême. Fold one long side in around the butter, fold the two short sides in, and then fold in remaining long side and roll like an eggroll. Press the meat together to enclose the stuffing completely. Repeat procedure until you have eight chicken rolls.
6. Have three dishes ready. In one, place about 1 cup flour. In the second beat 2 eggs, 1 tablespoon water, salt and pepper with fork until blended. In the third, place fresh bread crumbs. Roll stuffed suprêmes first in flour, then in egg mixture and then in bread crumbs. Refrigerate at least 1 hour until bread crumbs are set. (They can be frozen at this point; they must be completely thawed before cooking.)
7. Heat about 3 inches vegetable oil to 375°F. Deep fry suprêmes for 4 to 5 minutes. Drain on paper towels. Suprêmes may be kept warm in a 200°F oven for up to 30 minutes before serving. *Makes 4 servings*

Roller Tenderizer

No, this gadget is not a mini roto-tiller — it's a whiz at tenderizing tough meats. It has 12 rows of sharp, stainless-steel prongs that break down fibers as the tenderizer is rolled over the meat. The piercing pressure of the roller can be used to join several pieces of meat together into a "minute steak" or veal cube steak. Made in Canada, the 9-inch implement is sturdily constructed to handle the toughest cut of meat. Its handle is a durable white molded plastic and the roller head measures about 3½ inches wide. **To Use:** Roll back and forth over pieces of meat. Be careful not to cut holes in thin slices.
Approximate Retail Price: $10

Roll pronged tenderizer over meat; pound with two-headed tenderizer.

Two-Headed Tenderizer

Made of cast aluminum, the sturdy two-headed tenderizer has one flat side for pounding meat to the desired thickness and another, covered with raised metal studs, for breaking down tough muscle fibers. The double-edged head is attached to an 8-inch handle. **To Use:** Flatten meat with smooth side of pounder. Pound with studded side until tenderized. Use rapid, controlled motions to keep from tearing meat.
Approximate Retail Price: $9

CUTLERY CLASSICS

Shopping for good knives can make you feel like Goldilocks in a gourmet shop — looking for something not too cheap, not too dear, but just right. The salesperson waxes eloquent about Sabatier and Solingen, peppering the foreign names with references to carbon and tang. The blades all seem to look alike; the sharpeners look deadly. How's a shopper to deal with this confusion?

First of all, you do not need dozens of knives. Secondly, do not buy a name — Sabatier, Solingen, Sheffield or whatever; buy an individual knife to suit your needs. Some professionals claim all they need is a chef's knife and a paring knife. We think this duo is a little limited and have selected 5 types of knives as a basic "wardrobe": a chef's knife, a paring knife, a boning knife, a slicing knife and a serrated knife. Before discussing them individually, we'll take a look at the three main parts of any knife — the blade, the tang and the handle. While personal taste weighs heavily in choosing the right knife, the quality of those three parts is critical.

Blades

Using a dull knife is a dangerous, frustrating, tiring experience. A sharp knife is a pleasure to use, making cutting, slicing or chopping a speedy task. A blade's sharpness and ability to be resharpened are the keys to a knife's success. Knife blades come in stainless steel, carbon steel and high-carbon stainless. Stainless steel is the hardest and strongest of the three, making it the most difficult to sharpen and the quickest to lose its edge. Carbon steel is a soft metal that is easy to resharpen, but with the first cut of a

lemon or an onion a shiny new carbon knife will begin to blacken and stain. The advantage of stainless steel becomes obvious: Salty air and high-acid foods will pit and rust carbon steel while stainless remains impervious. Carbon steel requires much care to keep it clean and rust-free, but it keeps the keenest edge and is the cheapest of the three kinds of blades.

The most expensive type of knife is a combination of carbon and stainless steel with the cumbersome name of high-carbon stainless steel. These knives are the elite, combining the advantages of carbon and stainless and eliminating the disadvantages of both. They can cost almost twice as much as knives made of carbon steel.

Tang and Handle

Never buy a knife without first handling it yourself. It should feel comfortable in your hand. While you are hefting it in the store, examine the tang and the handle. The tang is the end of the blade that extends into the handle. It not only affects the overall sturdiness of the knife, but has a great deal to do with how the knife is balanced. A "full tang" runs the full length and width of the handle. A full tang is most important in the chef's knife for comfort during a long chopping session. No tang at all may mean the blade will come loose. Some knives have tapered tangs, appropriately called rattail tangs. The tang is usually held by rivets, which shouldn't stick up or be sunk into the handle. Knives without rivets are glued together and are not as sturdy.

For sanitary reasons, knives used professionally have to have plastic handles but plastic handles

can be slippery. We prefer the looks of wooden handles, which are often treated for sanitary purposes. Rosewood is a popular material for handles on quality knives. Not only is this material handsome, but the irregular grain makes it sturdy and secure to hold, even when wet and greasy. Even though some wooden handles have been made "dishwasher safe," we recommend washing knives by hand. The heat of a dishwasher does strange things to the blade: It makes the steel molecules go haywire, thus dulling and weakening the knife. Of course, nothing wooden should soak for long periods in water.

Most knife handles are wisely shaped. The curve near the lower back helps support and cushion the hand and a "shoulder" near the blade helps prevent dangerous slipping. Handles with finger grips are not necessary; the notches often are uncomfortable. Nor is it necessary for the handle to support the knife in the blade-up position. In fact, it is better not to be tempted to rest a knife blade-up.

As you hold different knives, think about how your hand will feel after a long chopping or slicing session. Comfort is the final test for buying a knife.

Five Basic Knives

There is an overabundance of handsome knives available for any use, from peeling asparagus to removing fish heads. We have selected five different types of knives as the components of a basic knife wardrobe. Together they will cover most everyday chores requiring knives. The knives pictured represent the features recommended for each type.

Chef's Knife

The chef's knife is the best chopper in the kitchen. A chef's knife's blade comes in all three kinds of metal and ranges in length from 7 to 14 inches. Most chopping calls for a gentle rocking motion, and a chef's knife is designed precisely for that. You don't hack away at food with a chef's knife; rather, hold the knife by the handle with one hand, steady the tip lightly with the fingers of your other hand and rock the blade up and down to chop or mince. For a more vigorous chopping technique, hold the knife parallel to the cutting surface — one hand on the handle, the other guiding the blade — and chop straight up and down. The handle should be high enough so that you do not rap your knuckles when chopping straight up and down. Chef's knives are about 2 inches wide at the handle and curve and taper gently toward the tip. Look for a thickening

Henckels high-carbon, Sabatier carbon, and Forschner stainless-steel chef's knives.

Hold chef's knife by handle, steady tip with fingers and rock blade up and down to chop parsley.

at the back of the blade near the handle to guard your hand against slipping. There should be a full tang, visible all around the handle. The rivets should be flush with the handle and hold the tang snugly.

This knife may be the most often used implement in the kitchen; it should fit comfortably in your hand. *Approximate Retail Price: $35.95 (Henckels); $19.95 (Sabatier), $12.95 (Forschner)*

Boning Knife

Not everyone needs a boning knife, as meats can be bought in almost any cut in the grocery store. However, if you have access to larger cuts of meat and want to bone them out, only a boning knife will do the job. Carbon steel may be a wise choice here: It won't discolor on meat, and razor sharpness is important when boning. Handles on boning knives usually are thickened near the blade to support the hand in the many positions required when breaking down meats. Blades are 5 to 6 inches long and very narrow. Boners come with rigid blades for larger meats and flexible blades for smaller pieces.
Approximate Retail Price: $6.25 (Sabatier); $9.95 (Chicago Cutlery)

Henckels (left) and Sabatier (right) boning knives.

CUTLERY CLASSICS

Paring Knife

The paring knife also is available in all three steels. Although it can double as a mini-chopper, a paring knife mainly is used to cut or pare food held in the other hand, and is often used on small items that need shaping or decorative cutting. Blades are generally 3 to 4 inches long, and a sharp, pointy tip is an asset. As the paring knife may be held in a variety of grips, even with the fingers on the blade, there should be no protective shoulders on the blade or handle.

Approximate Retail Price: $15.50 (Henckels paring); $9.95 (Sabatier paring); $8.50 (Sabatier sheep's toe); $12.95 (Henckels granny knife)

Left to right: Henckels paring, Sabatier paring and sheep's toe, Henckels granny.

Slicing Knife

A slicing knife is useful for cutting fairly even slices of any cooked meat. A slicing knife's blade is long and straight and only about 1 inch wide. Blades are most commonly made out of strong stainless steel. Some slicers have hollow ground ovals along the edge that help cut friction and can make the knife more useful for delicate items like pâtés. A slicing knife should have a shoulder or finger guard to keep your hand from slipping.

Approximate Retail Price: $12.25 (Sabatier); $33 (Henckels); $12 (Forschner)

From top, Sabatier slicer, Henckels slicer, Forschner slicer.

Serrated Knife

The scalloped, hollow ground edge of the serrated knife is ideal for foods that are hard on the outside and soft on the inside. Tomatoes, bread and baked potatoes pose special problems that can be solved by the serrated knife. Frequently, these knives are made out of stainless steel because they are used to cut acidic foods.

Approximate Retail Price: $17 (Forschner); $19 (L'affettatutto adjustable slicer); $4 (Nabel)

Top to bottom, Forschner roast slicer, L'affettatutto, Nabel bread slicer.

Zig Zagger

The strange double-edged, folded blade of the zig zagger simultaneously scallops and cuts fruit in half. Or it can be used to make a jagged grin on a pumpkin. You can cut decorative fruit halves with a sharp paring knife, but the zig zagger requires less skill. The 7-inch knife has a half-tang blade rather shabbily attached to a wooden handle. **To Use:** Holding the fruit at the top, poke the knife — blade down — into the fruit's equator. Keep the knife parallel to the table. Extract the knife and repeat the incision all the way around the fruit. *Approximate Retail Price: $2.25*

Zig zagger has a double blade for decorative cutting.

Poke zig zagger in and out to cut a jagged edge.

L'affettattuto

A fancy, almost gadgety slicer, the L'affettatutto (slice-all) has a sharp, serrated blade, a bar that controls the thickness of the slice, and a comfortable, unvarnished wood handle. The thickness bar can be adjusted to accommodate slices ⅛ inch to ¾ inch. Unless you position the food carefully, the slicing bar may hit the cutting surface before you finish slicing. **To Use:** Place food at edge of cutting board, adjust blade and slice. *Approximate Retail Price: $19*

Hold food on edge of cutting board when using the L'affettatutto.

Cheese Gouger

Well-aged Romano and parmesan cheeses are impossible to cut with an ordinary knife. The cheese gouger breaks these cheeses into chunks for convenient grating. An oyster knife would be a good substitute for a cheese gouger. The 4½-inch-long knife has a stainless-steel blade fastened to a knob-like wooden handle. **To Use:** Hold the gouger ice-pick fashion and plunge it into a hard cheese to break off pieces. *Approximate Retail Price: $2.50*

Use a cheese gouger to break off chunks of hard cheese.

CUTLERY CLASSICS

Cheese Cutter and Slicer

Port Salut, Muenster, Gouda, Swiss and other cheeses in the medium-soft to medium-hard range yield dainty slices to this 9½-inch cheese slicer. (Hard cheddars give it trouble, however.) The stainless-steel rod holds two wire cutters that can be tightened by a screw at the tip; the rod is fastened to a slender wooden handle. The wire can be badly bent if left to rattle around in a drawer, and the plastic wire guide makes this knife particularly fragile. The cheese slicer is a sturdier cheese cutter that can handle cheddars. **To Use:** For wire cutter, tighten the wires by turning the screw at the top. Draw the wire "blade" through cheese. For cheese slicer, draw slicer over top of cheese.
Approximate Retail Price: $3.25 (wire cutter); $4.50 (cheese slicer)

Cheese cutter and slicer.

Asparagus Knife/ Grape Peeler

Next time you lapse into Roman decadence and deliver the imperative, "Peel me a grape," you can hand your slave-for-the-hour this knife, confident that neatly peeled fruit will be forthcoming. This is the sharpest and most expensive peeler you will ever find, but it does not peel carrots or potatoes. Asparagus, eggplant, grapes and tomatoes are its forte. The German-made knife has a stainless-steel blade with a screw-controlled bracket attached to adjust the thickness and shape of the peel. Keep an eye on the detachable parts; they are tiny and easily dropped. **To Use:** Turn the brass screws to adjust the blade. Hold the peeler like a paring knife and draw the blade across the fruit or vegetable. For grapes: Peel from the stem end down.
Approximate Retail Price: $12

Asparagus and grape knife.

Frozen-Food Knife

This treacherous 11½-inch implement looks like the inside of the great white shark's mouth. Supposedly, the teeth gnash through solidly frozen foods, but we did not find the knife satisfactory. When we attempted to saw a block of frozen spinach into two pieces, the teeth became clogged with icy particles and the block remained intact after repeated efforts. However, the prongs on the tip can be used to break frozen vegetables as they cook, and the lightly scalloped edge can cut bread. The stainless-steel blade is attached to a plastic handle without a tang. **To Use:** We do not recommend cutting solidly frozen foods with any knife. Even this tool is not the answer, regardless of the Sabatier stamp on the blade. Let the food partially defrost before cutting.
Approximate Retail Price: $7

Serrated frozen-food knife could be used for bread or tomatoes.

Bar Knife

If your culinary escapades center exclusively around your home bar, this may be the only knife you will ever need. The bar knife is an 8½-inch-long, multipurpose tool that can replace a paring knife, a bottle opener — and a toothpick, when you're desperate. It is nicely constructed with a full-tang, stainless-steel blade. **To Use:** The straight, sharp side cuts fruit and vegetable garnishes for potent potables. The opener is perfect for beer bottles, and the prong at the tip deftly deposits olives into martinis.
Approximate Retail Price: $2.40

Bar knife opens bottles, spears olives and cuts fruit.

Steel and Stone Sharpeners

The traditional sharpeners are the round steel sharpener and the carborundum stone. Though they are of different material and different shape, you use the same basic movement with both of them. The tapered steel sharpener shown is about 20 inches long and has a wooden handle, a ring for hanging and a guard at the base of the handle. The guard is important because you draw the knife blade toward you as you sharpen. Steel sharpeners come in a fine grain for finishing and a medium grain for sharpening. Some are magnetic and realign the blade's molecules as they are used. High-carbon stainless blades benefit most from magnetic steel sharpeners. The carborundum stone shown is an inch-thick rectangle of silicon carbide, 6 inches long and 2 inches wide. It has a rough side for sharpening and a fine-grained side for finishing. Smaller, fine-grained stones of silicon dioxide, known as whetstones, can also be used for finishing. **To Use:** Start with either a medium-grained steel or rough stone. Rest the tip of the steel on a flat surface, holding the handle with one hand. Lay the stone, rough side up, on a flat surface. Holding the knife with the blade toward you, draw it up the sharpener at a 15 to 20 degree angle from the base of the blade to the tip. Turn the blade over and repeat. Do this rapidly and rhythmically until the blade is sharpened. For finishing on steel, use the same basic motion across a fine steel. For finishing on stone, or whetstone, the fine side of the stone may be lubricated with oil before you apply the knife. Guide the blade with your fingers as shown. Pressing lightly, move the blade up and across the stone from base of blade to tip. Use rotary movement when smoothing out an irregularity.
Approximate Retail Price: $11 (steel); $7 (stone)

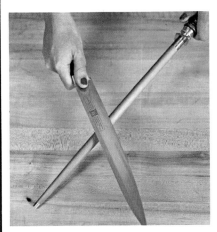

Draw blade up steel sharpener.

Oil may be used on fine side of carborundum stone for finishing.

CUTLERY CLASSICS

Zip-Zap Sharpener

Probably the easiest and most effective tool to use for sharpening good knives at home, the little Zip-Zap can be whipped out every time you pick up a knife. Unlike the steel, the Zip-Zap is moved along the blade of the stationary knife. The 5½-inch-long ceramic rod must be cleaned to take off the steel filing; soap and water and a scrub brush do the job. The sharpener can break if it falls onto the floor. **To Use:** Hold the knife to be sharpened stationary. Pass the sharpener back and forth at a slight angle over the knife's blade.
Approximate Retail Price: $3

Pass Zip-Zap back and forth to sharpen knife.

Crock Stick

Sharpening serrated and scalloped edges at home used to be impossible; but now the Crock Stick comes to the rescue. The contraption consists of a 7½-inch by 3-inch wood base with holes at one end for two 8¾-inch ceramic rods. Assembled, it looks like a rabbit-ear TV antenna with the ears askew. It does work, and the useful life of some of your serrated knives can be extended. For regular knives, we prefer the Zip-Zap or steel and stone. **To Use:** Slice straight downward toward the base of the sharpener, drawing the blade toward you from the handle to the point. Shift from one rod to the other to sharpen both sides of the blade.
Approximate Retail Price: $9

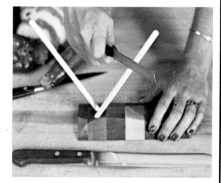
Slice down on Crock Stick.

Cutting Boards

Wooden cutting boards are the most fun to use and easiest on the knife, not to mention hand and arm. Wooden boards usually are thicker than synthetic boards and are softer than plastic or hard rubber, lessening knife impact. End grain cut boards are the best quality. Boards made of one plank may warp and split. Wood must be cared for and kept dry, even though most modern wooden boards are treated to resist moisture and bacteria. A warped board is useless; so it is important not to mistreat it by putting hot pots on it or otherwise subjecting it to extremes of temperature. Dishwashers should be avoided. Since we can't afford a genuine butcher's block — one of those handsome, thick wooden tables — we anchor our cutting boards to the counter by placing a damp towel under them. The one disadvantage of a wooden cutting surface is that it absorbs odors. You may want to keep a small plastic cutting board for pungent foods.
Approximate Retail Price: $6-$30 (wooden); $8- $20 (plastic)

Chop onion on plastic boards.

Slanted Knife Rack

Slanted construction provides knife blocks with a new angle — one that makes it easier for you to reach for the weapon of your choice. Now you have little excuse left to bang up the blades in drawers, since the slanted rack much improves upon the visibility and accessibility of standard blocks. This rack stands 10 inches high on a 5-inch-wide base; it holds eight knives and a steel or ceramic sharpener.
Approximate Retail Price: $20

Slanted wood knife rack.

Handcrafted oak knife block.

Knife Block

A classic knife block keeps knives safe and sound and within easy reach. This handcrafted oak block holds eight knives and one sharpening steel. It stands 10½ inches high on a 4½-inch by 5-inch base supported by non-skid rubber feet. The beauty of this model could dissuade you forever from the unhealthy practice of tossing the blades into a kitchen drawer.
Approximate Retail Price: $15

See-Through Knife Holder

One alternative to a knife block is a magnetic rack, but this can be a weighty and, if not hung properly, a dangerous item. Devotées of the magnetic rack tout the visibility of the knives arrayed along its length. To counter this argument, we present a see-through knife holder that allows you to select a blade without pulling out every knife. We only wish that this plastic box were larger: It will not hold blades longer than 6½ inches or wider than ⅜ inch. Six smaller knives will drop obligingly into the removable, slotted wood cover of this 7⅜-inch-high box.
Approximate Retail Price: $10

Knife blades are visible at a glance in the see-through knife holder, but the plastic box only holds small knives.

THE BLADE BOUTIQUE

When is a blade not a knife? When it is a custom-cutting edge. And these are blades designed for custom cuts of all shapes and sizes. Most of the items you'll find in "The Blade Boutique" are single-purpose, lightweight, manually-operated and relatively inexpensive. But in the grand finale we present some handsome heavy-duty equipment and a group of multipurpose machines that represent the ultimate, to date, in cutting edges.

We have assembled an interesting company: vegetable peelers — not just any vegetable peelers, but French ones — and garlic presses, those indispensable little tools that peel and mince garlic in one brief squeeze. There are citrus zesters and scorers for threads and ribbons of citrus peels. And a mushroom fluter that makes artwork of mushroom caps.

A cherry pitter in hand will give you the courage during cherry season to pit cups of cherries for fresh cherry pies, cherries jubilee, jams, preserves and Danish Cherry Soup. Fruits and vegetables other than cherries also crop up perennially with scores of seeds and cores — apples, pears, cucumbers and zucchini to name only a few. For these, too, we offer some shortcuts: an apple corer for apples and a zucchini corer for zucchini, as well as kernel cutters for corn and hullers for juicy strawberries. If you have ever tried to French-cut fresh green beans by hand you will appreciate the bean slicers which split the beans in one neat motion. These blades may seem overly specialized — but not when you're faced with bushels of abundance or an overzealous garden.

A radish rosette cutter not only produces roses of another name but sculpts citrus flowers as well. You can create drama in the round by scooping melons and potatoes with an assortment of melon ball cutters. And complete the plastic art of serving perfection with irresistible petals of butter — cut with a butter curler, of course. Whether you hanker after truffles or crave French fries, there's a blade to suit your taste.

Though the most fascinating blades are those designed purely for frivolous ends, cutters of serious intent also bear a special charm. Take the lyrically-named mezzaluna, for example. Its 10-inch curved blade, flanked by wooden handles, chops and minces with the efficiency of a chef's knife. But to wield this Italian classic you rock the blade back and forth on a flat surface, with a rhythm reminiscent of a folk dance. A German cabbage slicer, which is nothing more than two wooden slabs with cutting edges, has a similar provincial appeal. As does a French four-blade chopper that twirls through its tasks in a rustic wood bowl.

Of European origins, but by no means old-world, the food processor brings the newest and most dazzling set of blades to "The Blade Boutique." A machine that comes closer than anything else to replacing the chef in the kitchen, the processor cuts, slices, chops, minces, grates, purees, pulverizes, blends and grinds.

We welcome the relief the food processor offers from tedious chopping chores. But it will never flatter a radish as a spiral cutter does. Nor curl a strip of butter or flute a mushroom cap.

French Vegetable Peelers

These are all French versions of our standard vegetable peeler — quite an assortment. This style of peeler fits comfortably in the palm of your hand, and we found we had more control when peeling with the French peelers than with the standard peeler. Whatever its size or shape, a good vegetable peeler is a trusty kitchen companion. **To Use:** The French vegetable peeler is lightly drawn across the vegetable, as opposed to the shucking motion of the more familiar peeler. At first it seems much slower than the standard swivel-action peeler, but after a couple pounds of carrots and potatoes your speed will pick up. *Approximate Retail Price: $2 (all styles)*

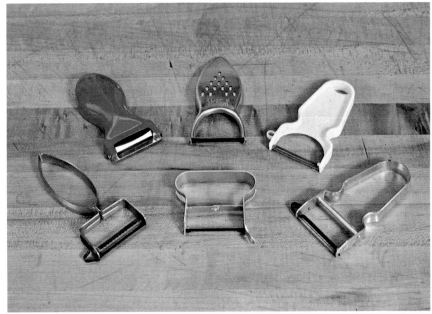

French vegetable peelers are drawn across food for controlled peeling.

Garlic Presses

The big news for many people who already use a garlic press is that it is not necessary to peel the clove! Divulge this to as many friends as possible and watch the light dawn in their eyes. Available in assorted shapes and sizes, all garlic presses serve the same purpose: reducing a clove of garlic to a grated or minced consistency. Some presses are more effective and simpler to clean than others. The Austrian-made, self-cleaning garlic press from Rowoco is the easiest to clean. It has a set of prongs that poke through the perforations when the handle is reversed. Most presses are made of cast aluminum, measuring about 7 to 8 inches in length. In all cases, garlic is forced or pressed through a perforated grate. Some presses have an additional insert to place over the holes to allow for a finer consistency. **To Use:** Place an unpeeled clove in the press and force the two handles together, squeezing the garlic essence through the perforated grate. The garlic does not have to be peeled; since the skin remains in the cup, you can skip that odious chore! For the self-

Garlic presses of various shapes mince unpeeled cloves.

Reverse the handles of the self-cleaning garlic press.

cleaning press, reverse the handles and force the plugged-up perforations over the little prongs. *Approximate Retail Price: $3 to $6.50; $6 (self-cleaning press)*
Helpful Garlic Hints:
• Buy loose, fresh garlic, not the packaged type, which is frequently old and stale.
• When sautéeing garlic, be careful

not to let it brown or burn, or it will turn very bitter and pungent.
• 1 medium clove garlic equals ⅛ teaspoon minced garlic.
• To remove the smell of garlic from your hands, rinse them in cold water, rub with salt and rinse again with cold water. Then wash with soap and water. Repeat if necessary.

THE BLADE BOUTIQUE

Citrus Zesters

One of the greatest little inventions of our time, a zester removes the outer skin, or zest (*zeste* is French for "peel"), of citrus rinds. Use a zester instead of those tiny holes at the end of a grater that seem to devour the zest and grate the white pulp and your knuckles too. Zesters come with either plastic, rosewood or beechwood handles. All are variations on the same theme: a stainless-steel head with five tiny, very sharp cutting holes that scrape off threads of zest. Save your sales slip and check the sharpness of a zester when you get it home; some lemon zesters are lemons and you can't tell from appearance. **To Use:** With the sharp cutting edges towards the lemon, lime or orange, run the zester down the side of the fruit in one motion to produce a thread-like strand of zest. Continue in this manner around the citrus until as much zest as needed has been removed. Citrus stripped of its zest should be sealed in a plastic bag and refrigerated to prevent it from drying out. Any zest not used in a recipe can be snugly wrapped and frozen. Also, a zester can be used to score carrots before they are sliced to make decorative carrot rounds.
Approximate Retail Price: $2.50

Citrus zester removes fine strands of lemon peel.

Run zester down side of fruit; chop strands to desired texture.

Citrus Scorer

The citrus scorer is a variation of the citrus zester. This device produces a thicker piece of lemon zest suitable for a martini or candied lemon peel. Available with black plastic, rosewood or beechwood handles, this device has a stainless-steel head with a single-pronged cutting edge. The citrus scorer can be distinguished from a mushroom fluter only by the fact that its cutting edge is on the side rather than the top of the steel head. **To Use:** Run the scorer down the side of the lemon, from top to bottom to produce one zest.
Approximate Retail Price: $2.50

Citrus scorer cuts strips.

Run scorer along side of lemon.

Cumberland Sauce

Zest of 1 orange
Zest of 1 lemon
1 cup port, Madeira or dry red wine
¼ cup currant jelly
¼ cup cranberry sauce
Juice of ½ orange
Juice of ½ lemon
½ teaspoon dry mustard
Pinch of cayenne pepper
Pinch of ginger

1. In a small saucepan, combine zest with port or wine and cook over a medium-high heat until the liquid is reduced to ⅓ cup.
2. Add currant jelly, cranberry sauce, juices, dry mustard, cayenne pepper and ginger. Cook over medium high heat until jelly is melted and sauce is thickened to desired consistency.
3. Pour into serving dish. This sauce is delicious served warm or chilled with chicken, turkey or ham. Refrigerate leftover sauce.   *Makes about 1 cup*

Citrus Spigots

Insert one of these little juice extractors into a citrus fruit and it will provide instant juice. As the lemon, lime or orange is squeezed, the juice drips out of the extractor. Both juicers are 3 inches long. One has a spiral insert tube; the other has a straight tube. **To Use:** Insert spigot in end of citrus. Squeeze as much juice as you need. Refrigerate fruit with spigot inserted.
Approximate Retail Price:$1.50 (both kinds)

Wooden Citrus Reamer

A replica of an 18th-century citrus reamer, this British-made model is not as neat as modern juicers. But what it lacks in efficiency, it makes up for in charm. The 6-inch-long beechwood reamer has deep ridges carved in its tear-shaped head. The handle fits as comfortably in the hand as the ridged end fits into a lemon. **To Use:** Cut end off lemon or other citrus fruit. Holding lemon over bowl, insert tip of reamer and turn.
Approximate Retail Price: $5

Insert spigot in lemon; squeeze to extract juice.

Place reamer in lemon and turn to extract juice.

THE BLADE BOUTIQUE

Mushroom Fluter

A careful scrutiny reveals this gadget to be a mushroom fluter, not a citrus scorer. The only difference between it and a citrus scorer is the position of the cutting edge. A mushroom fluter has its cutting edge on the tip of the stainless-steel head. You could use this gadget for both lemons and mushrooms but the angle of the cutting edge does make it perfect for mushrooms. The 6-inch-long mushroom fluter has a black plastic, nicely contoured handle that fits comfortably in your hand. Use this tool to decorate your next Tournedos Sauté aux Champignons with beautifully fluted mushroom caps. **To Use:** Clean the mushrooms with a mushroom brush. Place the fluter on the center of the mushroom cap's top, cutting edge down. Gently cut the edge of the cap in one motion. Repeat the procedure around mushroom cap at equally spaced intervals — and behold! A plain, ordinary mushroom cap turns into a work of art. We might add that this art, like any art, takes practice.
Approximate Retail Price: $2

Mushroom fluter looks much like a citrus scorer.

Cut mushroom toward edge.

Mushroom Brush

We paraded this discovery around to all our friends as though we'd discovered the Rosetta stone. You see, it solves the problem of how to clean mushrooms properly. Because mushrooms act like a sponge when put under water, they should not be washed. Instead, mushrooms should be brushed with a mushroom brush gently, so as not to bruise their delicate skin. This seems to be the only mushroom brush available. You probably could use a baby's hairbrush as a substitute. The mushroom brush has very fine, nylon bristles set in a piece of white, molded plastic. Before the discovery of this brush, we used rolls of dampened paper towels — very

A brush cleans mushrooms.

Use in Chicken Chasseur.

wasteful and messy. **To Use:** Lightly dampen the mushroom brush. Gently brush mushroom caps and dirt will stick to the brush. Rinse the brush after each use. Or, when preparing raw mushrooms for stuffing, dampen the mushroom brush with lemon juice and brush off the mushrooms, thus cleaning them and preventing them from turning brown in one easy step.
Approximate Retail Price: $3

Chicken Chasseur

½ pound mushrooms
1 chicken, cut into pieces
   Flour seasoned with salt and
     pepper for dredging
4 tablespoons butter, divided
2 tablespoons oil
¼ cup minced shallots or onion
¼ cup cognac or brandy
   (optional)
1½ cups chicken stock
¾ cup white wine
⅓ cup tomato paste
¼ cup chopped parsley
¼ teaspoon tarragon
1 teaspoon chervil
   Pinch of thyme
½ teaspoon salt
¼ teaspoon pepper
2 tablespoons flour
   Chopped parsley for garnish

1. Clean mushrooms with mushroom brush. Cut into quarters.
2. Dredge chicken in seasoned flour. Heat 2 tablespoons of the butter and the oil in a large frying pan or Dutch oven and brown chicken lightly.
3. Add shallots and mushrooms and cook until shallots are tender.
4. If using cognac or brandy, heat in a small saucepan and pour over chicken. Ignite carefully. Turn chicken in the flames.
5. Mix the stock, wine and tomato paste together in a mixing bowl and add to chicken when the flame subsides. Add parsley, tarragon, chervil, thyme, salt and pepper. Cover and gently simmer for about 45 minutes, or until tender.
6. With your fingers, combine remaining 2 tablespoons butter with 2 tablespoons flour. Mash together to make a paste.
7. Remove chicken to a serving platter and keep warm. Add butter and flour paste to the sauce in small bits, stirring constantly. Do not boil. Sauce will thicken in about 5 minutes.
8. Pour the sauce over the chicken and sprinkle with chopped parsley to serve.
Makes 4 to 6 servings

Butter Curlers

It is hard to believe that these strange, hook-like devices produce beautiful, delicate curls or shells of butter. They require patience to use, but they do, indeed, accomplish their artistic mission. The butter curlers shown have stainless-steel curved blades, with small teeth, set into a plastic or wooden handle. There are numerous sizes and shapes of butter curlers, some made completely of wood, others of metal. The basic procedure is the same with all models. The success of your butter curling venture depends entirely upon the consistency of the butter. It is simply a matter of trial and error. If the butter is too hard, it will not curl and will break off. If the butter is too soft, the blade will dig into the butter too deeply. Don't get discouraged. Jacques Pépin started out this way! It takes practice. **To Use:** Place butter curler, teeth side down, at the far end of a chilled stick of butter. Pull the curler toward you, producing a delicate butter curl. Place the curl in a bowl of iced water and continue quickly before the butter gets too soft. Whoever said "art endures" never sculpted butter.
Approximate Retail Price: $1 to $5 (depending on size)

Some butter curlers look like hooks, others like rakes or scoops.

Pull curler toward you.

THE BLADE BOUTIQUE

Cherry Pitters

Nothing could be more refreshing on a hot summer day than a cup of chilled cherry soup, laced with white wine and topped with sour cream. And nothing could be more exasperating than biting into a cherry pit! A combination cherry-olive pitter comes to the rescue. There are several styles; most work on the same principle. The small Westmark pitter, made of cast aluminum, measures about 7 inches long. As the handles, held together by a coil spring, are pressed together, a sharp cutting rod is forced through the cup holding the cherry or olive, thus poking out the pit. It does a neat job without tearing the fruit. This style also has a safety clasp to keep the instrument closed when not in use. We think it is an easy, inexpensive way to accomplish a rather tedious chore. Clearly, the only disadvantage is that it can only pit one cherry at a time. **To Use:** Unfasten safety catch. Place a cherry or olive in the cup and force the two handles together, poking the pit out through the cherry. The whole operation is much like punching a hole in paper to put in a notebook.

The larger cherry pitter shown is

an interesting looking gadget to clutter up your counter. Another Westmark product from West Germany, it accomplishes the same task as the small pitter, but much faster. It pits two cherries at a time, and the feeding and ejection are automatic. We pitted a pound of cherries in less than five minutes. This model is not hand-held; it measures about 10 inches high and requires some simple assembling. The pitter is made of rustproof aluminum and orange, unbreakable plastic parts. **To Use:** Follow the directions to assemble. Secure the cherry pitter to your counter by turning the lever on the side to attach the vacuum suction foot. Place a handful of cherries in the plastic tipping tray; position a bowl in front of the gadget. As two cherries fall into place, force down the round handle on top. This will pit the cherries, sending the fruit into the waiting bowl and the pits into the tray. We had fun using this gadget. But it does not work as well with olives as the small pitter. Olives have to be carefully positioned upright in the tray. Also, we found that some olives are too big for the tray's opening.
Approximate Retail Price: $4 (small pitter); $20 (large pitter)

Small pitter pokes out pits; large pitter does two at a time.

Danish Cherry Soup

4 cups fresh Bing cherries (about 2 pounds)
4 cups water
2 sticks cinnamon
½ lemon, sliced
2 tablespoons sugar, or to taste
Pinch of salt
1 tablespoon cornstarch
¼ cup water
1 cup white wine
Sour cream for garnish

1. Pit cherries, using a cherry pitter.
2. Cook 3 cups cherries in the 4 cups water until tender. Strain and reserve juice. Force the cooked cherries through a food mill, extracting as much juice as possible (or, with a food processor, process with the steel blade until pureed).
3. Add puree mixture back to cherry juice. Strain again, if desired, to get a perfectly smooth consistency.
4. Add cinnamon sticks, lemon slices, sugar and salt to cherry liquid. Simmer for 5 minutes.
5. Mix cornstarch with ¼ cup water and stir until smooth. Add to soup, together with the wine, and cook until clear. Add remaining cup of pitted cherries and cook until heated through.
6. Chill soup thoroughly. Serve each portion with a dollop of sour cream.
Makes 6 to 8 servings

Apple Corer

Obvious in its function, an apple corer is not as easy to use as it appears — it takes the aim of William Tell to remove the entire core in one motion! An apple corer consists of a 4-inch, trough-shaped stainless-steel blade with a sharp cutting ring on the tip attached to a 4-inch, wooden or plastic handle. Occasionally the corer goes off on an angle when you insert it, or the core is not perfectly centered in the apple, and some of the core is left behind. Further insertions will remove any leftover seeds and core. There are several models available, most of them comparable in performance. **To Use:** Place the apple on the counter and insert corer into the stem. Aim for the other end and rotate the corer as it goes through the apple. Extract the corer to remove the core. The neatly cored apple is ready.
Approximate Retail Price: $3.50

Apple corers hollow out apples.

Insert corer and extract core.

Spoon filling into cored center.

Brush with egg glaze.

Apple Dumplings with Rum Sauce

6 medium tart apples
Pastry for 9-inch two-crust pie
⅓ cup brown sugar
¼ teaspoon cinnamon
Pinch nutmeg
¼ cup raisins or currants
2 tablespoons butter
1 egg
2 tablespoons cream

1. Preheat oven to 425°F. Peel apples and core them with an apple corer.
2. Prepare pastry and cut into 6 equal pieces. Roll out each piece into an 8-inch circle. Trim the edges and save trimmings.
3. Mix sugar, cinnamon and nutmeg. Place apple in center of each circle. Fill center of each apple with about ½ tablespoon sugar mixture, add a few raisins, 1 teaspoon butter and another ½ tablespoon sugar mixture. Bring sides of pastry up and press circle firmly around each apple.
4. Roll out remaining scraps of dough and cut into small leaves. Place on top of dumplings. Arrange dumplings in an ungreased baking dish.
5. Combine egg and cream and whisk together until thoroughly blended. Brush dumplings with glaze.
6. Bake at 425°F for 40 to 50 minutes or until golden.
7. Serve warm with Rum Sauce. *Makes 6 servings*

Rum Sauce

½ cup whipping cream
2 tablespoons powdered sugar
1 egg
2 tablespoons rum

1. Beat cream until almost stiff. Add powdered sugar and beat until stiff.
2. Whisk egg and rum together until thoroughly blended. Fold into whipped cream. Serve immediately or refrigerate up to 1 hour.
Makes about 1½ cups sauce

THE BLADE BOUTIQUE

Strawberry Huller

We think strawberries deserve their own gadget! Better than a paring knife or your fingernails, the strawberry huller tweezes out the leaf without cutting the strawberry's flesh. The 2½-inch-long huller is made out of a single piece of stainless steel. **To Use:** Place the ends around the ring of leaves at the stem end and tweeze gently.
Approximate Retail Price: $.75

Hullers pluck out leaves.

Tweeze to remove stem.

Zucchini Corers

You planted an entire row of zucchini? You didn't know one plant could be so prolific, let alone eight plants, and your family is tired of sautéed zucchini three times a day? Our solution is to invest in a zucchini corer and serve stuffed zucchini for a change. You could stuff zucchini with ground meat mixtures or minced vegetables and bake them. Or stuff zucchini with cream cheese and slice into thin rounds for a raw appetizer. A zucchini corer can core any elongated vegetable, such as cucumbers, and works well on apples and pears, too. It has a 6-inch, trough-shaped stainless-steel blade on either a wooden or plastic handle. **To Use:** Select straight, firm zucchini or cucumbers, not too fat or too skinny. Cut off both ends. Insert the corer into the center of one end. Aim for the other end and rotate the corer as it passes through. Extract the corer, removing the pulp at the same time, and the vegetable is ready for filling.
Approximate Retail Price: $1.95 (plastic handle); $2.50 (wooden handle)

Corers hollow out zucchini.

Insert corer into trimmed end.

Extract corer to remove pulp.

Stuffed Zucchini Rounds

8 ounces cream cheese
2 to 3 tablespoons cream-style horseradish
⅓ cup ham, salami or pepperoni, finely chopped
2 tablespoons chopped parsley
3 tablespoons chopped chives
2 ounces chopped pimientos, drained
Pinch of salt
Dash pepper
5 small zucchini, cleaned

1. Mix the cream cheese with horseradish. Blend in the ham, parsley, chives, pimientos, and salt and pepper to taste.
2. Cut ends off zucchini and core with a zucchini corer.
3. Spoon the filling into the zucchini, forcing it into the center with each spoonful. Chill until ready to serve.
4. Score the zucchini with the tines of a fork. To serve, cut into ½-inch slices.
Makes about 10 appetizer servings

Note: Any leftover filling can be thinned down with a little cream and used as a dip for fresh vegetables or as a tangy salad dressing.

Radish Spiral Cutter

After several tries, we mastered the radish spiral cutter and glowed with pride. In theory the cutter reduces any solid fruit or vegetable to a delicate, spiral ribbon — the perfect garniture for a buffet table. We had the best success with radishes and firm pears. The radish spiral cutter consists of two pieces: a stainless-steel arm with a very sharp cutting edge attached to a plastic spiral; and a spindle that fits into the top of the spiral. **To Use:** Trim the stem and root from a large radish. Be careful when handling and inserting cutter — the blade is very sharp. Insert the spiral into the radish. Holding the radish firmly, turn the arm around and around, causing the blade to carve out a spiral shape. (Not all radish cutters come with a spindle to keep the cut radish spiral in place while you complete the job.) To produce a somewhat thicker spiral, exert downward pressure on the blade.

Approximate Retail Price: $1.50

Spiral makes radish curls.

Insert spiral into radish.

Turn cutter handle.

Radish Rosette Cutter

Compared to the spiral cutter, the radish rosette cutter is a simple, easy-to-use item. Crafted out of heavy-duty stainless-steel, it makes neat, attractive radish rosettes. You can decorate citrus shells, too, with the V-shaped cutting blade that makes fancy scalloped edges. **To Use:** Select rather large radishes. Trim off the stems and a bit of the root ends. Release the lever on the handle to open up the cutter. Position the cutting edge down. Center the radish, root end up, under the cutting edge. With a swift, decisive motion, force the cutting edge through the radish. Instant rosette! To scallop citrus shells, cut a lemon in half. Place the V-shaped edge of the cutter on the lip of the shell and press it closed to cut through skin. Continue around edge at equally spaced intervals.

Approximate Retail Price: $8

Radish rosette cutter turns trimmed radishes into flowers.

Force cutter through radish.

THE BLADE BOUTIQUE

Melon Ball Cutters

Imagine surrounding your next roast with delicately sautéed, golden-brown, fluted potato balls. The epitome of extravagance! A variety of melon ball cutters is available for shaping orbs of potatoes, melons and other produce. There are the traditional round cutters (ranging from ⅛ inch to 1¼ inches in diameter), oval cutters, and fluted cutters. Most have sharp, stainless-steel cutting edges fitted into wood or plastic handles. These cutters serve a variety of purposes. Besides scooping out decorative morsels of butter, carrots, apples, potatoes, melon and cheese, they can also be used to scoop out cherry tomatoes or, once an apple has been cut in half, to scoop out the core. **To Use:** Insert the cutting edge into the food, press in slightly, then rotate handle to dig out shaped pieces.

Melon ball cutters come in assorted shapes and sizes.

Approximate Retail Price: $1 to $5 (depending on size)

Krisk and Zipp Bean Slicers

No matter how good or how sharp your knife, cutting French-style green beans by hand is quite difficult. Even a bean slicer is slow going. So we were surprised at how fast the Krisk and Zipp slicers worked, even though they cut only one bean at a time. We French-sliced a pound of green beans in 13 minutes. The Krisk slicer strings and slices green beans in one swift motion. Made in Australia, it consists of a molded plastic handle and a stainless-steel cutting head. It also has an additional blade on the tip to cut off the ends of the beans. All the cutting edges are replaceable. The 1¾-inch by 1½-inch plastic Zipp slicer does not string the beans, but does cut them efficiently. **To Use:** Insert the bean in the Krisk funnel, or into either end of the Zipp; push the green bean through the cutter. Grasp the sliced green bean when it appears on the other side of the cutter and draw it straight through the blades.

Approximate Retail Price: $2.25 (Krisk); $1 (Zipp)

French-cutting green beans is easy with the Krisk or Zipp slicer.

Krisk slicer strings beans also.

Spong
Green Bean Slicer

A sturdy little machine named Spong, with a stalwart personality and a crank handle — how could we resist it? If you need to cut up large quantities of green beans, perhaps for fall canning, you'll enjoy this green bean slicer as much as we did. It does not French-style the beans, but cuts them into attractive ½- to 1-inch pieces with diagonally sliced ends. The well-built slicer is made of cast aluminum and stands about 8 inches high, taking up about as much room as a pencil sharpener; it fits securely on the counter with the aid of four suction cups. **To Use:** Place the slicer on any clean, smooth surface and secure by pushing the lever. If necessary, freshen the green beans by soaking them in cold water — firm beans cut very neatly. Then cut off tops and tails and string the beans. Feed the beans into the hopper, turning the handle as you do so. To get a long cut, keep the beans upright in the hopper.
Approximate Retail Price: $7

Spong slicer cuts diagonally.

Corn Cutter

We wouldn't bother using this 15-inch-long cutter on small quantities, but bushels and bushels of corn is another matter. The stainless-steel corn cutter has a long trough housing vicious little cutting blades and scorers. You can adjust the cutting head to remove either whole kernels or the meat of the kernels for cream-style corn. The cutter comes with a protective cover guard for the blades. **To Use:** For cream-style corn, remove the cover guard and loosen the blade screw on the underside to lower the blade completely. Set the cutter over a bowl and place a fresh ear of corn, small end forward, on the cutter. Push the cob over the scorers. Rotate the cob and repeat the procedure. Six or seven strokes will finish most ears. For whole kernel corn, replace the cover guard to cover up the scorers. Raise the blade fully and tighten the screw securely. Proceed as for cream-style corn, pushing against the blade only.
Approximate Retail Price: $8.50

Run ear of corn across stainless-steel corn cutter.

Pennsylvania Dutch Corn Relish

12 ears corn (6 cups kernels)
½ head cabbage (4 cups chopped)
4 medium onions (2 cups chopped)
3 small green peppers (2 cups chopped)
3 small red peppers (2 cups chopped)
4 ribs celery (2 cups chopped)
3 cups cider vinegar
1 cup cider or water

2 cups sugar
1 tablespoon powdered mustard
1 tablespoon celery seed

1 tablespoon mustard seed
1 teaspoon tumeric
1 tablespoon salt
1 teaspoon pepper

1. Cut corn off the cobs.
2. In a large pot or kettle, combine corn kernels with all other ingredients and cook for 20 to 30 minutes.
3. Prepare two-piece, self-sealing lids according to manufacturer's directions. Ladle relish into hot sterilized pint jars, leaving ¼-inch headspace. Seal jars and process 15 minutes in boiling water bath.
Makes about 5 pints

THE BLADE BOUTIQUE

Kernal Kutter

A good but rather messy cutter for small quantities of corn, the Kernal Kutter scrapes the whole ear at once. That's the theory, at any rate. In fact, it would take Popeye's strength to clean an ear with one swoop. The 10-inch gadget has a circular, ragged-edged, stainless- steel blade that expands as it is forced over an ear of corn. **To Use:** Cut the bottom end of a fresh ear of corn so it sits flat on the counter. Place the cutter over the top of the ear, grasp the handles with both hands and rock the blade back and forth while pushing it down the ear. *Approximate Retail Price: $3.95*

Kernal Kutter scrapes cob.

Cream-Style Cutter

Strictly for cream-style corn, this inexpensive cutter looks somewhat like a fish scaler. On one side of the cutter's head are 5 sharp prongs for scoring the corn; the reverse side is a scraper used to remove the meat of the kernal. The 5-inch easy-to- use cutter is made of stainless steel. **To Use:** Run the scorer down the length of the corn. Rotate the corn and repeat to score the entire ear. Use the scraping edge to extract the meat and juice. *Approximate Retail Price: $1*

Cream-style corn cutter.

Super Jolly

Who could frown on a gadget called "Super Jolly"? And the Super Jolly, we are relieved to report, just happens to be a jolly good gadget. It accomplishes three tasks, with three separate inserts. Super Jolly can quickly cut French fries, which neatly pop right through the French-fry grate; it can rice potatoes or puree cooked vegetables; and it can form gnocchi, little potato or semolina dumplings. Made in Italy, the 8-inch high, 8-inch long Super Jolly is crafted out of a cheery, bright orange, durable plastic — you were expecting maybe drab grey? **To Use:** Secure the Super Jolly to the countertop by turning the pressure lever at the base. Loosen the little white screw on top. With handle in upright position, insert the appropriate grate and tighten the screw to lock it into position. The pusher or press in the handle also comes with two different inserts. One is divided into sections which just fit into the French-

Super Jolly makes French fries, riced potatoes and gnocchi.

fry grate. The other is flat and is used with the ricer and gnocchi grates. Place the appropriate insert in the pusher. Lift the handle and feed the food into the container. Force the handle down to push the food through the grate. When making gnocchi, place the dough mix- ing gnocchi, place the dough mix- ture in the container, apply pressure on the handle and push out ½-inch-long pieces of dough. Cut off the dough pieces with the dull side of a knife blade and drop them into boiling water to make darling — oops, jolly — little dumplings. *Approximate Retail Price: $14*

Simplex French-fry Cutter

Yet another French-fry cutter, the Italian-made Simplex cutter vies with the Super Jolly for the cheeriest gadget award. Looking much like an old fashioned potato ricer, this cutter produces ½-inch-thick French fries. Crafted out of sturdy cast iron, it is covered with a bright orange enamel and measures about 10 inches long. The yellow cutting grate is removable for easy cleaning. **To Use:** Pull apart the two handles and insert a small to medium-sized peeled potato in the container. Push the handles together, forcing the studded pusher into the top of container and forcing the potato cuts out through the bottom. If the potato does not go through easily, reposition it in the container.

Approximate Retail Price: $13.50

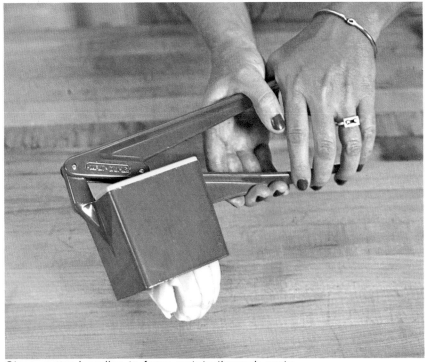

Close cutter handles to force potato through grate.

Pommes Frites

4 Idaho potatoes
2 quarts vegetable oil
Salt and freshly ground pepper to taste

1. Peel potatoes and cut into French fries, using a French-fry cutter. Rinse with cold water to remove surface starch and dry thoroughly on paper towels. Potatoes must be completely dry or they will not brown properly.
2. Heat oil in a deep fryer to 325°F. If you are using a basket, heat the basket. When heated, lift the basket and toss a handful of potatoes into it. Lower the basket and cook 4 to 5 minutes until the potato is soft but not browned. Be sure to lift the basket occasionally while cooking and shake it to prevent the potatoes from sticking together.
3. Drain cooked potatoes and spread them on paper towels. Cook the remaining potatoes. Let them cool at least 15 minutes or up to several hours before the second frying.
4. Shortly before serving, heat oil to between 375°F and 400°F. Place potatoes a handful at a time in the oil and fry for 2 to 3 minutes or until they reach desired brownness. Keep them warm in a 250°F oven on cookie sheets lined with paper towels. Make sure to bring the fat back to the correct temperature before frying each batch.
5. Serve as soon as possible with salt and freshly ground black pepper, if you like.   *Makes 4 to 6 servings*

Deep fry potatoes twice, till crisp and brown.

THE BLADE BOUTIQUE

Aspic Cutters

Cookie cutters for Munchkins? Possibly, but they are intended to cut truffle slices, pastry, pimientoes, thinly sliced carrot rounds, green peppers or stiffened aspic spread thin on a cookie sheet. The cutters in this tinned-steel, Italian set are rather large as truffle cutters go. Each of the 12 different shapes is about 1 inch in diameter. Other more intricate sets have up to 75 individual shapes, some as small as ¼ inch in diameter. Prices range as high as the truffles themselves.

To Use: Just like cookie cutters — only you don't flour them unless cutting pastry. Blot pimientos before cutting. The punched-out rounds of carrots can be used as decorations, along with the cut shape.

Approximate Retail Price $5

Cutters shape decorative pieces of aspic.

Truffle Slicer

With white truffles selling for $25 an ounce, piercing the flesh of one with an ordinary knife amounts to gastronomical sacrilege. An elegant, stainless-steel truffle slicer is a suitable instrument for slicing either the white, slightly garlic-flavored truffle from Piedmont in North Italy, or the less expensive (about $15 an ounce) black truffle from the Perigord district of France. The cutter has a 2¼-inch adjustable blade. Unless you are going to take up residence in the Piedmont and keep your own truffle-sniffer in the form of a trained pig or dog, you'll want to scatter your truffle slices carefully in a pâté or cut them into decorative shapes to grace an aspic-glazed dish. Canned truffles are available in gourmet shops, and some specialty shops import fresh ones. White or black, these subterranean fungi have a pungent fragrance and taste that can dominate less persistent flavors. A friend of our tried to freeze well-wrapped fresh truffles and found their odor permeated even the ice cubes.

Once upon a time, truffles were served as main dishes. Brillat-

Draw truffle lightly over blade to make thin slices.

Savarin, the 18th-century gourmand, mentions a Sauté of Truffles and Truffles à la Provencal. In the delightful translation by Anne Drayton, of Brillat-Savarin's *Philosopher in the Kitchen,* you'll also find a serious discussion of the erotic powers of truffles; the digestibility of truffles (thoroughly wholesome, taken in moderation — hardly a necessary caution, given their price today); and

the overall virtues of "the jewel of cookery."

To Use: Adjust the cutter blade according to the thickness of slices desired. Push truffle over blade to slice. Cut the resulting thin slices into decorative shapes with tiny aspic cutters or truffle cutters. This slicer also makes elegant curls of chocolate for a special dessert.

Approximate Retail Price: $6

Mezzaluna

Its lyrical name suggests a sprightly folk dance, but a mezzaluna looks like a potent weapon. Literally mezzaluna means "half-moon." Actually, the mezzaluna is Italy's answer to the 10-inch French chef's knife; it accomplishes the same chopping and mincing chores but in a different manner. The half-moon shaped knives have either a single or a double 10-inch curved stainless-steel blade attached to two natural wood handles that nestle nicely in the palms of your hands. Also available in smaller and larger sizes with carbon steel blades, mezzalunas are gracefully designed, easy to sharpen, easy to use, and strong enough to handle all heavy-duty chopping chores. The carbon steel blades will tarnish quickly. With a little practice, you can harness the mezzaluna's rhythmic, rocking motion. **To Use:** A mezzaluna can be used on any cutting surface. Place food on the chopping surface. Securely grasp the two handles in the palms of your hands, and rock blade back and forth over the food. Put it to good use chopping onions, parsley, prosciutto and fontina cheese for your next Linguini Carbonara.

Approximate Retail Price: $5 to $12.95, depending on size

Rock mezzaluna back and forth to chop prosciutto for Linguini Carbonara. Mezzaluna may have one or two blades.

Linguini Carbonara

½ **pound bacon**
1 **onion**
¼ **cup olive oil**
1 **small bunch fresh parsley**
¼ **pound Fontina cheese**
¼ **pound proscuitto**
1 **pound linguini**
4 **egg yolks, lightly beaten**
 Salt and freshly ground black pepper to taste
1 **cup grated Parmesan cheese, divided**

1. Cut bacon into 1-inch lengths and cook in a large skillet until crisp. Drain well on paper towels. Pour off most of the fat.
2. Chop the onion with a mezzaluna. Put the olive oil in the skillet and sauté the onion until tender.
3. Chop parsley, Fontina cheese and prosciutto with a mezzaluna and set aside.
4. Cook the linguini *al dente* and drain quickly. Pour into a heated serving dish.
5. Add bacon, onion, parsley, Fontina cheese, prosciutto, egg yolks and half of parmesan cheese to linguini and toss with a fork and spoon. Season to taste.
6. Serve immediately with the remaining Parmesan cheese on the side.

Makes 4 servings

THE BLADE BOUTIQUE

Rolling Mincers

Why use one cutting edge, when five or nine will work so much faster? That's the theory behind these two Italian rolling mincers. One mincer looks like a large, red plastic snail and has five stainless-steel, wheel-like cutting blades that rotate when you roll them across the counter. The 6-inch, rounded plastic case fits comfortably in the palm of your hand. This rolling mincer is one of our favorite kitchen toys — we used it to mince celery, green peppers, onions, parsley and mushrooms. To clean the mincer, you twist the white plastic knob on the side and remove the plastic axle; it comes apart for washing. The other rolling mincer pictured has nine stainless-steel, wheel-like blades attached to an axle on an 8-inch stainless-steel frame. You hold this mincer by its polished wooden handle to roll the blades across food. The nine-blade rolling

Multi-bladed rolling mincers take care of small chopping chores.

Roll mincer back and forth over food on cutting surface.

mincer does not come apart, but rinses out when held under running water. **To Use:** Place food to be chopped on a cutting surface. Some food, like onions, should first be cut into smaller pieces or slices. Roll the mincer back and forth

across the food to achieve the desired consistency. By the way, the blades are very sharp, so don't yield to the temptation to race the mincers like toy cars.
Approximate Retail Price: $3.95 (each mincer)

Wooden Bowl and Chopper

A variation of the mezzaluna, this French wooden bowl and four-bladed chopper is designed to chop smaller quantities of food. A couple of tablespoons of parsley, a few green onions or one hard-boiled egg for your next mimosa can be minced smartly with this implement. We liked the wooden bowl and chopper because food stays in the center of the bowl and does not spread all over the counter. When buying a bowl and chopper, make sure that the curve of the blade matches the contour of the bowl. This particular hardwood bowl is 6½ inches in diameter. The stainless-steel chopper has a wood handle. Both the chopper and the bowl are available in larger sizes. **To Use:** Place the food to be chopped in the bowl. Grasp the chopper

Wooden bowl and chopper work best when chopper is rotated.

firmly and start chopping, rotating chopper as you go to achieve desired consistency. The wooden bowl periodically needs to be oiled with salad oil to prevent it from dry-

ing out and to preserve the wood. Never put woodenware in the dishwasher!
Approximate Retail Price: $8.50 (bowl); $2.75 (chopper)

Cabbage Slicer

If you are of German ancestry, your grandmother probably used a paddle-shaped slicer like this to prepare cabbage for sauerkraut. The natural wood tool from West Germany brings us back to the basics of functional design and a simple, all-purpose slicer. A relative of the French mandoline, which has more cutting blades, the cabbage slicer is constructed from two pieces of wood fitted with 4-inch stainless steel cutting blades and attached with hinges to a 12-inch frame. To get varying degrees of thickness, the wooden inserts are raised or lowered, then locked into position by tightening the screws on the side. Not all cabbage cutters are adjustable, but we liked this versatile model. It does a beautiful job slicing cabbage for stew, zucchini for stirfrying, or potatoes for homemade cottage fries. The paddle handle on the slicer fits very comfortably in your hand. **To Use:** Loosen the screws on the side of the frame and adjust the wooden inserts to achieve the desired thickness. Tighten the screws and run food down the slicer washboard fashion. Be careful not to slice your fingers when you reach the end of the vegetable.
Approximate Retail Price: $16.50

Cabbage wedge is drawn across adjustable blade of slicer.

Swiss Wood Mandoline

This is the streamlined, *au natural,* version of the classic French mandoline. Because of its smaller size and lower price tag it will probably find its way into more kitchens than the more professional model. It slices, juliennes, and cuts French fries and Pommes Gaufrettes, but lacks the precision and speed of the large mandoline. Three wooden inserts, two of which are adjustable, fasten together in a 14½ inch wood frame. The mandoline has two stainless-steel cutting edges, one straight and one wavy. **To Use:** For slicing: Adjust uppermost screw on the side of the mandoline according to desired thickness. Tighten screw into position. Run food down straight edge blade or wavy blade.

For French fries: Adjust uppermost screw according to desired thickness. Slice potatoes. Collect potato slices and reassemble potato. Hold slices perpendicular to cutting edge and slice again to produce French fries.

For julienne: Follow same procedure as for French fries, but position blade in lower position to produce a thinner slice.

For Pommes Gaufrettes (waffled potatoes): Adjust lowermost screw on side and set blade to about ⅛

Run vegetables straight down on wavy blade of mandoline.

inch thick. Turn mandoline upside down and run potato across wavy blade. Discard first slice. Turn potato 90 degrees and slice again. Continue turning and slicing.
Approximate Retail Price: $14.50

THE BLADE BOUTIQUE

French Mandoline

If you yearn for evenly sliced spuds for Potatoes Anna and beautifully latticed potatoes for Pommes Gaufrettes, then the prowess of the French mandoline will be music to your ears. The professional mandoline, for the serious-minded gourmet, is an all-purpose slicing wonder. Made of heavy-gauge, nickel-plated steel with carbon steel cutting blades, this mandoline measures about 15½ inches in length and, when fully assembled, stands about 9 inches tall. The BIA Cordon Bleu model shown is also available with a metal carriage that holds the food being sliced and protects fingers. This classic mandoline accomplishes a variety of slicing chores with ease and precision: It slices thicknesses up to ⅜ inch and cuts varying sizes of matchstick or julienne strips. You can make thick French fries as well as delicately laced or waffled Pommes Gaufrettes. Surprisingly enough, the mandoline is not as difficult or complicated to use as it looks. First, get to know the four main parts:

● The large, uppermost plate, which is raised or lowered by the lever on the underside of the mandoline.

● The revolving cutting head attached to a handle on the side of the mandoline. The handle (a) can be positioned on either of two studs or just left hanging and not engaged. If it is positioned on the upper stud (b), the finer, julienne blade is engaged. If it is positioned on the lower stud (c), the French-fry blade is engaged. If it is just hanging, then neither blade is engaged and the mandoline is set up for basic slicing chores. Note: The large plate must be in its highest (thickest) position before the handle can be set or engaged.

● The middle-level plate holds the nonadjustable fixed blade.

● The waffled, lower plate is raised or lowered by the lever on the underside of the mandoline. Pommes Gaufrettes are made with this

Mandoline is a versatile slicer.

Use top plate for French fries.

blade. **To Use:** Pull out the collapsible legs and secure the mandoline on the table. To cut julienne or matchstick shapes: Raise the upper plate (1) to its highest position. Pull out handle on side and position it over the upper stud (b). The julienne blade is now in position. Lower the large plate by adjusting the lever on underside of large plate. Position plate according to whether you want fine or medium julienne cuts. (The first few slices will be a matter of trial and error until you get desired size.) Hold the food being sliced with the palm of your hand and push straight down. (It is helpful if food being sliced is trimmed so that it has a flat top and bottom.) To cut French fries: Raise the large plate (1) to its highest po-

sition. Pull out the handle on side and position it over the lower stud (c). Adjust the large plate (1) to its lowest position. Hold the flat-edged potato with the palm of your hand and push straight down.

To slice: Raise the large plate (1) to its highest position. Pull out the handle (a) on side and let it hang loose, disengaged. Lower the large plate (1) to the desired height (all the way down for the thickest, ⅜-inch slice). Hold food being sliced with the palm of your hand and push straight down.

To cut Pommes Gaufrettes (waffled potatoes): Disengage the handle on the side (a), so that it hangs down. Adjust the large plate (1) to the height of the fixed blade (2). Set the waffled plate (3) to a height of

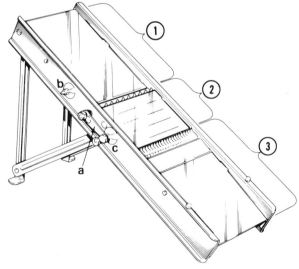
French mandoline: (1) upper plate, (2) cutting head, (3) lower plate, (a) handle, (b) julienne blade, (c) French-fry blade.

approximately ⅛ inch. This is the only cutting edge you will be using. Hold the potato with the palm of your hand and cut straight down. Discard the very first slice. Turn the potato 90 degrees and cut straight down again. This should produce a delicately laced Pomme Gaufrette. Turn the potato another 90 degrees and cut straight down again — to produce another waffled slice. (Note: If the slice does not hold together and is a mass of strings, it is too thin: Raise the blade. If it does not have the little holes or a waffled effect, then your slice is too thick: Lower the blade.) You'll be amazed how quickly you can master a classic French device like the mandoline. Use it for preparing any firm vegetable, such as beets, sweet potatoes, turnips, zucchini, cabbage, carrots or apples.
Approximate Retail Price: $105 (with guard)

Use only the waffled lower blade to make delicate Pommes Gaufrette.

Food Processors

The elegantly efficient Cuisinart food processor started the craze. Imported from France several years ago, it has been imitated by almost every small appliance manufacturer. Depending on the model and brand, a food processor can mix, blend, grind, slice, grate, shred, knead — and the list goes on. Above all, a food processor reduces the most time-consuming food preparation tasks to a matter of seconds. Indeed, specifying the length of time to process most foods is impossible because by the time you check the clock, it is too late. The sheer speed is the hardest aspect to get used to — but once you start using a food processor, you'll find it indispensible.

Safety practices should begin the minute you open the box: Be very careful of the razor sharp blades as you unpack them. Always handle them with care. Don't lose them in soapy water or store them where you might grab the blade accidentally. Be sure the blade has stopped moving before taking off the lid.

There are more than a dozen food processors on the market, and prices range from less than $100 to over $200 for home models. The discussion that follows is intended as a general guide to all processors; methods are similar for all models.

Basic Blades

Steel blade. Certainly the most versatile and frequently used blade, it chops, grates, minces, blends, purees, mixes and kneads. For the most part, the length of time the food is processed determines the consistency.
Slicing disc. Used for all slicing chores, the slicing disc can produce a julienne cut with a little maneuvering. All foods to be sliced are fed through the feed tube with the pusher. Foods must be cut into shapes to fit snugly into the feed tube.
Shredding disc. This disc produces shreds of food, though it looks like a grater. As with the slicing disc, all food to be shredded must be placed tightly in the feed tube and fed to the blade with the pusher. To produce long shreds, position the food horizontally in the feed tube.
Plastic blade. This is the least used blade, and some machines do not come with it. The plastic blade mixes soft foods such as mayonnaise, dressings, dips, omelettes, frostings and light batters. Use it to make egg salad, tuna salad and chopped liver; it produces a coarser texture than the steel blade does and does not create instant pâté.

Processor Techniques

Slicing raw meat with slicing disc. Use pusher to measure feed tube sized chunks of meat. Partially freeze the meat. With slicing disc in place, insert meat in feed tube, positioning meat so that it will be sliced against the grain. Exert firm pressure.
Mincing garlic with steel blade. Start the machine and drop peeled garlic through feed tube. Process 3 or 4 seconds.
Chopping onion with steel blade.

THE BLADE BOUTIQUE

Always peel and quarter onions; cut large onions into eighths. Never process more than 2 onions at a time. Drop onion into tube and turn top with quick on/off motions as fast as it takes to say on/off. Check consistency after three or four quick on/off turns.

Chopping hard vegetables with steel blade. Cut vegetables into 1-inch sized pieces and process with quick on/off turns.

Shredding cabbage with shredding disc. Cut cabbage into quarters and trim each quarter to fit in feed tube. Use medium pressure on pusher. Cabbage also can be sliced or chopped with the steel blade.

Slicing carrots and zucchini with slicing disc. Trim top and bottom of vegetables so they are flat. Using the pusher as a guide, cut the vegetables to the same height. Pack into feed tube as tightly as possible. Use firm pressure on pusher. To slice single carrot or zucchini: Place vegetable against right-hand side of feed tube so the motion of the blade keeps it upright. Vegetables may be positioned sideways in feed tube for rectangular slices.

Grating hard cheese with steel blade. Cut Parmesan or Romano into 1-inch cubes. With steel blade in place, turn on machine and drop cubes of cheese down tube at 2-second intervals. Process for 3 to

Food processors back row from left: Moulinex, Ronic, Waring, Cuisinart and Norelco. Front row from left: Omnichef, Hamilton Beach, General Electric and Farberware. Processors perform many cutting and slicing functions; many mix and knead doughs and grind meat too. Chefs are finding these machines indispensable.

Partially freeze salt pork or other meat before slicing.

To mince garlic, drop peeled cloves through feed tube.

To shred cabbage, cut into wedges to fit feed tube.

4 minutes until the cheese is powdery.

Julienne slicing with slicing disc. Trim zucchini, carrots, ham or cheese to fit sideways in the feed tube and slice. Remove all slices from machine. Keeping the pusher in place, pack the bottom of the feed tube with the slices perpendicular to the blade. Slice again, using moderate pressure.

Slicing mushrooms with slicing disc. Pack mushrooms sideways in feed tube as tightly as possible, keeping them horizontal to the slicing disc. Slice using light pressure.

Select perfect cuts for garnish; use rest in whatever recipe you are making.

French-cut green beans with slicing disc. Trim ends flat and cut beans to fit sideways into feed tube. Use moderate pressure to slice the beans.

To slice single zucchini, place it against side of feed tube.

To slice mushrooms, pack sideways in feed tube.

To French-cut green beans, fit them sideways in feed tube.

Minestrone

- ⅛ **pound salt pork, partially frozen**
- 1 **tablespoon olive oil**
- 1 **clove garlic, peeled**
- ¼ **cup fresh parsley (2 tablespoons chopped)**
- 1 **onion**
- 1 **leek**
- 2 **ribs celery**
- 2 **potatoes**
- 1 **small turnip**
- 1 **pound tomatoes**
- ¼ **small head cabbage**
- 1 **small zucchini**
- 2 **carrots**
- 2 **teaspoons basil**
- 1 **can (6 ounces) tomato paste**
- 7 **cups water**
- 3 **teaspoons salt**
- ½ **teaspoon pepper**
- ¾ **cup soup pasta**
- 1 **can (16 ounces) white beans**
  Dash tabasco (optional)
- 4 **1-inch cubes Parmesan cheese (½ cup grated)**

1. Using slicing disc, slice partially frozen salt pork. Put in a large pot with olive oil.
2. Using steel blade, separately process garlic, parsley, onion, leek and celery until chopped. Add them to the salt pork and olive oil and brown lightly.
3. Still using steel blade, separately process potatoes, turnip and tomatoes until coarsely chopped. Add to pot.
4. Using shredding disc, shred cabbage and add to pot.
5. Using slicing disc, slice zucchini and carrots. Add to pot, together with basil, tomato paste, water, salt and pepper. Simmer for about 1 hour.
6. Add pasta and beans to pot and cook for about 30 minutes longer. Taste and adjust seasoning. Add tabasco, if desired. Salt pork can be removed, if you wish.
7. Using steel blade, process Parmesan cheese until finely grated. Serve soup hot with grated Parmesan cheese.

Makes 8 to 10 servings

In our grandmothers' era, pots and pans — they are now called cookware — were strictly utilitarian. If Grandma was a city dweller, she probably bought her pots and pans in a department store where the selection was limited to cast iron and, later, aluminum. Otherwise, pots and pans of all descriptions were purchased haphazardly from traveling salesmen, pushcart vendors or mail order catalogues. Grandma "made do" with her pots and pans even when they became battered and lost their lids and handles.

But times have changed. Now that cooking is on the rise as a leisure time activity, we have begun to demand the same high quality, performance and good looks from cookware that we demand from sporting equipment, stereos and other gear. If you choose to spend long but enjoyable hours puttering in the kitchen, you'll want your pots and pans to be handsome, functional and durable. They should be easy to clean. Before you make an investment in high-quality cookware, consider the points we used in testing major brands.

Price: Even to buyers of the finest cookware, price is the first consideration. Be forewarned: Good cookware is never inexpensive and the steep prices of pots and pans, imports especially, can be shocking.

Use: The use a particular piece will get is something only you can determine and the frequency of use should certainly influence the price you are willing to pay.

Durability: Durability is a very important factor. Since there is no perfect material and since each has its drawbacks, check each piece of cookware for specific qualities: Will it chip? Discolor? Are the handles firmly riveted? Is it dishwasher safe? Can metal utensils be used without damaging the surface? Is the interior stain and scratch resistant? Does it tarnish?

Function: The architect Frank Lloyd Wright's dictum — form follows function — is also relevant to cookware. If the shape, material or design does not match the function, then that piece is neither useful nor well-designed. For example, if a saucepan has a short handle that

heats up quickly, or if the empty saucepan tilts on the burner, it is not functional.

The Best Cookware?

The answer to the question, "What is the best cookware?" is easy: there simply is no one best kind of cookware. There are over 20 brands on the market in a variety of materials and combinations, with new brands still arriving. With the possible exception of sterling silver (and silver pots are about as easy to find as 80 carat diamonds), copper generally is considered to be the best heat conductor — and efficient heat conduction is what stovetop cooking is all about. The heat conductivity and retention of all other metals are measured against copper. Aluminum, for which fantastic claims are made by manufacturers, conducts heat only 60 percent as efficiently as copper. Rolled steel, then enameled cast iron and, finally, stainless steel, the least conductive and slowest heating metal, round out the list in descending order of efficiency.

Stainless Steel

Certainly stainless steel is one of the most beautiful materials for cookware. No matter how you abuse stainless steel, it cleans like a dream and probably will outlive you. It will not chip, pit or rust and once washed, rubbing with a dry cloth brings out a rewarding shine. Most steel used for stainless cookware is called 18/8 which means it is 18 percent chromium, and 8 percent nickel and the balance is steel. The higher the nickel content, the better the cookware. Completely nonporous, stainless does not react with food acids, sulphurs or minerals, and will not harbor odors. Cooking at very high temperatures will cause a "heat tint" — a rainbow-colored swirl on the floor of the pan — but this is easily removed with any commercial stainless-steel cleaner.

To improve the heat conduction of stainless-steel cookware, manufacturers have added a "sandwich" bottom composed of either aluminum or copper bonded between two thinner steel layers. Sandwich bottoms greatly improve the heat conduction of the floor of pot; however, the sides and lids remain less efficient.

Three brands of stainless steel with sandwich bottoms stand above all others because of their higher nickel content. One brand, Alluminio Paderno, a professional quality cookware with an aluminum sandwich, is 18/10, or 2 percent higher in nickel content than American stainless. Made by an Italian firm, it is not widely distributed in the United States. Uginox, a French stainless-steel cookware, has large loop handles and a superb copper sandwich bottom. It is fabulous stainless cookware but we know of only one source, Bridge Kitchenware in New York, that carries Uginox. The third brand of superior stainless-steel cookware is Cuisinart.

Cuisinart

Several years ago, Cuisinart brought out a complete line of oven and stove top stainless-steel cookware. It has rapidly gained recognition and popularity because the flat aluminum sandwich bottom, set between two thin layers of steel, forms an extraordinarily efficient and responsive surface for sautéeing and frying. From the perfectly flat bottoms to the slightly domed lids, which sport polished wood, heat-resistant knobs, Cuisinart cookware exudes quality. Only such high quality could command the high price it fetches. The long steel handles, riveted with brass, are faced with glazed wood that is heat resistant up to 375°F. The pots are beautifully balanced and handles generally stay cool.

Cuisinart 4-Quart Sauté Pan

This is one of our favorite pans because it can be used both as a saucepan and as a skillet. Moreover, when there is a soup to be made, we reach for this saute pan because it holds a perfect simmer and the snug-sealing lid ensures minimal evaporation. The riveted wood handle makes lifting the filled pot an easy task. Invert the lid and it sits squarely on the kitchen counter, doubling as a spoon rest. Because the handle is wood, this pot and its cover must be washed by hand, but the stainless steel is so slick and highly polished that cleaning is never very hard. **To Use:** Wash with mild soap and hot water; dry thoroughly. Do not preheat this pan. When using it for sauteeing or frying, keep the food in the center, away from the slower heating zone

Cuisinart 4-quart sauté pan serves as saucepan or skillet.

around the bottom where aluminum ends and the single layer of stainless begins. Soak cooked-on food free with soap and hot water. If necessary, both inside and outside of pan may be scoured with fine steel wool. To restore high luster or remove head tint, use a commercial stainless cleaner, rinse well with hot water and rub dry with a soft towel. When dry, buff with a flannel cloth. *Approximate Retail Price: $50*

COOKTOP COLLECTION

Cuisinart 1 quart Double Boiler

The three pieces of this covered double boiler are priced separately and add up to a terrifically expensive pot! But it is the best double boiler on the market. Our reasons: the bottom of the boiler doubles as a 1½-quart saucepan with an aluminum sandwich bottom; the stainless-steel insert is a slow heat conductor and, as a result, the contents cook gently; and the insert is very wide, so the liquid can be stirred and removed easily. Further, the stainless steel will not react with highly acidic foods or egg yolks. The insert cleans beautifully and has no cracks or crevices in which egg yolks, for example, can collect. **To Use:** Wash with mild soap and hot water; dry thoroughly. Fill the boiler bottom with 1½ to 2 inches of water, which will heat the insert with the steam trapped between the two pans. Cover the bottom saucepan and bring the water to a boil. Then set the insert into the bottom and turn heat to very low. Always fill insert before placing it over bottom, or immediately upon setting it into place. This is an excellent utensil for one of the most classic and classy French sauces, Sauce Bearnaise.

Approximate Retail Price: $60

Sauce Bearnaise

- ¼ **cup white wine vinegar**
- ¼ **cup dry white wine or vermouth**
- 2 **tablespoons minced shallots**
- ½ **garlic clove, chopped**
- 2 **teaspoons dried tarragon, crushed**
- 3 **egg yolks**
- 6 **ounces unsalted butter, cut into tablespoons**
- **pinch salt and pepper**
- 2 **tablespoons fresh minced parsley**

1. In saucepan part of double boiler, combine the vinegar, wine, shallots, garlic and tarragon. Boil uncovered until the mixture reduces to 2 tablespoons.

2. Strain the mixture into a small cup. Press firmly on the solids in the strainer to extract all possible liquid. Discard solids.

3. Rinse the saucepan and fill it with 1½ to 2 inches of water. Cover and bring water to a boil.

4. Place the egg yolks in the insert, add the 2 tablespoons reduced liquid and turn heat to low.

5. Whisk until egg mixture turns pale.

6. Add 2 tablespoons of the butter and whisk until butter is absorbed. Add 2 additional tablespoons butter and whisk until absorbed. Continue whisking and add remaining butter, keeping the water in the saucepan at a low simmer. Check water occasionally.

7. When all butter is added, whisk until sauce is just hot. Add salt, pepper and parsley; stir well. Adjust seasoning to taste; serve immediately with meat, fish or vegetables.

Makes 4 servings

Boiler bottom used as saucepan.

Whisk eggs and butter in top.

Enameled Iron or Steel

Many cooks do not realize that the highly-colored porcelain-glazed pots and pans are actually made of glass baked over cast iron. Originally, vitreous enamel was used to make jewelry and decorative metal pottery. The origin is believed to be Byzantine and the process was used in Russia to make icons and jewelry during the 19th century.

In France, the process was called *cloisonné*.

The powdered glass used in the decorative arts fuses beautifully with cast iron at very high temperatures. The resulting surface is smooth, glassy, stain resistant and amazingly durable. Cast iron conducts heat relatively well, but heat-up is slow and not the best for quick sautéeing or browning. The enamel can chip and the close-grained cast iron can snap if dropped. The white porcelain enameled interiors may darken slightly from use with a metal whisk, but the dark color can be removed with a poultice of scouring powder and household bleach. Otherwise, you can sponge clean a porcelain-enameled pot and, unless the pot has wooden handles (some are removable), they are as dishwasher safe as any glassware.

Copco

The colorful Copco cast iron collection meets the basic needs of cooks with color-coordinated skillets, grills, omelette and crepe pans, sauté pans, casseroles and saucepans of various sizes. The line is intelligently and practically conceived with a durable high-quality enamel finish over cast iron bodies, and a ground iron plate on the bottom of each pan for added heat conduction and retention.

Copco cookware is a Danish import. Where wood is used with the cookware, it is polished teak, one of the hardest and most durable woods money can buy. The saucepans, especially, are reliable for cooking delicate sauces like Hollandaise or Béchamel, since they hold heat evenly and gently. Copco makes a good all-purpose skillet, called the chicken fryer, with an oven-proof, enameled cast iron handle and white interior. We do not, however, recommend this skillet for delicate sauté jobs like scallopine since heat conduction, while steady, tends to be slow. Four covered casseroles, in a range of sizes, are equally useful in the oven and on the stove. The handles on body and lid match at the sides but we find them difficult to handle once the pot is hot. The Copco omelette pan, unfortunately, has a short, tapered handle and a heavily weighted body, which make the pan difficult to grasp and turn and less than ideal for omelettes. What you're really paying for is the best quality enamel ware and great appearance.

Copco 5-Quart Covered Casserole

Here is a fine casserole with many cooktop uses, including soup, sauce and vegetable cookery. We do not recommend it for stews because the tapered form of the pot leaves a narrow floor without ample room for browning, nor does the white enamel promote browning. **To Use:** Wash with mild soap and hot water and dry thoroughly. Do not use abrasives such as steel wool on the porcelain. A nonabrasive sponge and dishwashing liquid will remove any cooked-on food. Both pots and lids without teak handles are dishwasher safe, although the cast iron plate will rust. If rusting occurs, clean with steel wool, dry, and oil lightly after each use. If staining occurs, prepare a bleach and scouring powder poultice, let sit overnight, and wash thoroughly.
Approximate Retail Price: $53

Copco 5-quart covered casserole.

Copco 3½-Quart Paella Pan

Paella, the glamorous one-pot Spanish dish, actually takes its name from the type of pan it's cooked in. The heavy iron-plate bottom of Copco's excellent paella pan keep the paella warm at a low, even temperature while diners are served. The pan is totally heat-proof, freeze-proof and dishwasher safe. The beauty of the pan, which comes in several colors, is that it makes as attractive a serving dish as cooking pot. **To Use:** Wash with mild soap and hot water and dry thoroughly. Paella pan may be used in the freezer, the oven and on the stovetop. Use steel wool only on ground-iron bottom if rust occurs. The open shape is great for serving pasta or spaghetti: just cook your sauce, reheat it in the paella pan and add the pasta. Toss, and *ecco!*
Approximate Retail Price: $45

Copco 3½-quart paella pan can be used on top of stove or in oven.

COOKTOP COLLECTION

Paella Valenciana

- ½ **pound fresh clams, scrubbed clean**
- ½ **pound fresh mussels, scrubbed clean**
- **2-pound frying chicken, cut into serving pieces**
- **1 cup all-purpose flour**
- ¼ **cup Spanish olive oil**
- ½ **pound shrimp**
- **2 2-ounce thawed frozen lobster tails**
- ½ **pound chorizo (Spanish sausage), cut into 1-inch pieces**
- ½ **pound ham, cubed**
- **2 cloves garlic, minced**
- **1 medium onion, peeled and chopped fine**
- **1 medium red pepper, seeded and cut into strips**
- **1 tomato, peeled, seeded and chopped**
- **3 cups raw rice**
- 6½ **cups cold water**
- ¼ **teaspoon saffron**
- ½ **pound green beans, cut into ½-inch lengths**
- **3 teaspoons salt**
- **Freshly ground black pepper to taste**
- **Parsley sprigs and lemon wedges for garnish**

1. Soak clams and mussels 30 minutes in cold water. Check to be sure all sand is removed from shells. Pull hairy beard free from mussels. Drain well and refrigerate.
2. Dry chicken carefully, then toss in flour. Heat oil in the paella pan and cook chicken, turning from time to time until lightly browned. Do not crowd chicken pieces; cook in 2 batches if necessary. Remove chicken and set aside.
3. Over medium heat, place shrimp and lobster in pan and stir-fry briefly just until the shells turn bright red. Remove and set aside.
4. Place sausage in pan, cook until most of the fat is rendered and sausage is lightly browned; remove and set aside. Preheat oven to 400°F.
5. Put ham, garlic, onion, pepper and tomato in pan and cook over medium heat, scraping the bottom with a wooden spatula to loosen the cooked-on food. Liquid will slowly evaporate and thicken.
6. Stir in rice, water and saffron. Turn heat to high and bring just to a boil, stirring. Place chicken and sausage over the rice, cover pan with foil and bake 20 minutes in the preheated oven.
7. Remove pan from oven, open foil and add clams and mussels hinged side down. Re-cover and bake 10 minutes.
8. Take pan from oven, open foil and add shrimp and lobster. Cover and bake 15 minutes longer.
9. Meanwhile, bring 3 quarts of salted water to a rolling boil. Add green beans and cook 8 minutes. Drain and run beans with cold water. Drain again.
10. When rice and seafood have cooked, stir well, season with salt and pepper. Add green beans. Garnish with parsley and lemon wedges.

Makes 8 servings

Le Creuset

This French import is perhaps the best-known name in enameled cookware. Le Creuset has been around for years and is consistently well-designed. Its quality is excellent, featuring great durability, and it comes in a huge variety of shapes and sizes, with a pot or pan for almost every kitchen need. The enamel finish guarantees reaction-free cooking and the brushed iron bases provide adequate heat conduction and superb retention.

Le Creuset has answered the problems posed by browning in some glazed enamel pans by designing skillets with a black, rough enamel interior finish. This black finish is chip resistant, almost nonstick and does improve heat conduction and browning substantially.

We feel that the Le Creuset cas-seroles with enameled cast iron handles are more versatile and functional than the saucepans with glazed wood handles. The wood, which begins almost at the edge of the pot, always burns, and the glaze eventually erodes. Furthermore, the all-enamel saucepans and cookware are freezer safe and ovenproof and clean beautifully in the dishwasher as well.

Le Creuset 10¼-Inch Oval Casserole

A marvelous pot for simmering, roasting or braising, the oval casserole provides a perfect snug fit for a small chicken, a veal or pork roast or a stew. You'll want to brown meat in another skillet, though. The lid has a small hole that allows some of the excess steam to escape and the oval dome promotes self-basting. We adore the little

To prevent braised foods from steaming, line Le Creuset casserole with parchment paper and set lid slightly ajar.

enameled cauliflower handles that are easy to grasp, won't burn like wood, and also make this casserole an unusual-shaped container for a French pâté. **To Use:** The lid creates quite a firm seal, so to prevent braised foods from steaming, we recommend that a sheet of kitchen parchment be cut into an oval, using the lid as a guide, and placed on the food in the casserole. Then the lid can be set slightly ajar, so that steam will escape. Never fear for the liquid, as the ground cast iron bottom keeps it at a perfect simmer. Clean the pan with mild soap and hot water; dry thoroughly. Both pot and lid are dishwasher safe. Use fine steel wool to take off any rust on the bottom. *Approximate Retail Price: $29.95*

Le Creuset Black Enamel Grills

A sensational idea — meat and fish grills designed especially for use on top of the stove. The principle is searing, an alternative to broiling and one the French use frequently. While other manufacturers make skillets with a grilled bottom, these grills are patterned after those used in French bistros. The meat grill has the characteristic grill markings, which elevate the meat above the fat and also give a decorative design. The fish grill is flat — a rectangular pan with a raised fish "eye" and "fin" pattern and no other markings. The removable, clip-in metal handles should be protected with a pot holder even though they take a long time to heat up.

If we could have but one, it would be the meat grill, which also grills fish. It cleans beautifully and the black, nonstick, slick surface does not absorb food odors. This grill, by the way, can double as a small broiler pan with excellent results. **To Use:** Wash with mild soap and hot water; dry thoroughly. Season the grill by placing it on top of a burner over medium heat for 5 min-

Le Creuset meat and fish grills are used on top of the stove.

utes; while hot, brush the grill with vegetable oil and turn heat to high until oil smokes; then turn heat off and cool grill completely. Wipe off excess oil. Once seasoned, preheat grill for best results, brushing lightly with oil or clarified butter before cooking. Cool grill before washing and remove cooked-on foods with a nonabrasive pad. *Approximate Retail Price: $19.95 (meat grill); $19.95 (fish grill)*

Grilled Rainbow Trout

2 small rainbow trout, cleaned, but with head and tail
Flour for coating (optional)
¼ cup clarified butter or olive oil
2 teaspoons lemon juice
Salt and pepper to taste
Parsley sprigs and lemon slices for garnish

1. Measure fish at thickest part. Plan to cook 10 minutes per inch.
2. Dust fish with flour, if desired, then dip into melted butter or oil. Sprinkle lemon juice on each side and slash in 3 places per side with a sharp knife, to aid heat penetration.
3. Preheat grill. Brush with butter or oil. Add fish and as soon as fish is seared, loosen with a spatula. Cook over medium high heat for half the total time indicated, then turn. Sear, then loosen and cook until done. Skin should be browned and crisp.
4. Transfer fish to a platter or dinner plate. Sprinkle with salt and pepper. Garnish with parsley and lemon slices. Serve with melted butter or with Bearnaise or Hollandaise Sauce. *Makes 1 or 2 servings*

COOKTOP COLLECTION

Le Creuset Chicken Fryer

"Chicken fryer" does not adequately describe the squatty shape of this pot, which has pouring lips on both sides, a short stubby handle and a bowler hat lid. Obviously, it is meant for sauté and frying and the high sides are intended to catch spatter. The black interior surface does promote browning and the chicken fryer is not limited to chicken. For stews, this is the ideal vessel — a good browning surface combined with an admirably tight lid. The handle and opposing enameled protrusion give solid support for lifting the pot into and out of the oven. **To Use:** Wash with mild soap and hot water and dry thoroughly. Both pot and lid are dishwasher safe. If rust forms on the iron bottom, remove with fine steel wool. The black enamel interior should be soaked clean and cooked-on food removed with mild soap and a nonabrasive pad. We have found another use for the 4-quart casserole base: It works

Depth of Le Creuset fryer prevents oil from spattering.

perfectly as a *bain-marie* or water bath pan, neatly cradling a 5- to 6-cup souffle dish with enough space left for the water to come halfway up the side of the dish. No other pan has ever worked quite so well as a *bain-marie*.
Approximate Retail Price: $39.95

Doufeu Oven

Braising has always been a versatile and economical cooking method. The word "braise" derives from the French for "hot coals." Originally, braised foods were cooked in a heavy pot over the coals; additional hot coals were placed on top of the pot, allowing long gentle cooking to take place. The doufeu is a pot made of enameled cast iron and designed and manufactured in France by Cousances to recreate the traditional way of cooking. But instead of hot coals, one places ice cubes in the doufeu's concave lid while the pot simmers on the stove. The ice helps steam to collect on the underside of the lid and drop back into the pot to baste the meat. The weight and thickness of the pot's cast iron construction promote even heating and retention; the tight-fitting lid minimizes evaporation. **To Use:** Brown meat or poultry in the doufeu. Add a small amount of liquid and the seasonings. Place lid filled with ice on casserole. Simmer over low heat on top of stove.
Approximate Retail Price: $59.95

Lid of Le Creuset doufeu pot is indented to hold ice cubes.

Dansk

Dansk makes extremely beautiful cookware and table accessories that have been popular forever, or so it seems. Almost every bride gets a lightweight Dansk casserole for a wedding present. Well, these pots really are handsome, but they're usually set aside in favor of sturdier equipment, once a cook gains experience. The four-pronged lid handle is hard to grasp with a pot holder. The lids do not fit properly; the lid on our Dansk casserole did a rhumba on the pot as we carried it across the room! The new "radiant heat" ground-iron bottom does help the previously dismal heat conduction and retention. But, the difference between the thick bottom and the thin sides makes cooking uneven.

Dansk Købenstyle 4-Quart Casserole

The classic Dansk enameled-steel casserole is available in a rainbow of colors. This pot goes from oven to table, then straight into the dishwasher. It cleans easily, will not retain odors and is stain-resistant. However, these casseroles chip easily and have limited stovetop uses. And you should be very careful about lifting the lid while the handle is hot. **To Use:** No seasoning is necessary. Cleanup is easy: soap and water or the dishwasher. Avoid using abrasive scrub pads on the enamel surfaces. Remove rust on the iron bottom with fine steel wool.
Approximate Retail Price: $36.95

Dansk 4-quart casserole.

French Steel

You have probably seen French steel cookware and wondered why it comes buttered in machine oil and cloaked in a plain brown wrapper. There are several reasons. First, French steel is inexpensive, so no extraneous costs go into packaging. Secondly, the coating of oil or lacquer prevents rusting. The oil or lacquer must be removed before this cookware can be seasoned and used. Getting rolled French steel cookware into usable shape may take several hours, but you will be rewarded by years of use. These inexpensive pans, if treated with respect, will last and last. Just ask any restaurateur whether his chefs like steel pans; the answer will be a resounding, "yes."

The medium-gauge steel is an excellent heat conductor; so standard French steel cookware includes large and small crepe pans, omelette pans, skillets of every description and specialized sauté pans.

French steel must be seasoned in the oven or on top of the stove. It should always be wiped and never washed because washing removes the seasoning. Cold liquids should never be poured into a hot French steel pan, nor should it be plunged into cold liquid while hot — it could deform or warp. If left untreated, these pans will rust, attracting greasy dirt that must be removed by washing. Then the pan must be re-seasoned; so handle with care.

French Steel 12¼-Inch Oval Skillet

Here is a great pan for browning roasts, fish, chicken or chops. Its long narrow shape is extremely convenient for pan frying a steak. The handle is long and curved but heats up rapidly; so use a pot holder. **To Use:** Read the manufacturer's instructions for removal of lacquer or machine oil. Scrub vigorously with a fine steel wool pad. Rinse in hot water and dry thoroughly. Rub with peanut or salad oil inside and out. Preheat oven to 500°F. Place skillet into oven, bake 30 minutes. Turn heat off and let skillet cool completely in the turned off oven with the door closed. When cool, the skillet is seasoned and ready to use. To season on top of stove, wash and oil as above. Place oiled pan on burner and heat gradually until the interior turns black.

French steel skillet is great for browning and pan frying.

This seasoning should be repeated after each use until the pan no longer loses its protective coating.
Approximate Retail Price: $15

Aluminum

Besides being attractive, aluminum is an excellent heat conductor, relatively lightweight, and was, until recently, inexpensive. Then along came the nonstick aluminum surface that wouldn't crack, chip or scratch and the price of aluminum cookware soared.

Aluminum cookware is made by stamping, pressing or casting. Cast cookware may have handles that are integral to the pot, or its handles may be of a different material and separately attached. The body of aluminum cookware is usually seamless. The gauge or thickness determines efficiency. The thicker and heavier the pot, the more even the cooking. But, the thicker the gauge, the more expensive the pot. Finished aluminum may be polished, brushed or buffed and each finish determines both the maintenance of the pot and the types of food that can be cooked in it.

The beauties of aluminum include fine heat conduction in the bottom, sides and across the cover of a pot. Food that is surrounded by even heat naturally cooks more evenly. Untreated aluminum, however, can discolor and pit when brought into contact with minerals in water and foods. The bright interior will inevitably turn a dull grey after a few months of use. High acid foods and those containing sulphur will discolor or absorb a metallic taste from interacting with the untreated aluminum. You should never cook spaghetti sauce, for example, in an untreated aluminum pot.

If pots become grey, simply boil with an acid solution — used lemon halves, vinegar or cream of tartar and water — then scour with fine steel wool. A bright surface should quickly reappear.

Leyse Aluminum

Leyse Aluminum Company makes a vast line of brushed aluminum cookware that is light- to medium-gauge, professional quality and still relatively inexpensive. Generally, this cookware offers good value and is ideal for the beginning or occasional cook who wishes to own reliable, good quality pots and pans without an enormous investment. Leyse makes a variety of saucepans in sizes ranging from ½ to 10 quarts, several skillets, omelette pans and double boilers. However, making stockpots and steamers is Leyse's forté.

Leyse manufactures 15 different stockpots, in sizes beginning at 8½ quarts and expanding to 80 quarts. Each has loop handles with aluminum rivets solidly placed. Lids do not fit snugly but they fit well enough for the purpose and the price.

Leyse Asparagus Steamer

Steaming is a healthy way to cook any vegetable, especially asparagus. This steamer is made of lightweight aluminum and holds approximately 2 pounds of asparagus. There is a basket insert designed to rest on the sides of the steamer for easy removal, but, unfortunately, no hook to pull the basket from the hot pot is included. The steamer eliminates the need to peel asparagus by cooking the thick stalks at a faster rate than the thinner tips. Even for use only at peak asparagus season — about 2 months each year — it makes a great low-priced gift for the asparagus aficionado. **To Use:** Wash with mild soap and hot water and dry thoroughly. Close vent. Fill bottom section with 1 inch of cold water. Prepare asparagus. Fill basket and insert. Cover and bring water to a boil. Open vent and cook.
Approximate Retail Price: $16

Leyse asparagus steamer.

Steamed Asparagus

**2 pounds fresh, thick
    asparagus
    Lemon to garnish
    Hollandaise, Maltaise or
    Bearnaise Sauce
    (optional)**

1. Buy uniformly large stalks with tightly closed buds. Cut or break off the tough bottoms. If desired, peel back two inches of fibrous end material with a sharp knife. Rinse well.
2. Tie asparagus into a bundle but leave one fat stalk free. Place into insert, cover and steam until barely tender, about 10 to 12 minutes. Test the loose stalk with the point of a sharp knife. If it pierces easily in the thickest part, asparagus is cooked.
3. Remove from steamer with tongs. Serve immediately, garnished with lemon, or with Hollandaise, Maltaise or Bearnaise Sauce.

Makes 4 to 6 servings

Leyse 20-Quart Stockpot

This is a basic stockpot and not all as large as it sounds. Suitable for stocks, soups or large quantities of spaghetti, it is also handy for lobster boils or shore dinners. The idea is to fill this pot all the way up, make a large quantity of stock at one time, and then decant and freeze the stock in convenient jars for use as you need it. This stockpot will cook stock very evenly and if the lid is left squarely on the pot, evaporation will be minimal. Open the lid away from you to avoid steam burns. This size pot cooks 5 to 15 quarts of liquid effortlessly and is still small enough to be stored in an apartment kitchen. The inside of the pot will discolor with use, and the lid may also discolor slightly. **To Use:** Wash with mild soap and hot water; dry thoroughly. This pot does not require seasoning. We do not advise cooking less than 3 quarts of liquid in this pot. To remove cooked-on food, soak in hot water and mild soap; then scour with a fine steel wool pad.
Approximate Retail Price: $36

Leyse 20-quart stockpot.

Brown Beef Stock

5 pounds beef bones
2 pounds veal bones
3 pounds beef, such as shank, neck or brisket
4 medium carrots, peeled
3 leeks, washed
1 whole onion, peeled and stuck with 3 cloves
1 unpeeled onion, halved
2 garlic cloves, unpeeled
1 bay leaf
8 sprigs parsley
10 black peppercorns

1. Place bones and meat on broiler tray and broil about 3 inches from flame about 20 minutes, turning meat until well browned.
2. Place meat and bones in stockpot. Cover with cold water by at least 2 inches (about 10 to 12 quarts). Cover and bring water to a gentle boil. Remove scum. Add the vegetables and remaining ingredients, cover and simmer gently 5 to 6 hours. Do not boil.
3. Strain stock and cool uncovered. Skim fat from the top or refrigerate the stock so the fat can be removed when solidified.
4. Stock is ready to use as a base for soups or brown sauces such as Madere. Add salt or pepper as desired. Refrigerate up to 3 days or freeze.
Makes about 8 quarts

Commercial Aluminum

The Commercial Aluminum Company makes two types of aluminum cookware that are widely used in professional kitchens. One is a medium-gauge, plain brushed aluminum line and the other is a heavier, non-reactive cookware known as Calphalon. The brushed aluminum cookware is bright, untreated, heavier than Leyse and accordingly more expensive. The pots have a feel of quality but the selection is limited to a few sizes of stockpots, colanders and omelette pans and a steamer, since the company concentrates on marketing Calphalon.

Commercial Aluminum 2-Gallon Stockpot

This versatile brushed aluminum pot with two firmly riveted loop handles is large enough for stews, soups and pasta for 6, yet is still small enough to fit into the oven. Unfortunately, it is not pretty enough to bring to the table, but it stores easily in a normal kitchen cabinet. The handles are large enough to grasp easily with pot-holdered hands and the lid strap also allows a firm grasp. **To Use:** Wash with mild soap and hot water and dry thoroughly. This stockpot does not require seasoning.
Approximate Retail Price: $26

Commercial Aluminum stockpot.

COOKTOP COLLECTION

Calphalon

Calphalon, a satin-finished, treated aluminum, is all the rage today. It will not chip, flake or rust and it is impervious to chemical reactions and metal utensils. It is heavy-gauge cookware with even heat conduction and is available in a sizes, including sauté pans, sauce-pans, stockpots and casseroles of every description. The handles, wide range of shapes, forms and made of tin-coated iron, are riveted to the bodies.

Commercial Aluminum does not make lids for Calphalon pans from the special non-reactive material. Instead, they top their chic black pots with plain old average-weight commercial aluminum strap-handled lids. We find it curious that this cookware, which is so expensive, should be topped with lightweight untreated lids.

In testing various Calphalon pans, we found that the bodies of certain sauté pans are lighter than others and that some tend to tip in the direction of the handle, which is actually heavier than the pan. Calphalon is almost as expensive as heavy copper and, although it has many endearing qualities, we think it is overpriced.

Calphalon 8-Inch Omelette Pan

In theory, this should be the perfect omelette pan, with gently sloping sides, fine heat conduction and some nonstick properties. However, in three tests our omelette stuck. The same omelette, however, did not stick to two other pans. The handle of this pan is very short. When we placed a handle mitt on it, the edges of the mitt singed over medium heat. Unlike larger Calphalon omelette pans, this one sits firmly on the burner. We tried to season the pan to see if that would alleviate the sticking problem but it did not. The pan must have had a few hot spots. **To Use:** Wash with mild soap and hot water and dry thoroughly. Pan does not require seasoning and is not dishwasher safe. Cool before washing.
Approximate Retail Price: $18

Calphalon 8-inch omelette pan.

Strawberry Jam Omelette

2 large eggs
1 teaspoon mayonnaise
    Pinch salt
2 teaspoons butter
2 heaping tablespoons
    strawberry jam
    Parsley for garnish (optional)

Swirl eggs over heat.

Place jam in center.

1. Beat eggs with mayonnaise and salt in a small bowl. Place dinner plate and the jam on hand at the stove.
2. Heat butter in omelette pan over medium heat until the foam subsides, but do not permit butter to brown. Pour eggs into the pan and swirl vigorously so that eggs begin to scramble slightly in the center and cook all over. The omelette will come together in one piece and should slide freely in the pan. Do *not* stir with a fork.
3. When omelette slides freely, but while eggs are still moist, place jam in center.
4. Fold the third of the omelette nearest you into the center, leaving a half moon of exposed pan bottom near the handle. Grasp the handle from underneath so that your palm is facing up. Slide the mixture to the edge of the pan on the side opposite the handle and ease it gently onto the plate, turning the pan over so that the omelette folds neatly in three as it moves onto the plate. Garnish with more jam or parsley. *Makes 1 serving*

Fold a third into center; flip omelette onto plate.

**Calphalon Half-Quart
Butter Warmer**

This is a cute little saucepan for making or warming clarified butter and for myriad other "little" tasks like melting jam, heating soup for one, warming a glass of milk or even flaming half a cup of cognac. **To Use:** Wash with mild soap and hot water; dry thoroughly. Take care pan does not tip over on burner when filled as it is very small and not well weighted. The handle heats up very quickly, so use a mitt. *Approximate Retail Price: $12.50*

Butter warmer is excellent for making clarified butter.

Clarified Butter

½ pound unsalted butter

1. Cut butter into chunks and place in saucepan.
2. Place over medium heat and melt but *do not stir.*
3. When butter is melted, turn off heat and let stand 5 minutes. Use a butter separator or skim off white foam and carefully pour out the clear yellow liquid and transfer it to a jar. Discard any milky residue left in the bottom of the pan.
4. Store in refrigerator. Clarified butter keeps indefinitely and is always useful for sautéeing or cooking meats and fish at high temperatures because the butter does not burn once the milk solids are removed.

Makes ¾ cup clarified butter

Firmalon

A new line of black, satin-finish, treated aluminum cookware, Firmalon, comes from Gourmet Limited. For our money, Firmalon is the new heavy-gauge aluminum star. This cookware, like the Cuisinart line of stainless steel, simply exudes quality. It is well designed both aesthetically and functionally. It is extremely heavy and thick. The nonstick, non-reactive coating is bonded with the metal so that this cookware will not chip, scratch or rust. Handle and pan are made in one piece and molded so that the handle sits high on the side, providing excellent balance. The handles are long and made of the same Firmalon material but rounded out with walnut. While the Firmalon will conduct the heat up the handle, the wood gives superb insulation. In addition, turning and maneuvering a pot with a long handle allows for a two-handed grip, which, any tennis player will tell you, is very steady indeed. The lids are made of untreated cast aluminum, but they are almost the same thickness as the body of the pot. When inverted, the lids sit flat on the counter. Lids fit inside the pot and the seal is very tight.

We feel the quality and performance of this cookware well command its price. When we made Crème Pâtissière, the basic French pastry cream, the Firmalon saucepan thickened the sauce quickly and evenly. Normally Crème Pâtissière takes 30 minutes or longer, but the Firmalon saucepan shortened the cooking time to 15 minutes.

Firmalon 1-Quart Saucepan

A kitchen basic is the only way to describe this superb saucepan. The cooking is so even and so smooth that it seems to happen all by itself. The treated surface, which is non-reactive, can be used safely with metal utensils. **To Use:** Wash with mild soap and hot water; dry thoroughly. Preheat pan over low heat about five minutes, then wipe pan inside and out with an oiled paper towel. Remove excess oil. After each washing, it is a good idea to wipe the walnut handles with a paper towel saturated with mineral oil to retain a smooth finish. Firmalon pans are not dishwasher safe. *Approximate Retail Price: $36*

Firmalon saucepan cooks Crème Pâtissière smoothly – a superb pan!

Crème Pâtissière

1 cup milk
1 cup half and half
5 egg yolks
⅔ cup sugar
½ cup flour
1 tablespoon Grand Marnier or other liqueur
1 teaspoon vanilla

1. Heat milk and half and half to lukewarm. Set aside.
2. Place yolks into saucepan and turn heat to low. Add sugar gradually, whisking continuously. Continue whisking about 3 to 4 minutes until the mixture thickens slightly. Add flour all at once, stir well and continue stirring to cook flour about 3 minutes longer.
3. Add milk mixture to egg yolk mixture, stirring until absorbed; then increase heat to medium and, stirring constantly, bring mixture just to the boil. It will be very thick with a pudding-like consistency. Whisk vigorously if any lumps form.
4. Whisk in the liqueur and vanilla. Remove to a clean bowl and cover tightly with plastic wrap. Cool to room temperature, then refrigerate. It will thicken slightly when refrigerated. Use to fill fruit tarts, cakes, eclairs or as a base for a sweet soufflé. *Makes about 2½ cups*

Copper

Silver aside, copper is the best metal for stove top cooking and once you have prepared veal scaloppine in a heavy copper sauteuse, you will know why.

Copper comes in many gauges. The lightest weights are used mainly for serving or presentation. Heavy-weight copper is used for serious cooking and no accomplished cook would be without it. Copper forms oxide in contact with air and oxides are slightly toxic and capable of discoloring food. So copper pots are always lined. Usually the lining is tin, which is easy to

use as a coating material since it can be brushed or poured into the pan and is compatible with most acidic foods. Recently, aluminum has been used to line copper; stainless steel also makes copper durable and in rare cases silver plate has been used. We can think of only one copper pan that remains unlined — a medium-gauge copper saucepan used exclusively to make sugar syrups. To keep copper bright, manufacturers have taken to glazing it with lacquer. It is important to remove the lacquer before the pan is subjected to heat, or a permanently spotted utensil can result. Lacquer is more frequently found on lightweight presentation

pans than on the heavy-duty equipment.

Tin is not very durable and the expense and trouble of retinning is one that a copper owner must face. Retinning should be done when the tin has worn so thin that the copper shows through. Do not mistake the darkened color tin assumes for a need to re-tin. With very heavy use, pots may need to be re-tinned as frequently as every 2 years, but this is rare. Tin linings do scratch and care must be taken with metal utensils used in a very hot skillet.

Stainless-steel lined copper is the most durable cookware and one of the most expensive. Stainless, as you know, is completely neutral and will not change the flavor of food or discolor it. It cleans beautifully and need never be replaced. However, stainless-steel linings slow down the conduction time and the copper's sensitivity to heat is largely lost. Also, we find that stainless-steel lined pans seem to be less copper and more steel.

The ultimate copper cookware is lined with silver plate. It is incredibly beautiful. It also is extremely durable and exciting to use, being supremely responsive to heat. Of course, it is lovely enough to bring to the table. Unfortunately, it is beyond the price range of most cooks and most normal people!

French Hammered Copper Evasee or Fait-tout

Fait-tout means "do-everything" and this tin-lined, slant-sided saucepan from BIA Cordon Bleu is an all-purpose pan indeed. A truly beautiful piece of equipment, in a shape used by French restaurants for concentrating or reducing sauces, this saucepan comes in various sizes and also in plain, heavy unhammered copper. The 2¼-quart capacity is perfect for making sauces because the wide top and narrow bottom promote evaporation. The handle, made of unglazed iron, is curved and very long so that two hands can be used to maneuver the pan. At first, hammered French copper may seem heavy, but it is surprising how quickly you become accustomed to its heft. **To Use:** Wash with mild soap and hot water and dry thoroughly. Never pre-heat a copper pan; it is not necessary. Never place an empty tin-lined copper pan over direct heat, as tin may bubble or crawl. Use on medium or low flame and heat gradually. For use on electric stoves, begin on low heat and increase temperature gradually. Do not use abrasives on tin lining. Clean with a nonabrasive sponge and mild soap.

Approximate Retail Price: $60

Hammered copper "fait-tout" is an all-purpose pan.

Sauce Madère

¼ **cup clarified butter**
½ **cup finely diced vegetables:**
     carrot, onion and celery
¼ **cup finely diced ham or beef**
3 **tablespoons flour**
4 **cups hot brown beef stock**
1 **medium tomato, peeled and**
     chopped
1 **large sprig parsley**
½ **cup Madeira**
     Salt and pepper to taste
3 **tablespoons butter, for**
     finishing sauce

1. Melt clarified butter in saucepan and heat until hot, but not bubbling. Add carrot, onion, celery and ham and cook over medium heat until brown.
2. Sprinkle vegetables with flour. Stirring constantly, cook until flour is browned and sticks to the pan bottom.
3. Turn off heat. Gradually ladle the hot stock into the vegetable mixture and whisk vigorously. Continue adding hot liquid and whisking until all liquid has been absorbed. Add tomato and parsley; stir and return saucepan to medium heat.
4. Bring to a simmer, then set pan slightly off center on the burner. Regulate heat to simmer sauce gently. From this point until the sauce is finished, do not stir. As sauce cooks, lift off the skin which forms on the surface. Simmer sauce 2 to 2½ hours or until reduced to 2½ to 3 cups. The consistency should be like heavy cream.
5. Remove sauce from heat. Strain sauce into a small saucepan, pressing vegetables to extract all liquid.
6. Sauce should measure 1½ to 2 cups strained. Set aside. Place Madeira in a small saucepan and reduce to ¼ cup over medium heat. Add reduced Madeira to brown sauce and cover with plastic wrap. Set aside until ready to serve.
7. Just before serving, reheat sauce and correct seasoning with salt and pepper to taste. Over low heat, whisk in additional butter. Adjust seasoning once again, if necessary. Serve immediately on beef or veal.

Makes 4 to 6 servings

COOKTOP COLLECTION

Cohr

At the time of the French Revolution, the aristocrats covered up their gilt furniture with white paint. Comes the modern revolution, we had better wrap up these fabulous silver lined pans in newspapers and stow them away in cardboard boxes! They are so beautiful, so extravagant and so aristocratic.

It is difficult to imagine that anyone would buy a whole set of silver-lined copper, but if you come into a fortune, head for the Cohr. Made by Danish Silversmiths, these pots were marketed several years ago by Georg Jensen with different handles. Today, the stainless-steel handles are beautifully wrought, stay cool and are long and very easy to grasp. There is a sublime, handcrafted look about these pots. They are surprisingly heavy, although not as heavy as hammered French copper. The lids too, are lined with silver and topped, with a small stainless-steel strap handle, which is actually smaller than it might be for easy handling, but quite in proportion from the standpoint of design.

Of course, you could never make eggs in a silver lined saucepan because they would turn grey. Nor is silver appropriate for any sauté which is deglazed with wine or vinegar — besides acquiring a metallic taste, wine or vinegar will pit the silver. For cooking, silver is a better conductor of heat than copper and the combination of the two is cook's heaven. Silver is extremely durable, although it scratches.

The way to justify the price of this cookware (if it is possible to justify) is to use it at table as well as in the kitchen. The pots double perfectly as presentation pans.

Cohr Butter Warmer

A little gem of a pot, this is a lidless, heavy copper pan with a pouring spout. We would not limit it to warming butter and would parade it as proudly as any silver sauceboat, antique or otherwise. It can go from low flame directly to the table, short-circuiting the warming-up-the-sauceboat routine (or worse, forgetting to warm up the sauceboat). The superior heat retentiveness of the copper/silver marriage will keep the Cohr warmer at an even temperature tableside. **To Use:** Wash with mild soap and hot water; dry thoroughly. Clean interiors with non-abrasive silver polish; then wash with mild soap and water and dry. Cohr includes a special sponge for cleaning. Do not place these pans on the heat while empty.

Approximate Retail Price: $36

Cohr silver-lined butter warmer.

Cohr 8-Inch Sauté Pan with Lid

What pleasure we derived from using this small saucepan to heat up a lobster bisque. It responded beautifully to the lowest flame. And what glamour! But it has serious uses, too. It is designed for high heat cooking and that's where it excels. The silver is specially bonded to the copper and follows the heat expansion perfectly. In addition to this size, Cohr makes a 10- and a 10¾-inch skillet, as well as a series of saucepans, several round gratins and a fondue pot that positively makes us drool. **To Use:** Follow directions for butter warmer above. Store these pots in the flannel bags in which they are packaged.

Approximate Retail Price: $78 (pan); $28 (lid)

Cohr silver-lined copper sauté pan responds to the lowest flame.

Copper Double Boiler

This is one of the most beautiful pieces of cookware ever to grace any kitchen stove or shelf. Unfortunately, the Korean-made double boiler's looks surpass its performance. It may be heresy, but we feel that the brass handles are too short and too skinny to grasp firmly when lifting and turning the heavy porcelain insert. What's more, the handles, both of them, get very hot. The insert conducts heat evenly, but slowly, and is impossible to cool quickly if your Hollandaise is curdling. The porcelain insert is narrow and deep; we found it difficult to stir in, since there is not a great deal of space. The boiler bottom does not double as a saucepan; so remember when purchasing this double boiler that it is for one and only one use. **To Use:** Fill bottom pot with 1½ inches cold water. Cover and bring to a boil. Water must not touch the insert. Place insert into bottom, place ingredients into insert and turn heat to low. Water must simmer to produce sufficient steam to heat the insert. To clean, allow insert to cool to room temperature. Wash with soap and water. Do not use abrasives on the outside of the boiler or the lid as they may cause scratches.
Approximate Retail Price: $48

Copper double boiler.

Lemon Curd

 5 egg yolks
 ½ cup sugar
 ½ cup fresh lemon juice
 2 teaspoons grated lemon rind
 5 tablespoons unsalted butter

1. Fill bottom of boiler with water. Cover and bring to a simmer.
2. Combine egg yolks and sugar in the insert, place onto boiler bottom and whisk until yolks are pale. Add lemon juice and rind. Change to a wooden spoon and stir, adding butter bit by bit and cooking until butter has melted. Check water from time to time to ensure that it does not boil.
3. Remove from heat and cool lemon curd, stirring until thick enough to coat a spoon. Remove to a clean dish and dot the top with small pieces of butter to prevent a skin from forming. Cool; then refrigerate until firm. When firm, serve spread on hot tea bread, or use as a base for lemon cream pie or as a filling for cake or sponge roll. *Makes about 1 to 1½ cups lemon curd*

Cobre

Cobre's tin-lined copperware includes a number of casseroles and frying pans, a colander, beating bowls, tea kettle and a champagne cooler. The last few items on the list give a pretty clear idea of what Cobre is all about — serving and decorative pieces rather than serious cookware. Both pots and lids are light-gauge copper with short, brassy handles. Use this cookware for finishing, serving, and over low heat only.

Cobre 2-Quart Casserole

This beautiful little pot will hold a casserole for two or a small portion of vegetables or soup. Use it over low heat or place it on a brazier for finishing off a sauce at table. Watch the intensity of the flame, however, as the copper is thin and lined with tin. **To Use:** Wash with mild soap and hot water; dry thoroughly. Cool to room temperature before cleaning. Do not use abrasives or steel wool on the smooth exterior.
Approximate Retail Price: $40

Cobre 2-quart copper casserole.

Beef Ragoût

1 pound lean beef, cut into
    1-inch cubes
½ cup flour
1 teaspoon salt
½ teaspoon pepper
1 tablespoon butter
1 tablespoon oil
1 clove garlic, minced
1 onion, chopped
1 can (16 ounces) tomatoes,
    drained and cut up, with
    liquid reserved
½ cup red wine
½ cup beef stock
¼ cup chopped parsley
1 bayleaf
1½ teaspoons basil, crumbled
⅛ teaspoon thyme, crumbled
1 turnip, diced
2 carrots, diced
1 potato, diced
¼ pound mushrooms, halved
    Chopped parsley for garnish

1. Dredge the meat in flour mixed with ½ teaspoon salt and ¼ teaspoon pepper.
2. Heat butter and oil in casserole and brown the meat on all sides. Lower the heat to medium, add garlic and onion and cook for about 5 minutes, stirring frequently.
3. Add tomatoes and tomato liquid, wine, beef stock, parsley, bayleaf, basil, thyme, remaining ½ teaspoon salt and ¼ teaspoon pepper, turnip and carrots. Cook uncovered for 1½ hours.
4. Add potato and cook 15 minutes longer.
5. Add mushrooms and continue cooking for an additional 15 minutes. Taste and adjust seasonings. Before serving, sprinkle with chopped parsley.

Makes 2 to 4 servings

Spring

Spring copper is Swiss-made and like all things Swiss it is durable, serious and very expensive. The reason for both the durability and the high ticket is the stainless-steel lining. In truth, Spring cookware is almost more stainless than copper. The essence of decorative, it is pre-lacquered and comes packed with a sachet of powder that you can dissolve in water to remove the lacquer finish. Once de-lacquered, the pan is ready to use. The copper will then tarnish and scratch but the stainless interior is practically impervious to anything.

Spring manufactures a very long list of restaurant equipment, gorgeous chafing dishes and myriad chafing dish braziers that are used by restaurants on their rolling carts. Spring even makes the carts.

Spring 8⅝-Inch Round Frying Pan

This pan is thin-gauge copper with a thick layer of stainless steel. It is surprisingly slow and insensitive for omelette making. The brass handle is long but gets hot as soon as the butter does. Omelettes cook slowly but evenly and do not stick. This would really make a lovely pan for potatoes cooked on top of the stove. It is ovenproof as well. **To Use:** Soak in hot water with the contents of the sachet dissolved. Soak 20 minutes or longer and check to be sure that the pan is completely submerged or brass handle will discolor. When dry, the pan is ready to use.
Approximate Retail Price: $55

Spring 8⅝-inch copper fry pan.

PASTRY PROVISIONS

In olden days, the mark of a good cook — and the aspiration of every new bride — was a flaky, delicate fruit pie. In many countries a girl was not even considered eligible for marriage until she could make a perfect pastry. Times have changed but pastry making is still a treasured art. And anyone with a little perseverance and a lot of patience can turn out praiseworthy pastries.

The word "pastry" has two meanings. In one sense, it refers to the dough itself, usually a mixture of flour, shortening, salt and water or other liquid. And in the other, it encompasses a wide range of baked goods, including cakes, cream puffs and Napoleons. Most often, a pastry is a dessert consisting of a crust and a sweet filling. But what would a beef Wellington be without its pastry jacket or a Quiche Lorraine without its pastry crust?

The making of pastry requires some skill and a modicum of patience. Many cooks find the process intimidating, because unlike other types of baking, pastry making is a precision operation. Certain rules apply and specific techniques must be mastered for perfect results. But there is no magic involved in turning out delicate pastries: The only essential ingredient is tender loving care. Pastry should be tender and flaky, and the key to pastry-making is a light touch. Too much flour will make the dough tough and too much liquid will make it soggy. In the initial step, fat is added to the flour and blended with the fingertips or with a pastry blender until small particles are formed, and many experts offer a dire warning against over-blending — the old-fashioned standards for particle size range from coarse crumbs to small peas. For flavor there is nothing quite like a pastry made with butter; however, fats such as lard and vegetable shortening make a very flaky short pastry. After the fat particles are coated with flour they must be bound together with a liquid. It is important to work quickly, so that the fat doesn't soften. Just enough liquid, a small amount at a time, is sprinkled over the flour to make a workable dough. The amount of liquid added will vary with the flour used. One of the main points to remember is not to overmix. Overmixing causes too much gluten development in the flour, which makes the dough tough and elastic and results in a tough pastry.

Once the liquid has been added, the mass of dough should be shaped into a ball and slightly flattened. Refrigerating the dough for a short time relaxes the gluten and allows the pastry to be rolled out much more easily. A formica or marble surface works best for rolling out dough. The marble is especially desirable for rolling out pastries with a high fat content since its cool surface prevents the pastry from softening too rapidly. You might want to roll out the pastry on a canvas pastry cloth, which can be floured to prevent sticking and washed for repeated use. Your choice of rolling pin should be a matter of comfort. Many European chefs swear by simple long wood cylinders without handles, claiming that these allow more sensitive contact with the dough, but most Americans are uncomfortable guiding this type of pin with their palms and prefer to grasp the handles of the thicker, conventional pin. To roll out pastry use short strokes and roll from the center out. Again it is important to work quickly so that the dough does not soften.

After the pastry has been rolled out it should be gently slipped into the baking pan without stretching. Glass or non-shiny metal pans bake pies perfectly; if using a glass baking dish it is usually necessary to lower the oven temperature slightly to compensate for the material's superior heat conductivity. For delicate pastries, especially those without a top crust, you may want to use a flan ring or a loose-bottom tart pan; then you can remove the ring or pan rim without disturbing the flaky crust and cut the tart easily into serving pieces. Before attempting any serious pastry making, check to see that your oven is calibrated correctly — an oven that is not accurate can produce disastrous results. Also, make sure that you match the recipe with the right size equipment.

Pastry shells can be baked either filled or unfilled. Baking unfilled shells is called "baking blind." To keep the empty shell from bubbling up and shrinking from the sides of the pan, it's necessary to pierce the pastry to allow steam to escape and to weight it either with dried beans or aluminum pie weights. The latter look like shiny little beads and they allow the shell to brown.

Applying the word "pastry" in its broader sense, we've stocked up on "Pastry Provisions" for cakes as well as pies and tarts. Cake making is an exacting art, but one easily mastered if you measure ingredients accurately and follow recipe directions to the letter. If you line cake pans with parchment paper the baked cake will slip right out.

Our assortment of unusual pans — including obsttorten and rehrücken forms — will tempt you to create a regal dessert and, perhaps, to crown it with creamy ribbons and rosettes piped with a pastry bag and decorating tubes.

We should warn you now: One way or another, the flaky tarts, heavenly moist cakes and super-rich cheesecake featured in this section are sure to swell your sweet tooth with pastry-making dreams.

Ball-Bearing Rolling Pin

Heavy-duty rolling pins used to be sold only to professional bakers, but now they are available for home use. If you are a serious baker, one of these pins will be a worthwhile investment. Manufactured by Thorpe, they have a steel rod with ball-bearings running through the heavy, hardwood cylinder and handles. The special ball-bearings never need lubrication. Cylinders range in length from 10½ inches to 18 inches. We recommend either the 12- or 15-inch one as the ideal size for home bakers. These have everything a good rolling pin should — excellent quality, construction and balance. We loved working with these pins on all types of dough. **To Use:** Place dough on lightly floured surface or pastry cloth. Flour the pin or use a floured pin cover. Roll the dough from center to edge. Lift pin and repeat. (Pushing the roller back and forth tends to stretch the dough too much.) Wipe clean with a damp cloth and dry after using.
Approximate Retail Price: $10.50 (12-inch); $12.50 (15-inch)

Tapered Rolling Pin

It is just plain hard to roll a circle of pastry or dough evenly. The middle always seems to be thicker than the edges. The French designed a tapered rolling pin to solve this problem. The hardwood pin is thick in the center and gently tapers to thinner ends. It has nice weight and balance and really lets you get a feel for the dough. **To Use:** Lightly flour rolling pin. On a lightly floured surface, roll dough from the center out, using the palms of your hand to push the pin.
Approximate Retail Price: $2

Rolling pins have diverse uses.

Straight Rolling Pin

The classic French rolling pin, without handles or ball bearings, is made out of a solid cylinder of wood. Once you get the knack of working it with the palms of the hand you can wield this pin more sensitively than the ball-bearing type. Its longer length, approximately 18 to 21 inches, makes it useful for rolling out long sheets of pastry, such as croissant dough. The pin is also handy for beating butter to soften it or for making a chilled pâté brisée more manageable. **To Use:** Place dough on lightly floured surface. Roll dough with pin using the palms of the hand to control the thickness.
Approximate Retail Price: $3.50

Marble Rolling Pin

Marble has always been prized as an excellent surface for working with pastry; it does not absorb fat or moisture and has a cool surface that keeps buttery dough from becoming soft and unmanageable. A marble rolling pin is usually used with a marble slab for maximum benefits. We especially liked marble for making very buttery, soft puff pastry. The pin's 10-inch rolling surface and weight (about 10 pounds) simplified this sometimes tricky task: The weight works to your advantage while rolling. **To Use:** Refrigerate rolling pin before using (30 minutes is sufficient time). Roll out pastry to desired thickness. Wipe pin clean after each use.
Approximate Retail Price: $75

Pastry Cloth with Frame and Rolling Pin Cover

Dough sticking to a cutting board and rolling pin rates right up there with traffic jams for total frustration. A well-floured pastry cloth and rolling pin cover definitely make the job of rolling out pastry less sticky. The extra flour acts as a buffer between pastry and rolling surfaces. We especially liked the Foley pastry frame because of its unique design: the pastry cloth, marked for 8- and 9-inch pies, is stretched between two removable wooden slats. Two long steel rods clamp on to the wood and hold it in place on the edge of a table or counter. The rolling pin cover simply fits like a sleeve over any medium to large rolling pin. **To Use:** Set pastry frame on a flat surface. Place the small loops of the metal rods upward over the ends of the wooden bar farthest from you. Place the opposite ends of the metal rods over the wooden bar nearest to you and hook them over edge of table or counter so that pastry frame stays in place. Slip cover over rolling pin. Sprinkle cloth with flour and roll covered pin across surface to coat both cloth and pin with an even film of flour. Roll out pastry. After each use, scrape off any excess flour and dried-on particles and store cloth and pin cover in a plastic bag. Slip cloth off frame to wash thoroughly.
Approximate Retail Price: $4.50

Pastry cloth and rolling pin cover prevent dough from sticking.

Electric Sifter

Even pre-sifted flour needs resifting for feather-light baking, and an electric sifter makes quick work of this oft-ignored step. Cordless and battery operated, it holds about 2 cups at a time, and stands 4 inches tall. A handy device for serious bakers! **To Use:** Lift up handle cover and insert size C battery (unit does not come with battery). Snap cover shut and switch on to use. It comes apart for easy cleaning.
Approximate Retail Price: $10

Battery-operated electric sifter.

PASTRY PROVISIONS

Pastry Blender

Although food processor owners are known to sing the praises of machine-mixed pastry, many bakers continue to advise that you blend the flour and shortening by hand to prevent the mixture from developing too much gluten. You can cut the shortening into the flour with two knives until the mixture resembles coarse crumbs. Or you can achieve the same texture with a pastry blender, which consists of about a half dozen curved wires attached to a handle. We found the Foley pastry blender, made in Hong Kong, to be not only the least ex-

pensive but also the best designed model on the market. The oval curve of the wires makes the Foley blender easier to use in deep bowls; the handle provides a comfortable grip and a thumb rest. **To Use:** Place flour and shortening in bowl. Grasp pastry blender and work shortening into flour, using an up-and-down motion, until mixture resembles very coarse crumbs. Do not overmix — shortening particles should remain separate within dough.
Approximate Retail Price: $3 (black handle); $2.50 (wooden handle)

Pastry blenders mix dough.

Pastry Crimper

If your tarts and pies have that sloppy, homey look and you want them to look neat and professional, consider a pastry crimper. While it is hardly a crucial item, the pastry crimper can be used to form a seal on double-crust pies and to neatly flute the edges of a pastry shell. At

first we found the crimper somewhat stiff and awkward to use, but with a little persistence and practice we were creating beautiful wavy rims on our pies and tarts. Made in France, the crimper is stainless steel and looks like a broad pair of tweezers with a serrated edge. **To Use:** Grasp crimper between fingers and squeeze gently around edge of pastry to form a decorative design.
Approximate Retail Price: $1.50

Pastry crimper flutes edge.

Pie Weights

Baking a pie shell without a filling is called "baking blind." You would use this method when you need a shell to hold an unbaked filling, or when pre-baking is necessary to prevent sogginess. It used to be that you had to line the unfilled pastry with parchment paper or aluminum foil and weight it with dried rice or beans. But now you can ensure that the shell will hold its shape during baking with pie weights. These aluminum pellets replace the rice or beans and come packed in 1- or 1½-pound plastic bags. We found them handy to use and very efficient. They absorb heat faster than either dried beans or rice and do not have to be removed half way through the baking in order to obtain a golden-brown crust. **To Use:** Line a tart

pan, flan ring or pie plate with pastry. Prick dough lightly with a fork. Line pastry with parchment paper or foil. Place pie weights in pan, spreading evenly. Bake until pastry is golden brown. Remove shell from oven and lift out paper and pie weights. (Be careful because weights will be hot.) Cool shell before filling.
Approximate Retail Price: $5 (1-pound bag); $6 (1½-pound bag)

Parchment Paper

Line a cake or bread pan with parchment paper before baking and delicate cakes and breads will slip right out without sticking. After removing the cake from the pan, simply peel off the paper. Parchment paper is also useful for baking blind or lining a casserole to eliminate

Pie weights are spread in parchment-lined pastry.

baked-on food. The paper is available in a roll in a handy dispenser box with a serrated metal cutting edge, or in sheets. We also have seen them packaged pre-cut for use in round cake pans. **To Use:** Trim parchment paper to desired size. Place in bottom of baking pan.
Approximate Retail Price: $1.50 (roll)

Blackbird Pie Funnel

You wouldn't want to bake four and twenty of these blackbirds in a pie, but one of them peeking through a crust keeps the filling from oozing out and releases steam through its beak. The 4-inch-tall, ceramic blackbird comes from England and eliminates the need to cut slits in a top crust. **To Use:** Line pie plate with pastry. Place blackbird in middle of dish. Arrange filling around bird. Cover pie and bird with top crust, letting the bird's head stick through the pastry.
Approximate Retail Price: $2.50

Place blackbird in pan; drape top crust over it.

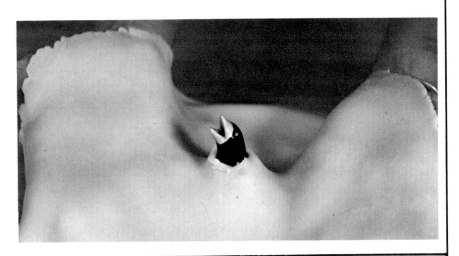

Rack Jack

This inexpensive, simple gizmo is worth owning. With it, you won't bake your face with a blast of oven heat, burn your fingers or singe potholders. The rack jack or oven stick is an 11-inch hardwood stick with a hook for pulling out the oven rack and a notched end for pushing it back. The rack jack comes with a hole for hanging; better yet, attach a magnet to the rack jack and stick it on the oven where it will always be in easy reach. **To Use:** To pull the oven rack out, hook the center of the oven rack edge and pull toward you. To replace rack, push with notched end of stick.
Approximate Retail Price: $1.25

Use rack jack to pull hot rack.

Pastry Piercer

Pastry piercers look like instruments from Kafka's *Penal Colony* but serve a benign purpose. They prick hundreds of tiny steam holes over sheets of pastry in a flash. Designed for piercing large quantities of dough, the all-steel roller has steel prongs encased in a steel frame and attached to a wooden handle. The less wicked-looking piercer has shorter steel prongs stuck in a wooden roller and attached to a metal handle. **To Use:** Roll out pastry. Roll pastry piercer over dough to make the desired number of holes.
Approximate Retail Price: $12

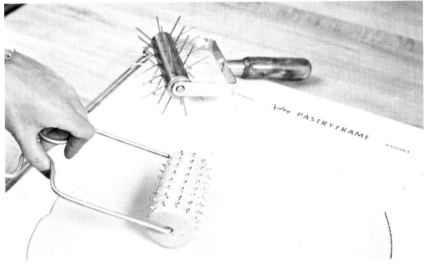

Pastry piercers prick dough to allow steam to escape.

Porcelain Quiche Dish

The traditional quiche, probably from the Lorraine area of France, is made with eggs, bacon, cream and no cheese. Through the years, creative cooks have added their personal touches to the savory custard pie and it has become a much-varied dish. Although a quiche can be baked in a pie plate, flan ring or tart pan, it takes on an air of sophistication when brought to the table in a white porcelain dish. French-made quiche dishes, from 8 to 11 inches in diameter, are crafted from highly glazed porcelain; their fluted edges shape the pastry decoratively. We prefer quiche in the smaller dishes because it is easier to slice and serve, but we loved the design and practicality of all the dishes. They also can be used for baking fruit desserts or simply as attractive serving vessels. The dishes shown can be used in a microwave oven. **To Use:** Line quiche dish with pastry. Bake and fill according to recipe directions. Cut into wedges for serving.
Approximate Retail Price: $18 - $22

Bake and serve Fresh Herb Quiche in a porcelain quiche dish.

Fresh Herb Quiche

Pâté Brisée (recipe follows)
5 slices bacon, cut into pieces
3 ounces Gruyère or Swiss cheese, thinly sliced
2 eggs
2 egg yolks
1½ cups whipping cream (or use half whipping cream and half light cream)
1½ tablespoon finely chopped fresh herbs (chives, rosemary, sage, basil, tarragon) or 2 teaspoons dried herbs
½ teaspoon salt
2 tablespoons butter

1. Prepare Pâté Brisée pastry shell. Allow about an hour to make pastry shell.
2. Preheat oven to 375°F. Cook bacon in skillet until crisp; drain. Scatter bacon in bottom of pastry shell. Arrange cheese over bacon.
3. In a mixing bowl, beat together the eggs, egg yolks, cream, herbs and salt. Pour egg mixture over cheese and bacon.
4. Dot with butter. Bake until top is golden and puffy and knife inserted in center comes out clean, 25 to 30 minutes. Serve warm or cold.
Makes 4 main-course servings

Pâté Brisée

1 cup all-purpose flour
⅛ teaspoon salt
5 tablespoons butter
2 tablespoons cold water

1. Place 1 cup flour and salt in mixing bowl. Cut in butter until small particles are formed.
2. Gradually add water and work dough into a ball.
3. Place on a lightly floured surface and knead gently several times. Dust with flour and wrap in a plastic bag; refrigerate about 30 minutes.
4. Roll out dough on lightly floured surface to ⅛-inch thickness. Roll dough around the rolling pin and unroll over a 9-inch porcelain quiche pan or loose-bottom tart pan.
5. Gently press dough into form, being careful not to stretch dough. Pass rolling pin over top to remove excess dough. Chill thoroughly.
6. Line the shell with parchment paper, allowing paper to extend over sides. Fill with pie weights or dried beans. Bake at 400°F 10 minutes. Remove paper and weights and bake 2 to 3 minutes longer. Cool slightly before filling.
Makes 1 9-inch pie shell

Loose-Bottom Tart Pans

An attractive tart is almost guaranteed when baked in a loose-bottom pan; the rim slips off after baking and the bottom holds the pastry for cutting and serving. The French-made, tinned-steel pans are available in an assortment of sizes. They are always round, range in depth from 1 to 2 inches and have fluted sides. Quiche, coffee cake and quick breads can be baked in these pans; a deep one can be used for cheesecake. **To Use:** Roll pastry to ⅛-inch thickness. Place dough over tart pan and gently ease the pastry into the pan, making sure that pastry is pushed into the fluted edges. Shell is ready to be filled or baked blind. After baking, place tart pan on a jar or can

After baking tart, slip rim off loose-bottom tart pan.

and let rim slip down. The tart is usually served on the metal liner.

Approximate Retail Price: $1.25 to $4.50 (depending on size)

Tartlet Tins and Barquettes

Many of us can resist a large, obviously sinful dessert, but will always fall for little, innocent-looking tartlets. Tartlet tins hold the pastry for irresistible dessert miniatures or bite-size appetizers. Crafted out of tinned steel, they are available in assorted sizes and shapes. Barquettes are merely oval or boat-shaped tartlet tins; they derive their name from the French word for small boat. Try making an assortment of fruit tartlets in various shapes and serve them after a special dinner on a tray with liqueurs and coffee. The pans are also perfect for baking mini-quiches, shells for pâté, or your own culinary creations. **To Use:** Set a cluster of empty tartlet pans or barquettes together on a counter. Roll out your favorite pastry dough and place over the tartlet tins. Pass rolling pin over tops to remove excess dough. Presto! Pastry for all the pans is cut at once. Press dough gently into pans, place them on a cookie sheet, and bake either filled or unfilled.

Approximate Retail Price: $.30 - $1

Drape tartlet pans with dough and pass rolling pin over tops to trim..

PASTRY PROVISIONS

Tartmaster

You can stamp out perfectly neat tarts or old-fashioned fried fruit pies with a tartmaster. It comes already assembled and is used very much like a cookie cutter. The sturdy metal form cuts, crimps and seals the dough in one movement. It should pinch the dough securely around the filling, but we found it necessary to pinch the edges of each tart together by hand in order to form a good seal. The tartmaster comes in two sizes, 2¾ inches and 4 inches in diameter. **To Use:** Roll out dough and top with small mounds of desired filling. Place another sheet of dough over top. Dip tartmaster in flour. Place over dough and firmly push down on

Arrange filling on dough, leaving space to cut with tartmaster.

knob. Remove excess dough and place tarts on baking sheet. To clean tartmaster, unscrew knob and

Push knob on top firmly to stamp out round tarts.

pull out fluted cutter.
Approximate Retail Price: $2 (2¾ inch); $3 (4 inch)

Kolacky Tart Cutter

Kolacky are delicate pastries prized by Eastern Europeans. They can be made with a yeast dough or with a tender and flaky pastry that literally melts in your mouth. You can fill them with either a fruit or a cheese mixture. When we first saw the kolacky tart cutter, we thought it was just a gimmick. But we later revised our judgment. The cutter conveniently shapes and cuts the pastry into perfect squares, with tabs at each corner that can easily be twisted pinwheel-fashion over the filling. All of our kolacky came out picture perfect. The cutter is a 3-inch square aluminum frame attached to a wood knob. **To Use:** Roll dough ⅛ inch thick on floured board or pastry cloth. Cut with floured tart cutter, removing the cutter gently each time. Place filling in center of each square. Bring tabs to center, overlapping slightly and press together.
Approximate Retail Price: $1.75

Kolacky tart cutters cut squares.

Fruit-Filled Kolacky

Pastry
  1 cup butter
  8 ounces cream cheese, softened
  2 cups all-purpose flour
1¼ teaspoons salt

Filling
  1 cup cooked prunes or apricots, finely chopped
  2 tablespoons sugar
  2 tablespoons butter
⅛ teaspoon vanilla
¼ teaspoon grated lemon peel

1. Cream butter and cream cheese until fluffy. Beat in flour and salt. Refrigerate 1 hour.
2. Prepare filling: Cook prunes or apricots, sugar, butter, vanilla and lemon peel over medium heat until thickened, about 5 minutes. While filling cools preheat oven to 400°F.
3. Roll pastry on lightly floured surface to ⅛-inch thickness. Cut with kolacky tart cutter.
4. Place 1 teaspoon cooled filling in center of each tart. Bring corner tabs to center, overlapping slightly, and press together.
5. Bake at 400°F until light brown, 12 to 15 minutes.   *Makes 2 dozen*

Flan Forms

A French flan is nothing more than a tart baked in a special metal form that has no bottom or top. The shell is made by fitting rolled out pastry dough into the ring; since the form has no bottom, the tart must be baked on a baking sheet. After baking, you slip the filled or unfilled pastry shell out of the ring on a plate. Flan forms are available in rectangular, square and round shapes, and are usually made of tinned or stainless steel. **To Use:** Place flan form on baking sheet. Roll pastry ⅛ inch thick. Place dough over mold and gently ease it into the ring, being careful not to stretch or tear dough. Pass rolling pin over top to remove excess pastry. Bake blind, or fill and bake. After baking, the form can easily be removed since the pastry shrinks. Blind-baked pastry shells freeze beautifully, so you can keep a few on hand for last minute filling.
Approximate Retail Price: $2 to $6.50

Flan forms come in various shapes and sizes; place dough in them and bake "blind" or filled on a baking sheet.

Fresh Cherry Flan

Pastry
  ½ cup butter
1½ cups all-purpose flour
  1 tablespoon sugar
  ⅛ teaspoon salt
  1 egg yolk, slightly beaten
  3 to 4 tablespoons water

Filling
  1 egg
  1 teaspoon water
  4 cups sweet cherries, pitted
  ½ cup sugar
    Granulated sugar

1. In mixing bowl, combine flour, sugar and salt. Use pastry blender to work butter into flour mixture until small particles are formed. Stir in egg yolk and water.
2. Form pastry into a ball and knead gently two or three times. Wrap in plastic wrap and refrigerate 1 hour.
3. Preheat oven to 350°F. Divide dough into two parts, making one part ¼ the size of the other. On lightly floured surface, roll larger part into a rectangle 16 inches by 6 inches.
4. Set a 14-inch by 4½-inch flan form on a baking sheet. Place dough over form and gently ease it into the corners, being careful not to stretch it. Pass rolling pin over top to remove excess pastry.
5. Mix egg and water. Brush lightly over bottom of flan shell, reserving some egg mixture for top.
6. Mix cherries and sugar. Fill shell with cherry mixture.
7. Roll out remaining dough and cut into ¾-inch lattice strips with pastry cutter. Arrange lattice strips over top of cherries, pressing down firmly at the edge. Trim off excess dough.
8. Brush lattice strips with remaining egg mixture. Bake tart until golden and cherries are tender, 40 to 45 minutes. Sprinkle tart with sugar during last 5 minutes of baking time. Remove from oven. Gently lift off flan form.
Makes about 10 servings

PASTRY PROVISIONS

Pastry Wheel

Consider the pastry wheel as pinking shears for dough. Several varieties of pastry wheels are available, but we liked an Italian-made cutter with a strong wood handle and a snugly set stainless-steel wheel. With one long sweep it cuts perfect "pinked" lattice strips. **To Use:** Grasp handle and press firmly with wheel on pastry — or pasta — to cut through dough.
Approximate Retail Price: $2

Pastry wheel cuts perfect lattice strips for Fresh Cherry Flan.

Goose Feather Pastry Brush

With goose feathers you can apply a thin, smooth glaze to puff pastry, cream puffs or brioche without leaving brush marks or drips. The brush is very flexible, allowing you to get into corners and do delicate edges better than with a regular bristle brush. The brushes are made in Hungary and the quills are intricately braided together to form the handle. **To Use:** Dip brush gently in butter or egg glaze and brush lightly over surface. Rinse the brush well after using and dry naturally.
Approximate Retail Price: $1

Flat Bristle Pastry Brush

Every cook needs a pastry brush — for basting a turkey, glazing bread or greasing a pan. A good pastry brush should be made out of natural bristles because these will remain soft and flexible. The bristles are fastened tightly to the wooden handle by a stainless-steel metal band. The brushes are available in various widths: Wider brushes are more efficient for applying large amounts of butter to pastries or for basting, while narrow ones are easier to use for small delicate jobs like glazing tarts. **To Use:** Dip brush in glaze, butter or whatever. Brush lightly over surface. Make sure to rinse the brush well after each use and allow it to dry naturally.
Approximate Retail Price: $1.25 to $2.95 (depending on width)

Goose feather pastry brush is good for applying delicate glazes.

Flat pastry brush butters phyllo dough for Greek Cheese Pastries.

Greek Cheese Pastries

- **1 package (8 ounces) cream cheese, softened**
- **4 ounces feta cheese**
- **1 tablespoon butter, softened**
- **1 small egg, slightly beaten**
- **1 tablespoon snipped parsley**
- **½ teaspoon dried mint leaves (optional)**
- **⅛ teaspoon freshly ground black pepper or to taste**
- **1 pound phyllo strudel leaves**
- **1 cup butter, melted**

1. Preheat oven to 350°F. Mix cheeses, butter, egg, parsley and mint. Season with pepper.
2. Cut phyllo leaves lengthwise into strips about 2½ inches wide. Stack and cover strips with a barely dampened kitchen towel to prevent drying.
3. Place 1 phyllo leaf strip on clean surface. Brush with melted butter. Place another strip on top. Brush again with butter.
4. Place about 1 teaspoon of the cheese mixture on a bottom corner of the strip. Fold adjacent corner over filling to form a triangle. Continue folding in triangles the length of the strip. (Fold flag fashion.)
5. Place triangle seam side down on lightly buttered jelly roll pan. Repeat procedure with remaining phyllo and filling. Brush tops of triangles with butter. Bake at 350°F until golden and crisp, about 20 minutes. Serve warm.

Makes about 45 pastries

Spring-Form Pan

A two-part spring-form pan solves the problem of removing cheesecakes and other delicate desserts from the pan after baking without having to invert them. You remove the rim of the pan and leave the cake intact. The grooved rim fits atop the ridged bottom and clamps shut. Release the clamp after baking, and the rim springs open, leaving the cake unsheathed on the bottom disc for serving. One of the most versatile models we came across is made in Germany of high-quality tinned steel. The pan comes with two extra interchangeable bottoms that can be inserted instead of the standard disc: a fluted tube excellent for pound cakes, and a fluted ring for molded salads and desserts. The pans are available in graduated sizes from 8 to 10 inches in diameter. **To Use:** Secure bottom of pan to rim by positioning in groove around base of rim. Lock clamp. Fill pan and bake. Remove rim by releasing clamp. Gently lift rim over cake. When using decorative bottoms, invert cake before removing rim.

Approximate Retail Price: $6

Spring-form pan has interchangeable forms: a fluted tube, a fluted base without tube and a flat bottom.

Release Chocolate Cheesecake from pan when cool by unlatching rim; see recipe on the following page.

Chocolate Cheesecake

Crust
1¼ cups chocolate wafer crumbs
5 tablespoons butter, melted

Filling
**3 8-ounce packages cream
  cheese, softened**
1 cup granulated sugar
3 eggs
**2 tablespoons creme de cacao
  or chocolate-flavored
  liqueur**
**8 ounces semi-sweet
  chocolate, melted and
  cooled slightly**
1 teaspoon vanilla
1½ cups dairy sour cream
**½ cup whipping cream,
  whipped**
**Candied violets for
  decoration**

1. Preheat oven to 350°F. Combine crumbs and butter. Press into bottom and about 1 inch up sides of a 9-inch springform pan. Refrigerate while preparing filling.
2. For filling, beat cream cheese and sugar until light and fluffy. Add eggs, one at a time, beating well after each addition. Beat in creme de cacao, chocolate and vanilla. Fold in sour cream.
3. Pour into crumb-lined pan. Place on baking sheet and bake at 350°F for 1 hour.
4. Turn off oven and cool cheesecake for 30 minutes in oven with door partially open. Remove from oven and cool thoroughly.
5. Cover cake and refrigerate in pan at least 8 hours. To serve, remove side of pan, pipe whipped cream through pastry tube on top of cake or mound in center. Decorate with candied violets. *Makes 16 servings*

Obsttortenform and Mary Ann Pan

The spongy yellow cakes positioned next to the fresh strawberries in the supermarket are baked in special pans. The pans produce cakes with shallow depressions designed to nestle fruit or cream fillings. If the form is straight-rimmed, the pan is called a Mary Ann pan; if the rim is flared and fluted, it's an obsttortenform. The pans are made of tinned steel and come in a variety of sizes. We like to fill the cakes with sliced strawberries, glaze them with jelly and then garnish with a decorative edge of whipped cream. **To Use:** Generously butter the obsttortenform or Mary Ann pans, being careful to get into all of the grooves. Pour batter into pan; bake until golden. Remove cake from pan and cool. Fill inverted cake with fruit.
Approximate Retail Price: $2.50 (Obsttortenform);$3.95(MaryAnn)

Obsttorte

2 eggs, slightly warmed
⅓ cup sugar
**¼ teaspoon vanilla or almond
  extract**
⅓ cup all-purpose flour, sifted

2 tablespoons melted butter
3 tablespoons kirsch
½ cup currant jelly
**1 pint fresh strawberries,
  sliced (leave one whole for
  middle of cake)**
Whipped cream for garnish

1. Preheat oven to 350°F. Beat eggs and sugar until very thick, about 5 minutes. Beat in vanilla. Fold in flour and butter.
2. Generously butter a 9½-inch obsttortenform, making sure to butter all indentations. Spread batter in pan. Bake at 350°F until top of cake is golden and springs back when lightly touched, about 15 minutes.
3. Remove cake from oven and invert pan on cooling rack; let cool 5 minutes. Gently remove cake from pan; cool.
4. Sprinkle depression of cake with 2 tablespoons of the kirsch. Heat jelly and remaining kirsch to boiling. Brush a thin layer of the glaze over the depression.
5. Arrange strawberries over glaze. Place whole strawberry in center. Spoon remaining glaze over strawberries; cool. Pipe whipped cream through pastry bag to garnish rim of cake. *Makes 6 servings*

Spoon glaze over obsttorte.

Pastry Bags

With practice and patience you can wield a pastry bag to decorate cakes, shape and fill cream puffs, stuff hors d'oeuvres, or pipe out fancy mounds of mashed potatoes. New materials such as nylon and plastic lined fabrics virtually have replaced the canvas of old-fashioned bags. The nylon bags are very flexible and allow for better control than either the canvas or plastic-lined bags. The plastic-lined bags, which get more flexible with use, are also easy to clean and are much less expensive than the French-made nylon ones. We recommend purchasing at least two sizes of bags, one 10- or 12-inch bag for working with small amounts of icing and a larger 21- or 24-inch one for piping potatoes or making cream puffs. In addition to the pastry bags you will need an assortment of metal tubes that fit inside the bag, along with a plastic coupler for holding the small tubes and enabling you to change tips without emptying the bag. The small tubes are used for intricate decorations

Use pastry bags and various tubes to decorate foods elegantly.

such as flowers and writing, while the larger tubes are nice for shaping cream puffs or ladyfingers or piping out broad borders of mashed potatoes. **To Use:** Screw ring off coupler and push the coupler down into the bag and through the narrow end. (A coupler is only necessary when using small tubes; large tubes will fit into the bag without extra support.) Insert a decorating tube over the coupler and screw on the ring. Fill bag and twist top. Press down to squeeze out filling.
Approximate Retail Price: $.35 to $5 (depending on size and material)

Rehrücken Pan

Rehrücken means "saddle of venison" in German and refers to the ridged, half-cylinder shape of the classic and elegantly rich Austrian cake baked in this pan. After the cake is unmolded, it is glazed with chocolate and decorated with almonds to resemble a deer's back. The ribs of the pan make it easy to slice the cake in uniform servings. Pans are available in various lengths from 10 to 14 inches and also can be used for nut breads, mousses and molded desserts. **To Use:** Butter rehrücken mold and sprinkle generously with bread crumbs. Fill mold with batter and bake. After baking remove cake from pan and cool.
Approximate Retail Price: $5 (14-inch pan)

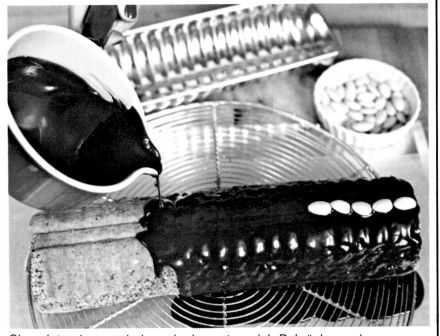

Chocolate glaze and almonds decorate a rich Rehrücken cake.

Rehrücken

Batter
Butter to grease pan
2 tablespoons dry bread
    crumbs
5 egg yolks
2 eggs
½ cup sugar, divided
5 egg whites
¾ cup whole almonds,
    unblanched, ground
2 ounces unsweetened
    chocolate, grated
½ teaspoon almond extract

Glaze
4 ounces sweet baking
    chocolate
2 ounces unsweetened
    chocolate
¾ cup whipping cream
2 to 3 tablespoons brandy
Whole blanched almonds for
    decoration

1. Preheat oven to 350°F. Generously butter a 4-inch by 14-inch rehrücken (deerback) loaf pan. Sprinkle with bread crumbs; shake out excess.
2. In a large mixing bowl, beat egg yolks and whole eggs with remaining ¼ cup sugar until pale and thick, about 5 minutes. Beat in almonds, chocolate and almond extract.
3. Beat egg whites until foamy. Gradually beat in ¼ cup of the sugar and beat until stiff peaks form.
4. Fold egg whites into yolk mixture. Do not overmix. Pour batter into prepared pan. Bake until cake is golden and springs back when lightly touched, 30 to 35 minutes.
5. Remove cake from oven and cool in pan 5 minutes. Gently take cake from pan. Allow to cool on wire rack.
6. For glaze, melt chocolates and cream in saucepan over low heat. Cook and stir until mixture is thickened, 3 to 4 minutes. Remove from heat. Stir in brandy. Pour glaze over cooled cake. (If glaze is too thick to pour, stir in another tablespoon or two of brandy.)
7. Decorate cake with row of almonds. Refrigerate 1 hour before serving.

Makes 14 servings

Straw Cake Tester

At first glance you may mistake this cake tester for a small whisk broom. Actually, it's a bundle of cake testers from Scandinavia; each is used to test a cake for doneness. The straws are bundled together and held at the top by a metal band. And since this cake tester is really too clever to hide away in a drawer, a ring has been attached so that the whole bundle can be hung on a wall. **To Use:** Twist off one of the strands near the band. Insert in middle of cake. If the straw comes out clean, the cake is done.
Approximate Retail Price: $2.50

Crinkle-Edge Loaf Pan

This pan looks like a cross between a loaf pan and brioche tin. Made of lightweight tinned steel, it has straight sides that flare out into fluted ends. Rich egg breads, nut breads and pound cakes look elegant when baked in crinkle-edged loaves with this pan. It comes in 1- and 1½-quart sizes. **To Use:** Butter pan. Fill with batter and bake.
Approximate Retail Price: $2

Crinkle-edge pan and straw tester.

Orange Glazed Pound Cake

Cake
½ cup butter
½ cup granulated sugar
2 egg yolks
1 tablespoon orange juice
¼ cup sour cream
¾ teaspoon grated orange peel
½ teaspoon vanilla
¼ teaspoon salt
⅛ teaspoon baking powder
⅛ teaspoon baking soda
1 cup all-purpose flour
2 egg whites

Glaze
½ cup confectioners' sugar
2 tablespoons fresh orange
    juice
1 tablespoon butter
1 tablespoon curacao or other
    orange liqueur
½ teaspoon zested orange peel
Slivered orange peel for
    garnish

1. Preheat oven to 350°F. Cream butter and sugar until light. Beat in egg yolks, orange juice, sour cream, peel, vanilla, salt, baking powder and baking soda. Beat in flour.
2. Beat egg whites until stiff peaks form. Fold into cake batter.
3. Pour batter into a well-buttered, 4-cup crinkle-edge loaf pan. Bake at 350°F until wooden pick inserted in center comes out clean, about 1 hour. Remove from pan. Cool on wire rack.
4. Prepare glaze: Cook and stir all ingredients for glaze in small saucepan. Heat to boiling. Pour over cooled cake.

Makes about 8 servings

THE BREAD SHOP

Baking a beautiful loaf of bread is truly one of the most satisfying accomplishments. The fragrance of bread hot from the oven is irresistible; the taste of the freshly-baked loaf slathered with butter is unforgettable.

We can thank the ancient Egyptians for making the first loaf of leavened bread. Bread remains the "staff of life" for many people and plays an important nutritive role in our diets. Almost every nation and ethnic group has its own hallmark loaf, and for many it is still a symbol of prosperity and good luck.

Recently, we have seen a marked revival of home bread baking. This has been motivated only partially by the desire for a product more flavorful and vitamin-rich than commercial brands. Many find baking to be a great way to relax. And the vigorous kneading yeast doughs require seems to dissipate everyday tensions! Moreover, the kneading provides results that mirror its psychological rewards: The dough is transformed from a sticky mass into a silken object so soft

THE BREAD SHOP

and smooth that you won't want to stop touching it.

The adventure of bread baking starts with the most basic ingredients: yeast, flour, salt and water. Yeast is a living organism that grows and multiplies, giving off carbon dioxide that literally "raises" the flour mixture. Yeast is available in two forms — dry and compressed. Dry yeast comes in sealed packages or in a sealed jar; it can be stored in a cool dark place or in the refrigerator and has about a 6 month to 1 year life span. Compressed yeast must be kept refrigerated and has a relatively short life span. Be sure to check the use expiration date stamped on the package before buying any yeast; the two types can be used interchangeably.

To start "growing," or activating, the yeast, you dissolve it in warm water or other liquid. The temperature of the liquid is important since the yeast will be killed if the liquid is too hot and it will not start to ferment if it is too cold; it should be between 100°F and 115°F. If you aren't sure as to how to gauge the temperature, you might want to invest in an "instant read" dough thermometer — you'll be able to use it again to check the rising bread.

The warmed, dissolved yeast "feeds" on the bread flour. The flour, when mixed with water or another liquid, becomes glutenous — or smooth and elastic. While this process is undesirable in pastry-making, it is essential to bread-baking. Gluten is a combination of two proteins present to some degree in all flour. All-purpose flour, which is a combination of hard wheat and soft wheat, has a high gluten content and is used most commonly in bread baking. Whole wheat and rye flours add additional flavor and nutritive value to the bread but the finished loaves usually are more compact because these flours contain less gluten and will not develop as much elasticity as all-purpose flour. Because flours vary in their abilities to absorb moisture and develop gluten, recipes usually don't specify exact amounts — you have to use your judgment in adding flour, based on the appearance of the dough.

Kneading develops the gluten in the flour and helps the dough to stretch evenly, giving the bread its characteristic light and airy texture. The dough begins as a soft sticky mass, but as additional flour is worked into it, the dough becomes elastic and smooth from the gluten that has been developed. A dough scraper is a handy device for working with the sticky dough until it becomes tough enough to knead by hand.

Once the dough has been kneaded it must be left to rise until doubled in bulk. Cover it loosely with a damp towel and set it in a warm place (about 80°F is ideal) away from drafts. You might want to adopt the French method for letting dough rise: They use reed baskets, called bannetons, which are lined with canvas, dusted with flour and filled with the dough. The basket shapes the dough and allows the baker to slip it easily onto a paddle and into the oven.

Professional bakers still bake their bread in specially designed ovens that circulate the heat evenly and produce a deliciously-thick crisp crust. Most of us don't have this kind of oven, but various aids are available for producing ideal crusty loaves. One of these is the baking stone — a hefty but handy item. Bread is baked directly on the preheated stone and the dry heat that rises from the stone creates a rich crust. Dark pans with a dull finish promote the same effect by absorbing heat rapidly and effectively — thus browning the crust quickly. Specially glazed clay loaf pans will perform the same magic.

Yeast breads are the baker's pride, but many of the utensils stocked in "The Bread Shop" also will produce beautiful quick breads — cornbread, nut breads, biscuits, muffins and all the other luscious loaves leavened with baking powder or soda instead of yeast. As their name implies, these breads rise quickly and require little mixing. So if your kneading arm is tired, you can still indulge in the homemade "staff of life."

Black Steel Baking Pans

The aroma that fills the air when bread is baking is irresistible. And an important element of successful bread baking is dark, heavy-gauge pans. The pans absorb the heat quickly, bake evenly and brown the crust. Black steel pans from Stone Hearth have been designed for function rather than aesthetic appearance, though they are quite handsome. Bread pans, loose-bottom pans, French and Italian loaf pans, cookie sheets, pizza pans and cake pans are just part of the available assortment. We include a recipe for a beautiful, crusty French bread that is about as authentic as you can make at home. **To Use:** Oil pans lightly. (For first time use, a little heavier oiling is recommended. The pans do not need to be seasoned.) Bake according to recipe directions. Because the pans absorb heat faster than shiny pans, it may be necessary to shorten your baking time. They are very hard to clean; we recommend soaking.
Approximate Retail Price: $13 (French bread pan); $12 (loaf pans); $3.75 (pie pan); $6 (cake pan)

Black steel pans bake evenly.

French Bread

> **1 package active dry yeast**
> **1 teaspoon sugar**
> **1½ cups warm water (105°F to 115°F)**
> **1½ teaspoons salt**
> **4 to 4½ cups all-purpose flour**
> **2 tablespoons cornmeal**

1. Dissolve yeast and sugar in warm water in a large mixing bowl. Let stand until bubbly, 8 to 10 minutes.
2. Stir in salt and enough of the flour to make a stiff dough.
3. Turn dough onto lightly floured surface; knead in additional flour until dough is smooth and elastic, about 10 minutes.
4. Place dough in oiled bowl. Turn oiled side up. Cover with a damp towel and let rise in a warm place until double.
5. Punch down dough and place on floured surface. Let rest a few minutes.
6. Oil two French bread pans. Sprinkle with cornmeal. Divide dough into two equal parts. Shape each piece into long narrow loaf, about 1 inch shorter than pan. Place dough in the molds; cover with towel and let rise until double.
7. Preheat oven to 400°F. When the loaves have doubled, make three diagonal slashes with bread slasher, razor or serrated knife on each loaf.
8. Bake at 400°F for 30 minutes. Mist loaves with water after first 15 minutes of baking to develop crisp crust. *Makes 2 loaves*

Bread Slasher

Here is proof that there is a gadget for everything. The bread slasher or *lame* is used to make slashes on the top of loaves of French bread. This allows the dough to swell up through the cuts during the first few minutes of baking, giving French bread its characteristic appearance. The thin blade is about 4½ inches long and tapers to a very sharp, curved end. A razor blade or the sharp edge of a metal scraper works equally well. **To Use:** With the blade held almost parallel to the bread, make slashes by drawing blade toward you in a swift, smooth, movement. Three or four diagonal slashes are usually made on the top of each loaf.
Approximate Retail Price: $2.50

Use bread slasher to cut characteristic slashes in French bread.

THE BREAD SHOP

Expandable Loaf Pan

The expandable loaf pan is a treasure for the cook whose special joy is baking. This Swiss-made, aluminum pan easily expands from 9 to 15 inches, allowing you to make different sized cakes and breads without buying extra pans. It is easy to clean and you'll never be caught without the right size pan. **To Use:** Use the pan as is or expand to desired length by gently pulling ends apart. The pan can be expanded even after you have poured in the batter or dough.
Approximate Retail Price: $8

Versatile loaf pan expands from 9 to 15 inches.

Metal and Rubber Dough Scrapers

Playing with pasta and bread dough is great fun and the dough scraper is a good addition to your baking gear. The metal scraper is made of two parts, a rustproof stainless-steel blade and a wooden handle securely riveted to the blade. Use the metal scraper to remass the dough while kneading. We prefer a scraper with a thin flexible blade, rather than the heavier gauge model, because of its greater control and maneuverability; it even allows you to spread a large amount of butter on pastry in one easy motion. If you hold the blade perpendicular to the work surface, it functions as a dough knife. The rubber dough scraper is U-shaped and has one rounded edge for working in a bowl and one straight edge for cutting and working on a flat surface. The flexible rubber scraper does a good job of incorporating flour into sticky batters such as Brioche and Baba au Rhum and scraping these out of the mixing bowl. Even though the straight edge of the scraper is not very sharp we had no trouble using it to cut through dough. **To Use:** For metal scraper, grasp handle and work flour into dough on floured surface by using an under and over wrist motion. After working with the dough, use scraper to clean the sur-

Use scrapers to handle dough.

face area. For rubber scraper, grasp straight edge in hand when working with dough or batter in a bowl; grasp rounded edge when working on a flat surface.
Approximate Retail Price: $1.50 (metal scraper); $1.50 (rubber scraper)

Pain de Mie and Pullman Pan

Close-grained bread with little crust makes the best canapes, croutons and fancy sandwiches. The French call this bread "pain de mie" and bake it in a pan with a lid instead of a conventional loaf pan. The most common form of pain de mie is the long rectangular loaf. (American bakers call it a pullman loaf.) Made of heavy-gauge black steel, a pullman pan is built with straight sides and a removable sliding lid. As the bread rises, it fills the covered pan and the bread is baked in a perfectly rectangular shape. Another type of pain de mie mold is long and cylindrical. Also made out of black steel, it has a hinged lid with a steel rod that holds the pan together while the bread bakes. It is perfect for making melba toast and cocktail breads. **To Use:** For rectangular loaves, grease the pullman pan, including the underside of the lid. Place dough in pan, making sure that bread does not fill loaf pan more than ⅓ full. Slide cover over dough. Let rise until pan is about ¾ full. Cover with lid and bake. Immediately remove lid and bread from pan. For cylindrical loaves, open the pan by removing the rod. Generously grease pan, including interior hinge area and steel rod. Place dough in lower half (the side with feet). Leaving pan open, cover

Cylindrical pain de mie and rectangular pullman pan.

dough with towel and let rise until double. Close pan and insert rod.
Approximate Retail Price: $17.50 (pain de mie); $12 (pullman pan)

Cocktail Pumpernickel Bread

1 package active dry yeast
1 teaspoon sugar

1 cup warm water (105°F to 115°F)
1½ teaspoon caraway seed
1 tablespoon cocoa
2 teaspoons salt

1½ tablespoons butter, melted
2 tablespoons light or dark molasses
2 cups rye flour
1¼ to 1½ cups all-purpose flour

1. Dissolve yeast and sugar in water in large mixing bowl. Let stand in warm place until bubbly, about 10 minutes.
2. Stir in caraway seed, cocoa, salt, butter and molasses. Mix in rye flour and enough of the all-purpose flour to make a dough that is easy to handle.
3. Knead dough on a lightly floured surface until elastic and no longer sticky, adding more flour if necessary.
4. Place in lightly oiled bowl; cover with damp cloth and allow dough to rise until doubled, about 1½ hours. (Rye flour rises slower than all-purpose flour.)
5. Punch down dough and place on lightly floured surface. Divide dough into three parts. (One part can be baked in pain de mie mold; the rest in regular loaf pans.) Preheat oven to 375°F.
6. For cylindrical pain de mie mold: Generously butter the interior and hinge area as well as the rod of the mold. Roll one part of the dough into a long narrow loaf. (This will be approximately ½ pound of dough.) Place dough in the bottom of pan and leave open. Cover with damp towel and allow to rise until doubled, about 1 hour. Close pan and insert metal rod. Bake at 375°F for 35 minutes. Remove pan from oven and open. Cool bread on wire rack.
7. For loaf pans: Generously butter two loaf pans, 5¾ inches by 3¼ inches. Place remaining bread into pans. Cover with a damp towel and allow to rise until doubled, about 1 hour. Bake at 375°F for 35 minutes.

Makes 1 small and 2 large loaves

Let Cocktail Pumpernickel rise in pain de mie; close pan to bake.

Brick Oven Bread Pan

Oatmeal Bread browns beautifully in a brick oven bread pan.

The brick oven bread pan simulates the interior of a stone hearth oven. The pan was designed and manufactured at the Alfred University College of Ceramics, utilizing a clay obtained from local sources in upstate New York. The clay surfaces were fired with a terra sigilatta coating that had been adapted from ancient Greek sources. The pan, which measures 8¼ inches by 4¾ inches, has straight sides and a wide lip on each end for ease in handling. Its coating allows the bread to rise and form a good crust evenly on all sides. We were truly impressed with the brick oven-baked bread. **To Use:** Before using the pan for the first time, it must be seasoned by rubbing the inside of the pan with vegetable oil and baking it at 250°F for 1 hour. Only then will the terra sigilatta coating perform well. Grease pan with butter. Use recipe calling for about 3 cups flour. Place shaped dough in prepared loaf pan. Let rise until doubled and bake according to recipe directions. Remember, pan is made of clay and can chip or break.

Approximate Retail Price: $9

THE BREAD SHOP

Oatmeal Bread

1 cup boiling water
¼ cup honey
1 teaspoon salt
1 tablespoon butter
½ cup quick-cooking rolled oats
1 package dry yeast
¼ cup warm water (105°F to 115°F)
2¾ to 3 cups all-purpose flour
Melted butter for glaze
1 tablespoon rolled oats for top

1. Combine boiling water, honey, salt, butter and ½ cup oats in large bowl; cool to lukewarm.
2. Dissolve yeast in warm water. Let stand until bubbly, about 10 minutes. Add yeast to oats mixture with enough flour to make a stiff dough.
3. Turn dough onto lightly floured surface; knead in enough additional flour to make dough smooth and elastic.
4. Place dough in oiled bowl. Turn oiled side up. Cover with a damp towel and let rise in a warm place until doubled, about 1 hour.
5. Punch down dough; divide into two parts. Shape each part into a rope about 10 inches long. Twist ropes together loosely. Place in buttered brick oven bread pan. Let rise until doubled, 45 minutes to 1 hour.
6. Preheat oven to 375°F. Brush dough lightly with butter. Sprinkle with oats. Bake until crust is well browned, about 35 minutes. Remove from pan; cool on wire rack. *Makes 1 (1-pound) loaf*

Banneton

French bake shops use coiled reed baskets called bannetons to hold and shape loaves of rising bread. The risen dough is turned out of the basket, upside-down, and slid into the oven to bake. The French line the bannetons with canvas, but we dusted ours with flour and enjoyed perfect results. The bannetons are available in two shapes, round and rectangular. We prefer the more traditional round shape. Both baskets produce 1-pound loaves of bread. Other sizes are available. When not in use, the banneton makes a nice addition to a basket collection; indeed, it makes a charming serving basket for the bread it shaped. **To Use:** Prepare bread dough according to your favorite recipe. (Use a recipe calling for about 3 cups of flour.) Knead dough and allow to rise until doubled. Generously flour banneton. Punch down dough and place in banneton. Cover and allow to rise until almost doubled in bulk. Turn bread out of banneton upside down onto oiled baking sheet. Let rise until doubled, then bake. A slight impression from the basket remains in the bread giving it a rustic look. *Approximate Retail Price: $15*

Herb Bread rises – and may later be served – in reed bannetons.

Herb Bread

1 package dry yeast
1 teaspoon sugar
1 cup warm water (105°F to 115°F)
1 teaspoon fines herbes
½ teaspoon dried dill weed
1 teaspoon salt
2 tablespoons melted butter
2½ to 3 cups all-purpose flour

1. Dissolve yeast and sugar in water in mixing bowl. Let stand until bubbly, about 10 minutes. Stir in fines herbes, dill, salt and butter. Stir in enough of the flour to make a stiff dough.
2. Turn dough onto lightly floured surface; knead, incorporating additional flour, until dough is smooth and elastic, about 10 minutes. Place dough in oiled bowl. Turn oiled side up. Cover with a damp towel and let rise in a warm place until double.
3. Place about 2 tablespoons of flour in the banneton. Shake and distribute the flour as evenly as possible. Punch down dough and form it into a ball. Place the dough, smooth side down, into the floured banneton. Press down firmly. Cover with a damp cloth and allow to rise until almost doubled in bulk, about 35 minutes.
4. Turn dough out of banneton onto a lightly oiled baking sheet. Slash the dough twice across the middle to form a cross. Allow the dough to rise until fully doubled, another 10 to 15 minutes.
5. Preheat oven to 375°F. Place bread in oven on rack placed in lower third of oven. Bake 30 to 35 minutes or until crust is golden. Cool on wire rack. The bread can be served in the banneton if desired.

Makes 1 (1-pound) loaf

Baking Stone and Wooden Paddle

Pizza may have had its origin in Italy but Americans have adopted it as a national favorite. One of the joys of a really good pizza is a crisp, chewy crust, but this is hard to achieve in a conventional oven. In Italy, pizzas are baked in large hearth ovens with stone floors. The Old Stone Oven baking stone, which measures about 16 inches in diameter, fits directly onto an oven rack and adapts the old-fashioned cooking method to home use. The stone is preheated in the oven while you assemble the pizza on the large wooden paddle that comes with the kit. The paddle is fashioned after one used by professional pizza bakers and allows you to shovel the pizza on and off the stone with ease. Dry heat rises from the stone during the baking process and bakes the pizza quickly, so that there is no chance of a soggy crust. The stone can also be used for baking hearty breads with a deep rich crust much like those baked in a stone hearth oven. **To Use:** Before

For crustier bread and pizza, bake on baking stone.

using the first time, the stone must be seasoned by washing in warm water (no detergent) and baking at 450°F about 30 minutes. This conditions and hardens the stone and improves its baking properties. The stone is durable but can break or chip if dropped. For baking pizza: Place seasoned stone in the center of the bottom rack in the oven. Turn oven to the highest temperature and heat 20 to 30 minutes. Sprinkle paddle with cornmeal. When stone is hot, slide the pizza onto it with the wooden paddle. When done, remove from oven with paddle. For baking bread: Place baking stone in oven and turn oven temperature to 375°F. Sprinkle paddle lightly with cornmeal and set risen dough on paddle. Let dough rise until doubled and then slide dough onto stone with paddle.

Approximate Retail Price: $25

Cool It Wooden Racks

Made by the Carmel Kiln Company, Cool It wooden racks come in two sizes: 11 inches by 19 inches and 10 inches by 14 inches. They are cleverly packaged in a canvas tote bag. Since wood does not conduct heat, the company feels that they have the perfect natural product for cooling breads and cakes. This theory works fine for breads but the wooden rungs are set too far apart to make them useful for holding cakes. The racks can be used as handsome trivets for casseroles and hot pots, or, better yet, they make attractive stands for potted plants. **To Use:** Rub racks with oil before using to cool baked goods.

Approximate Retail Price: $14

Cool It wooden racks can be used to cool baked goods or as trivets.

ROAST MASTERS

ROAST MASTERS

Certainly the cooking aromas of a succulent roast duck, a savory boeuf bourguignon or a juicy steak can rival those of pastries and breads. And, indeed, baking includes such methods of meat cookery as roasting, oven braising and broiling. All of these utilize the dry contained heat of an oven.

Roasting is the oldest form of cooking. But the modern oven offers some notable improvements over the original technique: You no longer have to keep turning the meat on a stick to get it to cook evenly and you can catch the juices in a pan placed beneath the roast. The tender results of oven roasting usually leave us quite content with this time-honored method. Recently, however, we came across a newfangled invention that makes all kinds of tantalizing claims. Called a vertical roaster, it is designed to hold meats, especially poultry, in an upright position. You stand the bird on a two-part, hourglass-shaped wire rack and place in a roasting pan; then you can rest a perforated pan filled with butter on top of the rack and the fat will drip down to baste the meat. We can't say that the results necessarily surpass other roast birds in our memory, but the rack is convenient. Because the poultry is held aloft, the juices collect neatly in the roasting pan, basting is effortless, and the rack holds the meat securely for carving. What we liked best, though, was the drama of marching the golden-basted bird, held upright on the vertical roaster, from oven to table.

To go from the apparently ridiculous to the certified sublime, we present a clay marmite, a deep earthenware pot that braises, bakes and simmers beautifully. A tradition so strong in France that a rich soup was named for it, the marmite holds heat snugly around its contents. The interior of the pot is glazed, but the exterior is not, and if you think the humble clay vessel lacks glamour, consider this: You're supposed to rub the unglazed surface with peeled cloves of garlic to season it with a film of the garlic's oil.

To braise a pot roast or stew in a marmite, you add liquid to the pot with the meat. To cook juicy, tender meats in the completely unglazed Romertopf clay pot, you literally infuse the vessel with water. The method lies somewhere between braising and roasting, has been used since Roman times, and is known simply as clay pot cookery. Before placing ingredients in the covered clay cooker, you soak the pot in water for 15 minutes. Then, as the pot — filled with meat, poultry, vegetables, fruit or even bread dough — heats in the oven, the water is released in a filmy vapor that mingles with the food's natural juices. The food comes out smelling and tasting wonderful — moist and succulent, but not overcooked.

There's more than one way to keep meat juicy in the dry-heated oven. So, as a counterpoint to the elegant earthenware pots, we include among our "Roast Masters" two inexpensive metal utensils. One is a set of trussing needles that we find indispensible. Once you've stuffed a bird or roast with a moistened savory mixture, you can fasten the cavity in the meat by inserting these short skewers and lacing them tightly together with string. It's as simple as can be — and it absolutely ensures that the stuffing, as well as the roast, will match the mouthwatering image around which many a holiday feast is planned. The other device is a larding needle, which you use to inject strips of fat into a lean cut of meat.

If, at this point, you feel too hungry to wait out a roast or a pot of braised meat, we suggest you turn to the quickest baking technique, which is broiling. And we recommend a great gadget to use with your steak, fish or chops. It's a water broiler, and it keeps the meat elevated on a rack placed atop a pan of water. The water catches spattering fat, and the meat broils conveniently to your taste. Indeed, the most significant items we've not included in this section are the ones you'll want to keep ever-ready — a knife, a fork and a warm dinner plate.

ROAST MASTERS

Clay Pots

The clay pot, one of the oldest cooking containers, is enjoying a revival. The Roman gourmand, Lucullus, advocated cooking in clay rather than metal. Today, there are several pots that pay homage to the ancient vessels. The Römertopf, which means "Roman pot," is a West German model made of unglazed porous clay (rather like a flower pot). Before using, the pot must be soaked in water 15 minutes to permit the clay to absorb moisture. Then, when you bake at a relatively high temperature, the heat from the oven causes the pot to release a thin vapor of steam, which bastes the food in its own juices. Roasts, poultry, fish and vegetables are some of the foods that adapt themselves well to clay pot cooking. The terra cotta Römertopf pots are available in five different sizes, each embossed with a rustic design. The clay pot can go from oven — or microwave — to tabletop. **To Use:** The first time used, soak entire clay pot in cold water 30 minutes. Soak 15 minutes before each subsequent use. Place ingredients in pot and cover. Place in cold oven and then turn to the desired temperature. For additional browning, remove lid 10 to 15 minutes before the end of the cooking time. Place pot on towel, not a cold surface, after removing it from oven. To clean, soak pot in hot water and scrub with a stiff brush to remove encrusted food. A little detergent is all right, but do not use cleansers — they clog the clay's pores. Avoid sudden temperature changes to keep pot from breaking: Don't put a hot pot on a cold surface or in cold water. Never, never set the pot on a burner or warming tray. The more you use the pot the darker it will become.
Approximate Retail Price: $20 (2-quart casserole)

Unglazed clay pot.

Soak pot for 15 minutes.

Serve food in clay pot.

Cornish Hen in Clay

1 cornish hen, thawed, (about 16 ounces)
3 tablespoons butter, divided
1 small onion, sliced
1 small eggplant (about 8 ounces) cut into ½-inch cubes
1 clove garlic, minced
1 small red or green pepper, cut into strips
4 ounces mushrooms, sliced
¼ teaspoon dried thyme
¼ teaspoon dried basil
¼ teaspoon salt
½ small lemon, sliced
¼ cup dry white wine
¼ cup chicken broth
   Snipped parsley for garnish

1. Soak clay pot and lid in water 15 minutes. Drain and wipe off excess water.
2. Rub hen with butter and place in clay pot.
3. In a skillet, cook and stir onion, eggplant, garlic, pepper and mushrooms in remaining butter until onion is tender, about 3 minutes.
4. Stir in seasonings and sliced lemon. Spoon mixture around hen in clay pot.
5. Mix wine and broth. Pour over vegetables.
6. Place covered clay pot in cold oven. Turn temperature to 450°F. Bake until hen is tender, about 1 hour. If crisper skin is desired, remove lid during last 10 minutes of baking time. Serve in clay pot or transfer to a platter. Garnish with snipped parsley. *Makes 1 or 2 servings*

Clay Marmite

How appealingly Gallic to rub the outside of a clay marmite with garlic before cooking — sort of a ritual gesture to the soul of French country cooking. A marmite is a straight-sided cooking vessel, made of either metal or clay. The clay marmite that we tried comes from the same area Picasso favored for his ceramics — Vallauris, in the south of France. The inner surface of the marmite is glazed to seal the clay, but the outer surface is left unglazed for total heat absorption. If you rub the outside with garlic cloves, the garlic oil will form a fragrant glaze. Once heated, earthenware keeps contents hot for a long period of time. Available in several different sizes, we recommend the smaller marmites for baking vegetable casseroles, such as ratatouille, and the larger ones for hearty soups and stews. Of course, they also make lovely serving pieces. **To Use:** Place ingredients in marmite and set it in a cold oven, then turn to desired temperature. Avoid sudden temperature changes to keep pot from breaking. Do not scour with cleansers.
Approximate Retail Price: $10

Rub clay marmite with garlic.

Cooking Thermometers

The sign of a professional chef is the slender gauge he or she carries in an upper apron pocket to check instantly the temperature of a roast or a sauce. Home cooks will find this instrument especially useful for meats and poultry. Unlike conventional meat thermometers, it does not remain in the meat throughout the cooking period; you insert it after roasting to confirm doneness. This means that you have to use it in conjunction with a chart of cooking times and a reliable oven thermometer — you wouldn't want to remove the roast too frequently to check it, and once the meat is overcooked, the thermometer would be useless. But this method offers two advantages: the slender "instant-read" thermometer doesn't poke a big hole in the roast, and, because it doesn't remain in the meat, it can't conduct heat to the desirably-rare center.

Taylor Instruments makes two professional food thermometers with shatterproof, moisture-resistant, 2-inch glass dials that have easy-to-read numbers. One thermometer indicates Fahrenheit temperatures from 100 to 225 degrees; the other registers centigrade from 10 to 100 degrees. The thermometers have thin, 5-inch stainless-steel stems. The centigrade thermometer would be useful if you cook with European recipes. Cuisinart makes a similar thermometer with a 2-inch dial and a slender 6-inch, stainless-steel stem. Called a meat/yeast thermometer, it registers from 50 to 250 Fahrenheit degrees — low enough to check yeast dough, yogurt and cheese as well as meat. **To Use:** The Taylor and Cuisinart thermometers can be checked and adjusted for accuracy: Holding the thermometer by the tines of a fork, dangle it in boiling water without touching the bottom of the pan. It should register 212°F or one degree less for every 1000 feet above sea level. The thermometer can be reset by rotating the hex nut under the dial head. Or you can remember the discrepancy and take it into account when checking temperatures. The thermometers should not be plunged into hot substances without warming them in warm water. For cooked foods, insert thermometer into food for a quick reading; remove thermometer after checking. For roasts, insert in the thickest part of the meat, away from fat and bone; remove after checking.
Approximate Retail Price: $14 (Taylor); $14 (Cuisinart)

Test oven temperature with the folding thermometer; test foods with "instant-read" gauges.

Folding Oven Thermometer

Taylor's excellent, accurate oven thermometer comes in a folding stainless-steel case that doubles as a stand. Standing, it measures 5 inches high; folded for storage, it's a compact 5½ inches by 2 inches. This is a mercury thermometer — more reliable than the bi-metal spring type — that registers in 25-degree steps from 100°F to 600°F. The silver mercury stands out against a yellow background and is easy to check. **To Use:** Open case so that thermometer stands on perforated base. Set in oven near cooking area in use. You could use it to check oven hot spots, as well as to keep tabs on the temperature while cooking.
Approximate Retail Price: $8

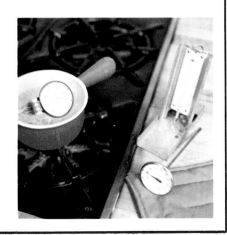

Vertical Roaster

The "Eiffel Tower" design of the vertical roaster lets you cook meats, poultry and shellfish in an upright position. Special wires hold the meat or poultry aloft and sear it inside during the initial high-temperature roasting time, thus preventing some of the natural juices from escaping. Composed of two stainless-steel cone-like sections, the vertical roaster comes with a special basting tray and eight skewers for kebabs and chops. Does vertical roasting make food taste better? We cooked two chickens side by side, one in the vertical roaster and one by the conventional method and our results were pretty much the same. While the food itself never touches the pan beneath, any excess juice or fat collects in the pan and can be used for delicious gravies and sauces. After roasting, place the meat on a platter (still on the roaster), garnish, and bring it to the table. It is easy to carve vertically-held poultry. **To Use:** Set bottom of roaster in baking pan. Place unstuffed poultry on the bottom cone of the roaster. (It will not handle stuffed birds.) Replace the roaster ring cone. Fill the baking pan with about ¾ cup of water and place the entire pan on the lower rack of the oven. Always have some liquid in the roasting pan to prevent burning. To baste: Slice four ½-inch cubes of butter and place them in each of the four sections on the baster tray. Place baster tray on top of roaster and continue cooking. Remove the baster tray after the butter has dripped through. To cook kebabs and chops, string the meat on the skewers and hang them from the top ring of the roaster.

Approximate Retail Price: $16

Roast duck on vertical roaster.

Carve duck on roaster cone.

Duckling à l' Orange

Duck
  1 duck (about 5 pounds)
  ½ teaspoon salt
  ⅛ teaspoon pepper

Sauce
  2 oranges
  1 lemon
  ½ cup sugar
  2 tablespoons white wine
      vinegar
  ½ cup dry white wine
1½ cups chicken broth
  1 tablespoon arrowroot
  ¼ cup orange-flavored liqueur
  ¼ teaspoon salt or to taste
  ⅛ teaspoon pepper or to taste
      Parsley for garnish

1. Preheat oven to 450°F. Season the cavity of the duck with salt and pepper. Set bottom of vertical roaster in roasting pan. Place the duck on the roaster through the neck opening. Tuck excess skin over the top and down inside the roaster. Place top ring of roaster over the tucked-in skin. Put about ¾ cup water in the roasting pan.
2. Bake on lower rack in 450°F oven for 15 minutes. Reduce temperature to 350°F and bake until juices of duck run clear when tested with a fork, about 1 hour and 15 minutes. While duck is roasting, start making sauce.
3. Remove peel from oranges and the lemon with vegetable peeler and cut into very thin strips, or use citrus zester. Reserve peel. Section one of the peeled oranges to use as a garnish and squeeze the juice from the remaining orange and lemon. Reserve juice.
4. Place sugar and vinegar in saucepan and cook over medium heat until sugar is golden. Stir in reserved orange and lemon juice and heat through. Reserve.
5. Remove duck from oven. Place duck and roaster on serving platter. Keep warm while making final sauce preparations.
6. Pour off fat from roasting pan, reserving the juices. Add wine and broth to juices in pan and cook over medium heat 5 to 10 minutes.
7. Mix arrowroot and orange liqueur. Stir into the broth mixture. Heat to boiling. Reduce heat and simmer until mixture is reduced by half. Stir in the sugar-vinegar mixture and the orange and lemon strips. Season to taste with salt and pepper.
8. Brush duck with sauce. Garnish platter with parsley and reserved orange sections. Serve remaining sauce with duck. *Makes 4 servings*

Trussing Needle

A neatly trussed bird keeps its shape while cooking and makes a nice presentation. A trussing needle is just a large, 6- to 9-inch version of a sewing needle. No fancy stitches are required. **To Use:** Thread needle with a long piece of string or twine. With the stuffed or unstuffed bird breast side up, push needle through one wing section, the loose neck skin, and then through the other wing. Pull the string tight and secure it; cut string. Thread needle again, if necessary, and push through the lower part of the back next to the tail. Go through the loose skin under the end of the breast with the needle. Secure with a tight knot.

Approximate Retail Price: $1.95

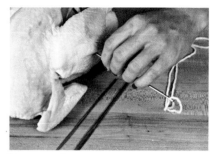
Use trussing needle with string.

Turkey Lacers

Turkey lacers make the job of sewing up the cavity of poultry so much easier that you will wonder how you ever got along without them. The stainless-steel skewers don't break and can be used over and over again. They come six to a card and a small amount of string is supplied for use the first time. We also find them useful for skewering and broiling small appetizers such as chicken livers and for securing the stuffing in whole fish. **To Use:** Stuff cavity of poultry with dressing. Place skin flap over dressing. Push skewers through the skin flap on one side and thread through to other side. Repeat at ½-inch intervals. Depending on the size of the fowl, it may not be necessary to use all of the skewers. Lace string around skewers, starting at top, and tie in a knot. After roasting, withdraw pins to release lacing.

Approximate Retail Price: $1

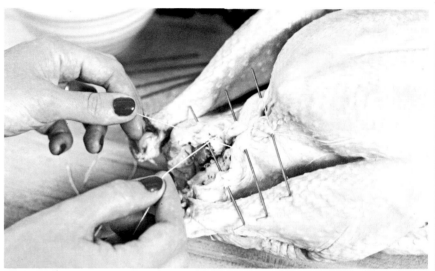
Turkey lacers neatly tie up dressed poultry: Jab skewers through skin flaps and lace together.

Lardoir

Larding needles inject lard into tough cuts of meat to make them tender. Since slow, moist cooking seems like a better, less caloric way to prepare tough cuts of meat, we suggest another use for a lardoir: Use it to poke savory bits of herbs, meat, nuts or vegetable mixtures into roasts. **To Use:** Press filling into groove of needle, making sure the cylinder is pulled back to the handle. Jab the needle into the meat using a twisting-turning motion. Press the cylinder against the meat and hold it in place with a finger while removing the lardoir with a firm swift motion.

Approximate Retail Price: $2.95

A lardoir can be used to insert strips of ham into a pork roast.

ROAST MASTERS

Roast Pork
with Apricot Glaze

¼ **pound boiled ham**
4 **pounds pork loin**
½ **teaspoon salt**
¼ **teaspoon pepper**
½ **teaspoon rosemary,**
   crumbled
¼ **teaspoon thyme, crumbled**

Glaze
6 **ounces dried apricots**
¼ **cup brown sugar or honey**
2 to 3 **tablespoons Dijon-style**
   mustard
¼ **teaspoon nutmeg**
⅛ **teaspoon mace**
¼ **teaspoon salt**
   Pinch of cayenne pepper
   Chopped parsley to garnish

1. Cut ham into thin strips to fit in lardoir. Insert ham strips into pork loin with lardoir at regular intervals, so that cut pork loin will display an interesting cross-sectioned pattern.
2. Heat oven to 325°F. Rub loin with salt and pepper and sprinkle the top with rosemary and thyme.
3. Put loin on a rack in a shallow roasting pan. Roast uncovered for about 1½ hours.
4. Meanwhile, in a small saucepan, cover apricots with water and cook until tender. Pour off excess water.
5. In a blender or food processor fitted with the steel blade, combine cooked apricots, brown sugar or honey, mustard, nutmeg, mace, salt and cayenne pepper. Blend until apricots are pureed.
6. About 30 minutes before loin is completely cooked, coat meat with a thick coating of glaze. Finish roasting meat. (Meat is done when meat thermometer registers about 170°F.)
7. Before serving, sprinkle pork with chopped parsley. *Makes 6 to 8 servings*

Water Broiler

Smokeless, spatterless broiling and ease of cleaning distinguish the water broiler. A beautiful, heavy-gauge stainless-steel pan fitted with a removable grill, the water broiler holds a small amount of cold water, which catches dripping fat and prevents it from smoking or spattering. When not used for roasting or broiling, the 12-inch-wide pan doubles as a serving dish for such specialties as paella or eggplant parmigiana. The grill also makes a handy cooling rack by itself. The 15-inch stainless-steel tongs that come with the pan are called a Forkula; they are designed to facilitate lifting and turning meat. **To Use:** Fill pan with about ½ inch of cold water. Place grill on top of pan and arrange the meat to be broiled or roasted on top of the grill. Place water broiler under oven broiler. To use tongs, insert one set of tines between bars of the grill and underside of meat. Close tongs and lift. Cleanup is easy with this trio since there is no baked-on grease to remove. Simply wash in hot, soapy water.
Approximate Retail Price: $25

Enjoy smokeless, spatterless broiling with the water broiler.

It comes as a surprise to most people to learn that a good piece of fish is *never* fishy. People who were raised in coastal states are likely to be more familiar with the various types of fish than inland dwellers. However, the increased popularity of fishing as a sport is working to reduce that disparity.

Many fish fans are becoming as adept as fishermen at cleaning and filleting their catch. Sometimes this skill can save some money at the fish counter; sometimes it's the only way to ensure that the fish will be prepared the way you like it. A big fish knife is a terrific aid — it can be used to remove heads, tails and fins of even the largest fish and to cut neat fillets without tearing the flesh. A smaller, all-purpose fish knife is great for cleaning, scaling and filleting such freshwater specialties as lake trout. The household scalers we show may be a bit small for the biggest catch, and they may not be necessary if your fish vendor is especially thorough, but, more often than not, they're

handy for removing the scales that the vendor's electric scaler misses. We have found it useful to keep a tweezers in our kitchen for the purpose of removing stray bones.

To store fresh fish, always remove any paper wrapping as the paper tends to stick to the fish and dry it out. Rinse fish in cold water, pat it dry, place it on a plate, and wrap loosely with plastic. Or, prepare a bed of cracked ice (a small broiler pan will do nicely), set the fish on ice and cover either with a damp towel or loosely with plastic wrap. Here are a few tips for freezing fresh fish: Always remove head, gills and guts before freezing as these are breeding grounds for bacteria. Scale the fish; rinse and pat it dry, then wrap tightly in plastic and cover the plastic with a second wrapping of aluminum foil. Freeze fish whole, or in filets. Be sure to put a date on the package; it is not advisable to use fish which has been frozen longer than one year.

Those who appreciate fresh cherrystones and oysters on the

half shell will learn to master the clam and oyster knives especially designed for opening shells and cutting the meat inside free. A word of caution: Always wrap your hands very well with a layer or two of towels before wielding a clam or oyster knife; fresh clams or oysters can be tough to open and nasty cuts can occur if you don't take proper precautions. For the novice, a claw-like clam opener is safer than a clam knife. The Shrimp Kleener, on the other hand, makes easy work of slitting the shrimp shell and carving a channel above the intestinal vein, so that the vein can be removed simply by running the shrimp under cold water. Always store cleaned and cooked shrimp loosely wrapped, with at least one or two holes in the wrapping through which air can circulate; otherwise, the gases given off by the shrimp can become trapped in the wrapping and cause spoilage. Store clams and oysters in a dry bowl covered by a cold, damp towel; put the bowl in a large plastic bag with several holes in it.

There are many exciting ways to cook fish — almost as many ways as there are fish varieties. Fish can be broiled, poached, grilled, baked, braised, fried or steamed. Fish cooks quickly and it is often overcooked, which is a shame, for a piece of properly-cooked fish is one of the tenderest, juiciest foods imaginable. A good way to ensure that fish will not be overcooked is to test for doneness as follows: Pierce the raw fish gently once or twice with the sharp tip of a fish knife or paring knife; there will be some resistance. Then, while the fish is cooking, pierce it the same way and you'll know when the fish is done because the knife will not meet resistance.

It's gotten to the point where good cooks have as many fish stories to tell as the fishermen themselves. And once you get hooked on the fruits of the sea, as well as their complement of paraphernalia, you'll find yourself talking less about the ones that got away — and more about the ones you savored.

PICK OF THE CATCH

Fish Knife

Every fisherperson and fish aficionado should arm themselves with this superb 15½-inch-long knife. Its stainless-steel serrated blade is perfectly mated to the task of removing fish heads, and it will not rust in salty sea air. The sturdy black plastic handle sheaves a ¾ tang; finger ridges provide a great grip for slippery slicing. Legend has it that the extended handle butt was designed for breaking open sea chests filled with gold. Less romantically, we found the knife performed well on all cutting chores that require a serrated blade. **To Use:** Handle with great respect and caution — this is a large, sharp weapon.
Approximate Retail Price: $18

All-Purpose Fish Knife

Its versatility makes this a strange-looking knife and one useful to own. The 6-inch sharp cutting blade slices, bones and fillets fish with ease. The serrated edge accomplishes scaling. And the scoop-like cup at the end of the black plastic handle removes viscera. If you can buy only one fish knife, choose this nicely balanced model by Sabatier. **To Use:** Slit the fish and scoop out viscera. Use the serrated blade edge for scaling fish, the cutting blade for boning, filleting or slicing.
Approximate Retail Price: $10

You can use either a large fish knife or a fish knife/scaler to clean fish depending on the size of the catch; the scoop-handled all-purpose knife removes the viscera too.

Fish Knife/Scaler

Trout could go from stream to fry pan with the aid of this 6½-inch knife, which combines scaling and slicing functions. However, don't count on it as an all-purpose parer; the scalers will inhibit finger mobility. **To Use:** Use notched edge for scaling, curved tip to dress fish, smooth blade for slicing and cutting.
Approximate Retail Price: $2

Dressing a Fish

The art of dressing a fish usually involves scaling, boning and filleting. It is not as difficult or time consuming as you might think. Here are some simple instructions:
1. Rinse the fish. (Since it is going to be skinned and filleted, it does not have to be scaled.) Lay the fish on its side on a cutting board.
2. To remove the head, slide a sharp knife under the bone near the gills and cut off the head.
3. Cut along the backbone down the entire length of the fish.
4. With a sharp knife, follow the central bone closely into the cavity of the fish, leaving as little meat as possible on the bone. Following the contour of the rib cage, lift up and remove the fillet as you cut.
5. Cut under backbone, close to the bone in the same manner. The central bone is now on top of the knife.
6. Again, follow the contour of the rib cage, lifting up the backbone as you progress, leaving as little meat as possible on the bone.

Remove head with knife.

7. It may be necessary to remove the small side bones from center of fillets with tweezers. (You can feel the bones by running your finger from the head down to the tail of the fillet.)

8. To skin fillet, place it skin side down on your cutting board. Starting at the tail, grasp the skin in one hand (or hold it with a towel if it is too slippery) and slide your knife in between the skin and the flesh. Cut forward from the tail in a back-and-forth movement, scraping the flesh from the skin. Remove the skin and discard. If fillets are not skinned, prevent them from curling while they cook by lightly scoring the skin side with your knife, making cuts ½ inch apart and less than $\frac{1}{16}$ inch deep.

Cut along backbone.

Follow contour of rib cage.

Cut between skin and flesh.

Fish Scaler

Even if you don't dress your own fish, a fish scaler is handy for removing scales missed by the fishmonger. A stainless-steel shoehorn-shaped scaler from Sweden accomplishes the task with 35 sharp perforations. It's easy to guide with its 5-inch handle, but the scales scatter all over. Less effective but somewhat neater, an aluminum model features a 4-inch double-edged serrated blade positioned at the bottom of an inch-deep rectangular container. Snap a plastic cover over the top of the container and most — but not all — scales will be trapped within. **To Use:** Grasp the fish securely by the tail (not as easy as it sounds, we realize) and run the scaler toward the head. Repeat around the fish until all scales are removed. Rinse the fish and the scaler under cold running water.

Approximate Retail Price: $2.50 (Swedish stainless-steel scaler); $6 (aluminum scaler)

Grasp fish by tail and run fish scaler toward head, against the scales. The covered sealer (right) will catch removed scales.

PICK OF THE CATCH

Fish Poacher

A fish poacher could be considered a one-pot campaign against the gastronomic sin of dried-out, over-cooked fish. Long, narrow and fitted with a rack, the poacher befits the noble dimensions of a large whole fish, allowing it to simmer stylishly in a shallow depth of court bouillon. While the bouillon heats to barely a boil — just a faint, lazy bubble — the fish lies on the poacher rack and cooks to tender perfection, absorbing the fragrance of the seasoned liquid and yielding none of its own precious juices.

A small fish will, of course, accept the indignity of being poached in any shallow covered vessel. It's only the length of a really big catch that demands a poacher. Prices on this item range from less than $50 for an aluminum model to over $300 for a copper showpiece. Aluminum is the least preferred material because it tends to discolor the cooking broth; copper is unnecessary because the simmering liquid will heat evenly regardless of the

Stainless-steel fish poacher has rack with handles and a tight-fitting lid; lower whole fish into Court Bouillon and poach very gently.

metal's conductivity. An 18-inch-long Italian stainless-steel poacher does the job perfectly. Its rack has two handles that are easy to grasp with potholders to lift out the fish; the lid fits securely — an important consideration in fish poaching. For a once-in-a-lifetime lucky catch — up to 36 inches — or if you don't wish to invest in a poacher, you may be able to rent a suitable

model at a gourmet cookware store. **To Use:** Prepare court bouillon, which is usually composed of water, fish stock, clam juice or wine seasoned with vegetables, herbs and spices. Place whole fish on rack (cheesecloth may be used on rack to prevent sticking) and lower it into slightly-cooled liquid. Bring to a simmer, cover and poach.
Approximate Retail Price: $50

Poached Fish with Caper Hollandaise Sauce

1 whole (2 to 3 pound)
    whitefish or red snapper

Court Bouillon
 8 cups water
 4 cups dry white wine
 ½ cup white vinegar
 2 onions, chopped
 3 carrots, chopped
 1 rib celery, chopped
 1 bayleaf
 1 tablespoon salt
 6 peppercorns
 3 sprigs parsley
 1 teaspoon thyme
 1 teaspoon tarragon

Caper Hollandaise
 8 tablespoons butter
 3 egg yolks

 2 tablespoons lemon juice
 ⅛ teaspoon salt

 Dash pepper
 2 tablespoons capers

1. In fish poacher without the rack, combine all ingredients for Court Bouillon. Bring to a boil and simmer for about 30 minutes. Let bouillon cool to lukewarm.
2. Measure the depth of the fish at its thickest point. Allow for 10 minutes of poaching per inch of thickness.
3. Place the fish on rack and lower it into the poacher.
4. Bring Court Bouillon to a simmer on medium heat. As soon as broth begins to simmer, reduce heat to low, set cover ajar and poach fish 10 minutes per inch of thickness.
5. When fish is done, lift out rack and carefully transfer fish to serving platter. Cut away skin on the top side of fish.
6. For Caper Hollandaise, heat butter in small saucepan until it begins to bubble. In blender or food processor with steel blade, combine egg yolks, lemon juice, salt and pepper. Blend for several seconds until mixture is thick and creamy. With machine on, slowly add hot butter in a thin, steady stream. Do not add milky residue left in bottom of butter. Blend until butter has been incorporated.
7. Drain capers and rinse with cold water. Pat dry and add to sauce. To keep warm until ready to serve, set sauce in a pan of warm water. Serve with poached fish. *Makes 4 to 6 servings*

Clam Openers

Hard-shell clams, known to East-erners as quahogs, are among the stubbornest critters on the face of the earth. If you have ever strug-gled to pry open their tightly clamped shells and felt their deter-mined resistance, you will under-stand the need for a clam opener. The 7-inch-long Super Shucker consists of two stainless-steel jaws: a spoonlike piece that holds the clam securely in place and a rip-pled, contoured blade. As the two plastic-clad handles are pressed together, the sharp rippled blade is forced between the halves of the shell, spreading them apart. An ad-vantage of the Super Shucker is that it only spreads the shell and does not cut through the body of the clam; the clam remains intact for

appetizing eating. In contrast, the 7¾-inch Hoffritz clam opener holds the clam in its curved nickel steel bottom jaw and, when you squeeze the handles together, the stain-less-steel blade passes between the halves of the shell and slashes the clam as well. **To Use:** Always wash and scrub clams with a brush. Let them rest before opening — they tighten up under stress. If you place them in the refrigerator for an hour or so, they will relax their grip. Open clams over a bowl to save the tasty clam juice. Place clam in spoonlike piece of the shucker. Guide the sharp blade between the two halves of the shell. Get a good grip and squeeze the handles to-gether to open shell. (If they are not going to be served raw, you can speed up the process by steaming clams for a few minutes; they will

Use Super Shucker to open clams.

open up in the pot. Discard any that do not open — they are bad.) Add clam juice — or liquid from steam-ing — to chowder.
Approximate Retail Price: $5

Clam Knives

A clam knife is nothing but a blunt-nosed, blunt-edged sturdy knife de-signed for prying into the affairs of clams. Both knives shown have stainless-steel blades about 3½ inches long. One has a rounded handle with the blade set into it; the other has an ordinary paring knife handle with a half tang. Both re-quire a little more clam-opening skill than the Super Shucker. The best trick is to let the bivalves relax in the refrigerator for an hour before open-ing — that way they won't clam up! **To Use:** Holding clam over a bowl, insert blade between the shells. Work it back and forth into the shell

Insert knife into shell and cut hinge muscles; scrape clam into bowl.

and twist the handle to pry open, cutting through the first upper mus-cle that holds the shell shut. Then cut the second upper muscle.

Scrape out the clam. Protect hand holding clam by wrapping it in a kitchen towel if desired.
Approximate Retail Price: $2

Block Island Quahog Chowder

**24 large hard-shell clams
    (quahogs)
¼ pound salt pork, diced
 1 cup chopped onion
 3 cups cubed raw potatoes
¼ teaspoon pepper
½ teaspoon dill
   Pinch thyme
 2 cups heavy cream
   Chopped parsley for garnish**

1. Open clams and reserve juice. Measure juice and add enough water to equal 3 cups.
2. In a large saucepan or kettle, sauté salt pork over low heat until crisp and golden. Pour off all but 1 tablespoon of fat.
3. Sauté onion in pan drippings until translucent. Add potatoes and clam liquid and simmer until potatoes are tender. Skim fat, if necessary.
4. Chop clams or grind coarsely.
5. Add clams, pepper, dill, thyme and cream to broth. Cook over low heat for about 10 minutes. Taste and add more cream if desired. Sprinkle with chopped parsley and serve. *Makes 6 to 8 servings*

PICK OF THE CATCH

Oyster Knives

Oysters are the ugly bivalves with pearls inside — sometimes. They're also valued for their succulent flesh — which is not easy to get at either. The irregular shaped shell makes it hard to insert a knife. Most oyster knives are short and sharp-tipped and feature a hand guard to protect you from both the blade and the ragged-edged shell. The oyster knife shown with the unstained handle is 6 inches long; the one with the stained handle is 5 inches long. They both work as well as anything, but sheer brute force remains the most important factor in opening an oyster. **To Use:** Like

Insert knife into oyster; scrape whole oyster into rounded shell.

clams, oysters will relax if refrigerated. Hold the oyster with the rounded shell beneath and carefully force knife point under the upper, flatter shell. Once the knife is in, twist it and run it between the shells, cutting the muscles. When the shell is open, detach any remaining muscle. Scrape whole oyster into rounded shell to chill and serve raw with lemon.
Approximate Retail Price: $2.50

Oyster Loaf

2 dozen oysters (1 pint, shucked)
1 loaf French bread
1 stick butter
1 clove crushed garlic
1 tablespoon chopped parsley
1 cup ketchup
2 tablespoons horseradish
1 tablespoon lemon juice
1 teaspoon Worcestershire sauce
Dash tabasco

1 cup corn meal
2 cups vegetable oil

½ teaspoon salt
2 dill pickles, thinly sliced

1. Shuck oysters and reserve.
2. Slice bread lengthwise and hollow it out, leaving a ¾-inch shell.
3. Melt together the butter, garlic and parsley, and brush the bread with this mixture. Toast at 300°F for about 25 minutes.
4. Meanwhile, combine the ketchup, horseradish, lemon juice, Worcestershire and tabasco to make a sauce.
5. Dredge the oysters in the cornmeal and fry in hot oil just until brown. Drain and salt.
6. Place the oysters in the lower part of the warm, toasted loaf. Spoon the sauce over and top with sliced pickles. Replace the top part of the bread and cut the loaf into serving portions. *Makes 4 to 6 servings*

Shrimp Kleener

Beautifully contoured in stainless steel, the Shrimp Kleener was designed to shell and devein shrimp. But the 7-inch-long tool is dull-edged and deveins better than it shells. The handle's textured surface does provide a firm grip. **To Use:** Grasping the handle with the wide edge upright, poke the pointed end between the shell and the flesh at the head end. Run Shrimp Kleener back towards the tail, following the outer curve of the shrimp. This should both split the shell and partially remove the vein; use the tip to remove any remaining vein.
Approximate Retail Price: $4

Poke pointed end of Shrimp Kleener between shell and flesh to split shell.

Flaming Shrimp de Jonghe

2 pounds fresh shrimp
1½ sticks butter
3 to 4 cloves garlic, minced
2 tablespoons chopped parsley
¼ cup chopped green onion
1 teaspoon chervil
½ teaspoon tarragon
Pinch nutmeg
½ cup brandy or cognac
¾ teaspoon salt
¼ teaspoon pepper

1. Shell and devein shrimp without removing tails.
2. In a large skillet, heat butter and add shrimp, garlic, parsley, green onion, chervil, tarragon and nutmeg. Sauté until shrimp are pink and tender.
3. In a small saucepan, heat brandy or cognac. Pour over shrimp. Ignite, shaking the pan gently until the flames die out. Season with salt and pepper. (Note: If a heavier sauce is desired, add 1 cup of heavy cream after flaming and seasoning and heat thoroughly. Serve with toast points or toast cups.)

Makes 6 servings

Scallop Shells

Centuries ago, scallop shells were carried by pilgrims as a symbol of homage to their patron, St. Jacques. Today the shell has secular import for seafood-lovers who savor a creamy dish of Coquilles St. Jacques — scallops cooked in a sauce and baked and served in the lovely, curved scallop shells. Pretty as they are, however, the natural shells tend to frustrate chefs by rocking and tipping when filled and placed on a baking sheet. More stable and less fragile are the porcelain scallop shells from B.I.A. Cordon Bleu. Both natural and porcelain shells are about 5 inches wide, and either can be used to bake and serve seafood other than scallops, as well as vegetables au gratin. **To Use:** Make sure natural shells will hold fairly level before filling. Place shells on baking sheet and fill with Coquilles St. Jacques or other food; bake according to recipe. Porcelain shells are dishwasher safe. Natural shells must be handwashed to reuse.

Natural scallop shells or porcelain ones can be used for dishes like Coquilles St. Jacques.

Approximate Retail Price: $.50 (natural); $5 (porcelain)

Coquilles St. Jacques

1 pound scallops, rinsed
1 cup dry white wine
1 bayleaf
1 onion, sliced
1 sprig parsley
½ teaspoon salt
Pinch pepper
3 tablespoons butter
2 to 3 green onions, sliced
1 clove garlic, minced
4 tablespoons flour
1 cup milk
2 egg yolks
1 teaspoon lemon juice
Pinch nutmeg
½ cup shredded Swiss cheese

1. In a saucepan, combine scallops, white wine, bayleaf, onion, parsley, salt and pepper. Bring to a boil, reduce heat to simmer, cover and cook for 3 minutes. (Reduce cooking time if using small bay scallops.)
2. Drain scallops and reserve liquid, which will measure about 1½ cups. Discard bayleaf, onion slices and parsley. Return broth to pot; boil until reduced to 1 cup.
3. In another saucepan, melt butter and cook green onions until tender. Add garlic and cook for 1 minute. Whisk in flour and cook for 2 minutes, stirring constantly. Add hot broth, stirring to mix.
4. Combine milk and egg yolks. Add some of the hot sauce mixture to the egg-milk mixture. Then pour the egg-milk mixture into the sauce. Cook over medium heat until thickened, stirring constantly.
5. Add lemon juice and nutmeg. Taste and adjust seasoning.
6. If using large sea scallops, cut into slices. Add scallops to sauce.
7. Place scallop shells on a baking sheet. Distribute scallop mixture among 6 scallop shells. Sprinkle shredded Swiss cheese on top and bake at 400° F for 5 to 10 minutes until bubbly. If desired, brown quickly under broiler.

Makes 6 servings

PICK OF THE CATCH

Escargot Equipment

When is a snail not a snail? When it's cooked in a delectable butter sauce and blessed with the French name, escargot. Appropriately, it acquires a full wardrobe of paraphernalia in the process. Usually served as a first course, escargots are almost always purchased canned rather than fresh and restored to separately-purchased shells for baking. The shells can be either natural or porcelain. The natural shells are huge and can hold two snails and a generous amount of butter; the porcelain ones, somewhat smaller, are less fragile and do not retain the odor of garlicky snail butter the way the natural ones do. You can buy the porcelain shells individually; the natural ones are often sold in a set of 12 with a can of 24 snails.

An enameled cast iron escargot dish by Le Creuset holds six shells in separate indentations to facilitate baking and serving. Other models, in various materials, hold 12 shells. If you're using the larger, natural shells, be sure the indentations on the dish you buy are far enough apart to hold them.

How do you extract an escargot from its curved habitat? With specially-designed tongs and fork, of course. Stainless-steel tongs, 6½ inches long, fit around the hot bubbling shell while you pick out the snail with a dainty, two-tined 6-inch stainless-steel fork. Ah, delicious! And what elegant showmanship!

To Use: Stuff shells with butter, garlicked or not. Insert the snail and

Stuff shells with butter.

Insert snails in shells.

Arrange on dish.

Hold snails with tongs and spear with fork.

top with more butter. Arrange shells in escargot dish, bake according to recipe you are using, and serve hot. Hold tongs with curved edge down. Force handles together to spread tongs and fit them around a hot shell; relax your grip and tongs will hug escargot. Pick out snail with

snail fork and enjoy; then tip butter into escargot dish, sop it up with French bread — and enjoy again! Wash shells to reuse.
Approximate Retail Price: $8 (natural shell set with can of snails); $1.75 (porcelain shell); $8 (escargot dish); $2.50 (tongs); $1 (fork)

Escargots Bourguignon

2 dozen canned snails
¼ cup dry white wine
⅜ pound butter (1½ sticks)
3 cloves garlic, minced
1 green onion, minced
3 tablespoons chopped
    parsley
Salt and freshly ground
    pepper to taste

1. Wash snails well in water and drain thoroughly. Soak snails in wine while preparing butter. (Soaking helps remove the briny taste and adds flavor.)
2. Cream the butter and add remaining ingredients.
3. Drain snails. Place about ½ teaspoon of butter mixture in each shell. Push snail, rounded side first into the shell. Pack another teaspoon or so of butter mixture into shell. (If you are using natural shells, insert two snails per shell and position double the amount of butter in each shell accordingly.) Place on snail plates.
4. Bake at 400° F for 12 to 15 minutes. Serve bubbling hot.
Note: Always serve escargots with crusty French bread, so that you can use it to soak up the delicious snail butter poured out of shells into snail dish. A dry white wine is the perfect accompaniment.   *Makes 4 to 6 servings*

MOLDED ART

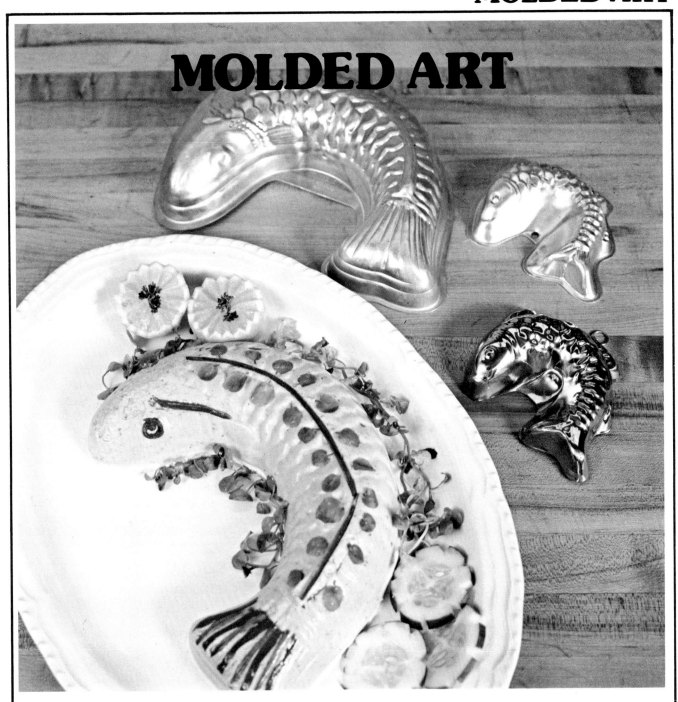

In the art world, there is a French term, *trompe l'oeil,* that translates literally to "fools the eye." It is the style in which painters create the illusion that something is real rather than two-dimensional. At one time or another, we have probably all been fooled by what looked like gorgeous wood paneling, but which was actually painted on the wall, or by a spectacular marble column that turned out to be pastiche.

Molds are the *trompe l'oeil* tools of culinary artists. By placing salmon mousse in a mold shaped like a fish and decorating it to look real, for example, the chef "fools the eye" of diners — and tempts them all the more. The better and more finely wrought the mold, and the more successful we are in decorating the molded food, the more fabulous the effect.

Whether it is an ordinary gelatin dessert or an ethereal mousse of some exotic gamebird, molded food never fails to inspire wonder. Perhaps it arouses our sense of romance or mystery, since until the moment when we actually taste

MOLDED ART

the artful fare we're never really sure what the sculpted mound consists of.

Molds have been used for centuries, especially by French chefs. Finely detailed antique molds, which come in myriad shapes and sizes, are among the most precious possessions of any kitchen connoisseur. Today molds are made of many materials, including tin, stainless steel, aluminum, copper, porcelain and glass. For candy-making and sugar work, there are even flexible plastic molds intricately stamped with the forms of flowers, animals and people.

Many molds, especially those made of copper and copper alloys, have a two-fold decorative value. They can be hung on kitchen walls to be admired, and their bright charm creates an atmosphere of warmth. For those who are concerned with maintaining copper, a special non-toxic lacquer can be applied to keep molds shiny through a lifetime of use.

There are as many foods that can be molded as there are shapes and sizes of containers. Those of us who may be frustrated by our inability to draw or paint will derive satisfaction from the experience of sculpting food, which requires only a minimum of dexterity and virtually guarantees superb results. All you need is patience and a good recipe to produce an elegant product.

Molded foods may be cooked or uncooked and served hot or cold. Mousses and salads are among the more familiar chilled delights. You may be less familiar with the spectrum of pâtés and terrines which are baked in special molds and served cold. Once you start exploring the possibilities, you'll recognize one marvelous fact: The attractiveness of molded foods obscures their often simple preparation. You can entertain a luncheon crowd with simple chicken salad shaped to resemble a regal roast chicken. Or, you can use a special mold to relieve a lot of the worry involved in

baking a pâté wrapped in pastry.

The English are great advocates of steam molding and their scrumptious plum and persimmon puddings, served at Christmas time, are famous examples of the art. Steamed pudding molds are filled with a treasury of ingredients, and then set into a pot that contains a small amount of water. As the water boils, the steam heats the mold to cook the food.

Ice cream molds are called bombes, as are the desserts they hold. There is a temptation to pronounce this word BOMB-BAYS, but the correct French pronunciation is BAHM-BB. A classic bombe consists of ice cream molded around a soft center — making it a French cousin of our Baked Alaska. There can be two or more ice cream flavors molded in a bombe but the center is always a surprise.

A Bombe Diplomate, for instance, is vanilla ice cream with a maraschino and candied fruit center; Bombe Médicis, is cognac-spiked ice cream with a raspberry center; and Bombe Strogoff is peach ice cream with a champagne-flavored center. Once unmolded, bombes can be elaborately decorated with flourishes of whipped cream and bouquets of fruit. Bombe molds come in every shape under the sun and always serve to create a spectacular impression.

The carving of ice sculpture is an art unto itself and traditionally has remained the domain of the professional chef. But now there are ice molds that produce the same fabulous effect without the skill needed for carving or the investment of time. A wonderful ice sculpture can begin with the mere turn of the tap needed to fill an ice mold with water before freezing. Later you can peel off the mold — *et voilà*! You'll have a dramatic centerpiece for a party or holiday buffet.

The only requirements for molded art are a good imagination and a few hours of time. But the effect will "fool the eye" of the beholder into believing you've been cooking and sculpting all day.

Hinged Pâté Molds

A pâté may be as smooth and un-complicated as seasoned, ground chicken livers, or as formidable as a whole breast of duck sandwiched in a mixture of ground meats. Regard-less of ingredients or consistency, it is simply a fresh meat loaf known by its French name. Food pro-cessor owners have discovered how easy it is to mimic the French. And now another dimension of the pâté mystique falls prey to imported gadgetry: With a hinged-con-struction mold, you can bake the pâté en croûte — which means "in a crust," — and serve your humble meat loaf encased in a glorious golden puff. Or, with an alternate bow to tradition, you can sheathe the loaf in strips of bacon. Either way, the glamorous preparation easily comes free from the mold when you release the hinged sides.

The two fluted sides of a three-piece tinned steel oval pâté mold fit snugly into the curled lip of the flat bottom; you insert the sides and clamp them together with four alu-minum clips, then line with pastry and fill with meat. The mold shown is 6 inches long; a 9-inch size is also available. The 10-inch rectan-gular pâté mold produces a long, slender loaf that's easier to slice and serve than the oval; two metal pins secure the L-shaped sides to the bottom and the waffled tinned steel impresses a pretty pattern on the pastry. You can purchase this mold in sizes up to 14 inches long. **To Use:** Assemble either mold and line with pastry or bacon. Fill with meat mixture and arrange over-hanging pastry or bacon over top. Bake and cool. Unhinge mold and slice pâté.
Approximate Retail Price: $11 (oval mold); $12 (rectangular mold)

Pâté en croûte molds release the pate without damaging the crust.

Terrines

A pâté cooked and served cold in its baking dish is called a terrine; the baking dish bears the same name. Classic covered terrines, made of glazed earthenware, oven-proof porcelain or enameled cast iron, come in various shapes and sizes. Le Creuset flame and white enameled cast-iron terrines measure 10½ inches long by 4 inch-es wide by 3 inches deep and hold 4 cups of pâté; they're available in other colors and in a 6-cup size. Important features are snug-fitting lids with steam holes and easy-to-grasp flared handles. **To Use:** Line terrine with bacon or strips of fat. Pack filling into terrine and cover. Place in a large pan and add a 3-inch depth of boiling water. Bake according to recipe. Remove terrine from oven, lift off cover, remove from water bath and allow to cool. Refrigerate. Slice to serve.
Approximate Retail Price: $25

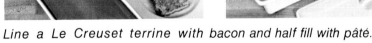

Line a Le Creuset terrine with bacon and half fill with pâté.

Add ham strips and cover with pâté; fold bacon over.

MOLDED ART

Country Terrine

1 pound sliced bacon
¼ cup brandy
1 slice smoked ham, (about 4 ounces), cut into ½-inch strips
1 medium onion, chopped
2 cloves garlic, crushed
2 tablespoons butter
1 pound boneless pork (half lean and half fatty), ground
8 ounce boneless veal, ground
4 ounces chicken livers, coarsely chopped
¼ cup toasted coarsely-chopped walnuts
2 eggs
1 teaspoon salt
½ teaspoon dried thyme
½ teaspoon dried savory
⅛ teaspoon ground allspice
⅛ teaspoon ground cloves
⅛ teaspoon ground nutmeg
⅛ teaspoon freshly ground black pepper
1 bay leaf
1 thyme sprig (optional)

1. Place bacon in skillet. Cover with water and simmer 10 minutes. Drain; pat bacon dry. Pour brandy over ham strips and allow to stand while preparing remaining ingredients.
2. Sauté onion and garlic in butter until tender, 2 to 3 minutes. Mix onion mixture with all the remaining ingredients except bay leaf and thyme sprig. Drain ham and pour reserved brandy into meat mixture. Mix thoroughly.
3. Preheat oven to 350°F. Arrange bacon slices across bottom and up sides of 4-cup terrine, reserving 1 or 2 slices for top. Spread half of the meat mixture in terrine. Arrange ham strips lengthwise over meat. Cover ham with remaining meat mixture. Fold bacon over top. Lay bay leaf and thyme sprig on top. Cover top of terrine with lid. Place terrine in baking pan and add boiling water to pan to a depth of 3 inches. Bake until juices run clear and meat shrinks away from sides of mold, about 1½ hours.
4. Remove terrine from oven and lift off cover. Cool slightly. Remove from water bath and place foil over top of terrine. Weight the foil-covered terrine with a brick or other heavy object. Refrigerate at least 24 hours before serving. To serve, remove weight and foil. Cut terrine into slices. Terrine is traditionally served with French bread and tiny sour pickles called cornichons.
Makes 8 to 10 servings

Fish Molds

The sign of Pisces brings cool elegance to a summer buffet in the form of a luscious chilled salmon mousse. Decorations can be positioned in the mold before the mousse is added, but eyes and gills may slip while you're filling the mold; it's easier to apply your artistic talents after the fish has been unmolded. An aluminum Mirro mold measures 11 inches from head to tail and holds 6 cups. Smaller molds of aluminum and tin-lined copper are 5 inches long and hold single 6-ounce servings. When you're not fishing for culinary compliments, you can hang all three molds by attached hooks to brighten kitchen walls. And if you're truly hooked, you can use all three molds for hot baked dishes too. **To Use:** Oil the molds before filling with either cold mousse to be refrigerated or a hot dish to be baked. If a chilled mold sticks, cover it briefly with a warm, damp towel; then run knife around edges.
Approximate Retail Price: $3 (large Mirro aluminum); $1.50 (small Mirro aluminum); $8 (6-ounce tin-lined copper)

Small aluminum and tin-lined copper molds hold 6-ounce servings; large mold holds 6 cups of Salmon Mousse.

Salmon Mousse with Dill Sauce

First Layer
1½ packages unflavored gelatin
¼ cup white wine
½ cup boiling water
2 cups cooked salmon, cleaned and flaked
½ cup mayonnaise
4 ounces pimientoes
2 tablespoons grated onion
2 tablespoons capers, chopped
2 tablespoons lemon juice
1 teaspoon salt
A few drops tabasco
½ cup whipping cream

Second Layer
1 large or 2 small cucumbers, peeled and seeded
½ package unflavored gelatin
8 ounces cream cheese
¼ teaspoon salt
Dash pepper
½ teaspoon cream-style horseradish

Dill Sauce
1 egg
1 cup sour cream
½ cup plain yogurt
1 green onion, minced
1 tablespoon lemon juice
½ teaspoon salt
⅛ teaspoon pepper
Pinch sugar
1 to 2 tablespoons fresh dill weed or 1 tablespoon dried

Garnishes
Green onions
Pimientos
Olives
Watercress
Lemon halves or wedges
Cucumber slices

1. For first layer, soften gelatin in wine; then add boiling water and stir until gelatin is dissolved. Set aside.
2. Using a mixer, blender or food processor, combine salmon, mayonnaise, pimientoes, onion, capers, lemon juice, salt and tabasco. Add gelatin mixture in a slow, steady stream and mix until thoroughly blended.
3. Whip the cream and fold it into the salmon mixture.
4. Pour mousse into an oiled 6-cup fish mold and refrigerate until firm.
5. For second layer, shred or grate cucumber and drain in a colander, reserving cucumber liquid. Add enough water to liquid to make ¼ cup and place in small saucepan.
6. Soften gelatin in reserved liquid. Stir over low heat until gelatin is dissolved. Set aside.
7. Soften cream cheese and add to gelatin mixture. Mix in salt, pepper, horseradish and cucumber. Stir until blended.
8. Pour mixture into mold to cover salmon mousse and refrigerate two hours or until firm.
9. For Dill Sauce, beat egg until thick and lemon-colored. Add remaining ingredients and stir until blended. Refrigerate until ready to serve.
10. Unmold mousse onto serving plate and decorate. Surround with watercress, lemon and cucumber and serve with Dill Sauce. *Makes 8 servings*

Chicken-in-Aspic Mold

You needn't bother with the aspic — a plain salad, mousse or liver pâté will easily hold its own as a conversation piece when served in the shape of a chicken. The 9-inch-by-5-inch French tinned-steel mold holds one quart and comes with a stand to hold it level in the refrigerator or oven. The mold's smoothly contoured drumsticks and breast release food easily. **To Use:** Oil the mold before filling with cold mixture to be refrigerated or hot mixture to be baked. If chilled mold sticks, cover it briefly with a warm damp towel; then run a knife around edges if necessary.
Approximate Retail Price: $13

Chicken-in-aspic mold shapes an entree of Chicken Mousse.

MOLDED ART

Chicken Mousse with Lemon Dressing

2 tablespoons butter
2 tablespoons flour
½ cup chicken stock
½ cup milk
1½ envelopes unflavored gelatin
¼ cup dry sherry
2½ cups chopped cooked chicken
1 tablespoon lemon juice
½ teaspoon paprika
1 teaspoon dry mustard
Pinch nutmeg
¼ teaspoon salt
Fresh black pepper
1 cup heavy cream, whipped

Lemon Dressing
1 cup lemon yogurt
½ cup mayonnaise
3 tablespoons lemon juice

Garnish
Lettuce leaves
Avocado, watermelon and cantaloupe cubes
Grapes
Watercress sprigs, if desired

1. In saucepan, melt butter over low heat. Whisk in flour and stir to blend, about 2 minutes.
2. Combine chicken stock and milk and add to flour mixture, stirring constantly with a whisk until thick and smooth.
3. Soften gelatin in sherry and add to the sauce. Cook and stir until gelatin is completely dissolved.
4. Add chicken, lemon juice, paprika, mustard, nutmeg, salt and pepper. Mix thoroughly. Refrigerate until mixture begins to set.
5. Fold cream into slightly set mixture.
6. Lightly oil a 1-quart chicken mold. Turn mousse into it and refrigerate until firm.
7. To make Lemon Dressing, combine all ingredients and refrigerate.
8. Unmold Chicken Mousse onto serving plate lined with lettuce leaves. Surround with fruit and watercress. Serve with Lemon Dressing.

Makes 4 to 6 servings

Steamed-Pudding Mold

Yuletide plum pudding like the one cherished by Tiny Tim can be steamed beautifully in this pudding mold. And the covered mold will serve other puddings and other occasions as well. The 1½-quart, tinned-steel tube mold comes from West Germany, stands about 6 inches tall and measures 6 inches across. Its swirl-embossed bottom and sloping sides produce an attractive tube-shaped pudding. The same mold is also available in 1- and 2-quart sizes. **To Use:** Grease mold, pack with pudding and cover with lid. Hold the sides of the mold as you lower it into a large pot, as the lid handle will not support the weight of the pudding. Fill pot with water to half the depth of the mold. Simmer until pudding is done, lift out mold and remove lid. Cool and unmold pudding. Dry mold thoroughly after washing or it will rust.
Approximate Retail Price: $11

Steamed Carrot-Apricot Pudding is made in a steamed pudding mold.

Steamed Carrot-Apricot Pudding

Pudding
 2 cups grated carrots
1½ cups chopped dried apricots
1½ cups golden raisins, cut into pieces
 1 cup chopped suet
 ½ cup brown sugar
 2 tablespoons honey
 2 cups flour
 1 teaspoon baking soda
 2 teaspoons baking powder
 ½ teaspoon salt
 1 teaspoon cinnamon
 ½ teaspoon cloves
 ½ teaspoon nutmeg
  Grated rind of 2 oranges

Hard Sauce
 8 tablespoons butter
 1 cup powdered sugar
 ⅛ teaspoon salt
 1 teaspoon vanilla
 2 to 3 tablespoons orange liqueur, brandy or rum or 1 egg yolk
 Candied orange peel (optional)

1. Combine all ingredients for pudding in a large bowl and mix together until thoroughly blended.
2. Pack into a greased 8-cup steamed pudding mold with lid.
3. Cover and lower mold into a large pot. Fill pot with water to half the depth of the mold. Cover pot and bring water to a boil. Lower heat and keep water at a simmer for entire steaming time. Steam for 2 hours. You may have to add more water to maintain depth during steaming. (Note: For a smaller pudding, this recipe can be cut in half.)
4. To make Hard Sauce, cream butter and mix in remaining ingredients until blended. Place butter mixture in serving dish and sprinkle with candied orange peel. Refrigerate until hard.
5. Unmold pudding and serve warm with Hard Sauce.

Makes 10 to 12 servings

Ice Cream Mold

With a decorative ice cream mold, you can dress up ordinary ice cream and transform it into a fancy dessert. In fact, when molded with a soft filling, ice cream takes on a French name and is called a bombe. Layer two or more flavors of ice cream or sherbet to produce an interesting cross-section, or add a little spirit to the cream with a dash of fruit liqueur. The combo possibilities are endless. The classic 5-inch-square tinned-steel mold shown holds about 3 cups and imprints the ice cream with a fluted motif. Its graceful sloping sides are riveted and welded together to prevent leaking and its tightly-fitted lid protects contents during freezing. The same model comes in sizes from 1 cup to 6 cups. **To Use:** Fill with a single flavor of softened ice

A 3-cup mold makes a special dessert of ice cream and liqueur.

cream or layers of several flavors. Cover and freeze. Dip mold in cool water and unmold onto serving dish; return unmolded ice cream to freezer for an hour before serving. *Approximate Retail Price: $9*

Grand Marnier Ice Cream Mold

 1 quart French vanilla ice cream
 ½ cup Grand Marnier
 5 oranges
  Mint leaves
  Grated orange rind

1. Slightly soften ice cream. Stir in ¼ cup of the Grand Marnier until blended. Pour into ice cream mold and cover. Freeze for several hours, or overnight, until firm.
2. One hour before serving, cut oranges into sections, peel and seed. Pour remaining ¼ cup Grand Marnier over orange sections and refrigerate.
3. About one hour before serving, unmold ice cream. To unmold, dip mold in cool water a few seconds, dry, and invert onto a serving plate. Run a knife around the edges of the mold to break suction, if necessary. Return unmolded ice cream to freezer.
4. To serve, surround mold with orange sections. Garnish with mint leaves and grated orange rind.

Makes 4 to 6 servings

MOLDED ART

Ice Sculpture Mold

Few monuments are as eye-catching as a sculpted block of ice — and few are as easy to construct. With a special kit, you can "cast" your objet d'art by filling a pliant blue plastic mold with water and freezing it overnight. Two narrow wire supports hold the mold suspended in a cardboard box while it freezes. The shapes the molds come in suggest the innocence of the art: They include a duck, a single penguin or a grouping of mother and baby penguins, a polar bear, a dolphin, a seal, a frog and a Christmas tree. Surely a child would love to see one of these 9- to 10-inch-tall creatures centered in a birthday party punch bowl. Adults can point to the sculpture's functional aspect — keeping food and beverages chilled — while smiling inwardly as guests acclaim the frozen masterpiece. **To Use:** Be sure your freezer has enough room to hold the box the mold comes in, as this will hold the mold while it freezes. Wash mold with warm soapy water before using; rinse and dry thoroughly. Turn mold upside down and insert two wires through reinforced circles in the base. Suspend mold in box by hooking wires over edges, so that mold hangs free. Fill mold with water to just below wires. Place in freezer overnight or until solidly frozen. Remove sculpture and let it sit at room temperature for a few minutes. Slip out wires and gently peel off plastic mold.

Approximate Retail Price: $7

A festive dolphin ice sculpture is made in a blue plastic mold.

PALATE TEASERS

PALATE TEASERS

Ever since man began to putter around in his leisure time, he has searched for the ideal object with which to putter. Inventors have found their widgets and wherewithal, gardeners their acres of tools. And cooks have found their gadgets.

Every connoisseur of our acquaintance, regardless of age or cooking ability, boasts some collection of esoteric equipment. Some are displayed, not without pride, as a chaos of tangled handles, with all the organization of a bowl of spaghetti. Others are jealously guarded and carefully wrapped in plastic bags to guard against dust and corrosion. There are cooks who actually use their specialized gadgets; yet they do not love them any more than the cooks who just stow them away and take them out only to cast a fond glance. For a true gadget lover, possession is nine-tenths of the fun.

Will Rogers once said, "I never met a man I didn't like." Well, that's the way most of us feel about kitchen gadgets. We would go so far as to speculate that the reason for this affinity has something to do with toys — and something to do with play.

All the "Palate Teasers" we have selected have a playful dimension. They all perform some function rather effectively — but they turn the culinary labor into a game.

Take the Bel Cream Maker, for example. It's the only gadget we know of that's designed to make cream, and it will make any kind of cream you desire — from a thin liquid for coffee to thick crème fraiche to fresh delicious whipping cream. And the great joy of this plastic mechanism is that it turns butter and milk into the more elegant stuff by means of a simple little pump. Once you start pumping, you'll find yourself, like Tom Sawyer, besieged with offers to help.

Bigger, but no more complex, the tomato pureer will also keep you puttering for hours — ostensibly to make tomato puree for cooking or canning, but really because cranking the handle of the bright plastic machine offers such fascinating results.

Anyone who played Lord High Executioner as a child will delight in two egg-eating aids: With an egg topper or egg cutter, you can lop off Humpty Dumpty's head with nary a care for all the king's men. If playing with dolls was your youthful obsession, you'll undoubtedly fall for the tiny cloth caps fastidiously stitched to garb lemon wedges. If a doll's house once intrigued you, you'll grow enamored of the Magic Mop, a small-scale item designed to whisk fat off the surface of food.

Every kindergarten has its sensuous crowd — the kids who can't be distracted from finger paints or sand castles. For this group, grown up, we present the sausage stuffer. You can't use it without getting your fingers sticky from mixing and shaping the meat. But, on the other hand, you can't make sausage links without it.

Other toys, too, have distinctive rationales. A swinging mesh ball slings over the side of a pot to keep herbs and spices suspended in a soup or sauce. A 7-in-1 cup, which we'd buy for its name alone, actually has seven functions — straining, separating eggs, skimming gravy, measuring liquids, dispensing syrups, clarifying butter, and funneling liquids.

Perhaps one of the juvenile pleasures dedicated cooks remember most fondly is playing with their food — naturally enough. So we conclude with two gadgets, the egg slicer and the egg wedger, designed to do just that. Regardless of what they say about the appealing symmetry of neatly sectioned hard-cooked eggs, we know in our heart of hearts that we could be persuaded to throw away all of the tempting yellow and white slices but we'd never part with the slicers themselves.

Bel Cream Maker

For over 40 years the British have been enjoying fresh, thick double cream, pouring cream, whipping cream and creme fraiche made with the Bel Cream Maker. This 8-inch-high durable plastic gadget consists of a pumping mechanism and a clear jar. It works on a pressure principle, blending and aerating a mixture of butter and milk as it's pumped. **To Use:** For 8 ounces of cream, combine 4 ounces of milk and 4 ounces unsalted butter, cut into pieces, in a saucepan. Heat slowly until butter melts. Do not let mixture boil. Pour the hot mixture from the saucepan into the cup on top. Pump the handle up and down to emulsify butter and milk; chill cream in jar. Be careful not to raise pump all the way, as it may stick; adjust piston inside if it sticks. The cream maker comes assembled and can be taken apart for cleaning after use. A helpful instruction booklet and recipes for various types of cream are included.
Approximate Retail Price: $14.50

The Bel Cream Maker.

Bouquet Garni Bags

What will they think of next? We never thought tying a mixed herb bouquet in a piece of cheesecloth was any big deal. But if you did, these tiny bouquet garni bags are now at your disposal. A Rowoco product, the set includes 10 washable cotton bags, each about 2½ x 3½ inches in size. **To Use:** A bouquet garni usually includes 2 sprigs of parsley, a small bay leaf, and ⅛ teaspoon thyme. Pieces of celery, garlic or scallions may be included. Fill bag and tie drawstring. Place in soups, stews, sauces. Remove bag, empty herbs, and wash to reuse.
Approximate Retail Price: $2 (set of 10)

Wonderball

A 2½-inch, round ball consisting of two stainless-steel, fine mesh hemispheres joined by a hinge is billed by Taylor and Ng as the Wonderball. Open the ball and fill it with herbs, spices or tea; then suspend it by its hooked 7-inch chain over the rim of a pot. The Wonderball's contents will season a sauce or soup, or infuse a pot of tea. Our only criticism is that the little hinge joining the two hemispheres could be sturdier. The mesh is fairly fragile. Don't let it bang around in a drawer full of utensils and gadgets. You might want to store the Wonderball in its box instead. **To Use:** Fill ball with bouquet garni, spices or tea. Or use it to cook or color

Bouquet garni bags and Wonderball.

eggs, or fry shredded potato balls.
Approximate Retail Price: $3

Lemon Wedge Bags

Strange that these esoteric touches of elegance should be called lemon panties! But that's how they're known to devotees of squirtless lemon wedges. The washable cotton bags with elasticized edges come 25 to a set from Rowoco. **To Use:** Slip bag over lemon wedge, so that elastic edge hugs rind. Then squeeze to your heart's content — with nary a drop catching you in the eye!
Approximate Retail Price: $3 (set of 25)

Bags hold lemon wedges.

PALATE TEASERS

Egg Topper

Once you've tried an egg topper, any other means of getting at a soft-boiled egg will seem quite uncivilized. Not a cutting device, the 3½-inch-long aluminum topper cups the small end of the egg, gently taps it and lifts it off. **To Use:** Place metal cup over small end of egg. Pull knob on top and release; then pull and release again. Vibrations from the spring-action hammer neatly top the egg. No ragged shell and no burned fingers!
Approximate Retail Price: $3.50

Egg topper has spring-action hammer that strikes egg to remove top.

Egg Cutters

Armed with these cutters, Gulliver would have tipped the Lilliputians' civil war in favor of the Small-Endians. Both the orange plastic Zyliss cutter and the stainless-steel cutter lop off the small ends of soft-boiled eggs, but neither works as neatly as the egg topper. **To Use:** Fit Zyliss cutter over small end of egg; force handles together. To open Zyliss cutter for cleaning, turn the little black button to "V"; to close, turn button to "U." To use stainless-steel cutter, fit ring over small end of egg and squeeze the handles together; repeat several times.
Approximate Retail Price: $6 (Zyliss); $6 (stainless-steel)

Plastic Zyliss and stainless-steel cutters remove egg tops.

Egg Rings

To dazzle guests at Sunday brunch, you might serve toast rounds layered with creamed spinach, topped with a perfectly-round fried egg and drizzled with Mornay Sauce. But to accomplish this well-rounded dish, you'll need an egg ring. We tried two models. The first is a heavy-duty stainless-steel ring, only 3½ inches in diameter, with a handle that folds to facilitate storage. The second, a deluxe model that's more cumbersome to store, is made of chrome-plated steel and measures about 4 inches in diameter; its spiral-knobbed handle flares away from the ring to prevent it from heating up while the egg is cooking. **To Use:** Butter or oil the egg ring, place it on a griddle or pan and break an egg into the center. When the egg is cooked or ready to turn, remove the ring — and behold! A beautiful round fried egg.
Approximate Retail Price: $1

Ring shapes fried eggs.

Eggs Provencal

1 egg
1 tablespoon water
1 cup fine, dry bread crumbs
½ teaspoon salt
¼ teaspoon pepper
6 slices eggplant, 4 inch-diameter, ½ inch thick
¼ cup olive oil
1 clove garlic, minced
6 thick slices tomatoes, 4-inch diameter, ¼ inch thick
6 eggs
3 tablespoons butter

Hollandaise Sauce (see Index)
Chopped parsley for garnish

1. Beat egg and water together.
2. Combine dry bread crumbs, salt and pepper.
3. Dip eggplant slices first in egg mixture, then in crumbs.
4. Fry eggplant slices in hot olive oil until golden brown and tender. Remove from pan and keep warm.
5. Add garlic to skillet and sauté 1 to 2 minutes. (Add more olive oil to pan if necessary.) Add tomato slices and sauté lightly.
6. In the meantime, pan fry eggs in butter, using egg rings.
7. To assemble, top each eggplant slice with a tomato slice and a fried egg. Top each serving with a generous dollop of Hollandaise Sauce and sprinkle with chopped parsley. *Makes 6 servings*

Egg Slicers

A prosaic hard-boiled egg always seems so much more tempting when it's cut neatly into slices. Kids always perk up at the sight — especially when they get to wield the egg slicer themselves. And adults are no less vulnerable — when the slices are arrayed on a salad plate or buffet. Westmark's slicer, made of heavy cast aluminum with stainless-steel wires, delivers a bonus: its ridged cup is designed to hold eggs positioned either lengthwise or crosswise, for either round or oval slices. The two-part handle of this 8-inch-long tool has a locking mechanism to fasten it shut when not in use. **To Use:** Unfasten the locking mechanism on the end of the handle. Place the egg in the cup and force the two parts of handle together to slice egg completely. Release handle, which will spring open due to spring-action construction, and remove sliced egg. The slicer easily washes clean.
Approximate Retail Price: $3.25

Egg wedger and egg slicer.

Baked Egg and Onion Tart

Pastry
1½ cup flour
Pinch salt
8 tablespoons butter
4-5 tablespoons ice water

Filling
Dijon-style mustard
6 hard-cooked eggs, sliced
5 tablespoons butter
2 large onions, sliced
½ teaspoon tarragon, crumbled
½ teaspoon salt
¼ teaspoon pepper
¼ pound mushrooms

Custard
2 eggs
1 cup heavy cream
¼ teaspoon salt

⅛ teaspoon pepper
⅛ teaspoon nutmeg

½ cup shredded Swiss or Gruyère cheese

1. Prepare pastry. (See Index, Pâté Brisée recipe, for method.) Roll out and line a 10-inch quiche or pie plate. Chill. Prick bottom with a fork and line shell with foil or parchment paper. Fill with dried beans, rice or pie weights.
2. Bake at 400°F for 10 minutes. Remove foil and weights and return to oven for 8 to 10 minutes longer, until lightly browned. Let cool 5 minutes and coat with a thin layer of Dijon-style mustard.
3. For filling, slice hard-boiled eggs and set aside.
4. Heat 4 tablespoons butter and sauté onions until tender. Add tarragon, salt and pepper and cook 2 to 3 minutes.
5. In a separate pan, heat remaining tablespoon of butter and sauté mushroom until browned and all liquid has evaporated.
6. For custard, combine eggs, heavy cream, salt, pepper and nutmeg and mix until thoroughly blended.
7. To assemble, arrange alternate layers of onion mixture, sliced eggs and mushrooms in baked shell. Pour custard mixture over all and sprinkle with shredded cheese.
8. Lower oven to 375°F and bake 35 to 40 minutes, until top is puffy and lightly browned. *Makes 6 to 8 servings*

PALATE TEASERS

Egg Wedger

The Westmark egg wedger takes the perfect symmetry of an egg one step further, splitting the ovoid into six equal parts. Great for garnishing a julienne salad or garlanding a mousse. Made of aluminum with stainless-steel wires, the 7-inch-long wedger locks shut when not in use. **To Use:** Unfasten the lock on the double handle. Place a hard-cooked egg upright in the cup. Force the handles together to completely wedge the egg. Or, if you desire a partially-wedged egg, to be filled, don't push the cutting wires all the way through. For a quick luncheon, partially wedge an egg and set it on a bed of lettuce. Open the wedged "cup," fill it with a scoop of chicken salad and garnish plate with cucumber slices and cherry tomatoes.
Approximate Retail Price: $4

Bird's-Nest Maker

The purpose of this French gadget is so frivolous that we're almost ashamed to admit our fondness for it. It is designed to shape and fry little "nests" of shreddable, starchy foods like potatoes, carrots, yams and turnips, so that you can achieve the height of serving elegance — edible baskets in which peas, purees and other foods can nestle on the plate. You can definitely live without this device, but it's great fun to use and the results are always impressive. The bird's-nest maker consists of two wire baskets, 3 inches and 4 inches in diameter, attached to 13 inch-handles that are held together by two tiny removable clamps. You line the larger basket with shredded food, insert the smaller basket, clamp the two together and plunge into bubbling oil to fry a crisp, golden nest. Noodles or a slice of bread will also curl into a basket shape when fried thus, and the bird's-nest maker is available in larger sizes. **To Use:** In a deep fat fryer, heat about 3 quarts of oil to 375°F. Peel and shred four medium potatoes — one potato for each basket. Rinse shredded potatoes until water runs clear; pat dry in a dish towel. Dip the empty bird's-nest maker into hot oil to prevent fried food from sticking later. Line the larger basket with a ⅜-inch-layer of shredded potatoes; insert smaller basket and clamp in place. Plunge baskets into hot fat and fry until potatoes begin to turn golden brown; then remove from fat and unmold nest by unclamping baskets and tapping on counter. Let nest drain a few moments; then plunge it back into the fryer to brown on all sides (you can hold them below surface with a skimmer). Drain nests well on paper towels and fill with fresh green peas, potato puffs, creamed chicken or ham, curried shrimp, cold mayonnaised scallops, or sautéed mushrooms. Keep empty baskets warm on a baking sheet placed in 120°F oven until you're ready to fill them.
Approximate Retail Price: $15

Bird's-nest maker fries potato baskets; fill wire basket with shredded potatoes and fry in hot oil.

7-in-1 Cup

Gravy separator, batter or syrup dispenser, egg separator, strainer, butter clarifier, funnel and measuring cup — those are the seven functions of this little cup. Made of clear, dishwasher-safe Lexan with a white plastic strainer insert on the top, it is 4 inches tall and 3¾ inches in diameter and holds 1 cup of liquid. A valve and opening toggle in the bottom enable it to do its more interesting jobs. **To Use:** As a gravy separator, pour gravy, or other liquid into cup with valve closed. Allow a few seconds for fat to settle on the top; then pull toggle open, allowing fat-free liquid to flow through spout at bottom. Close valve just before fat reaches opening. To use as a butter clarifier, pour slightly melted cooled, unsalted butter into the 7-in-1 cup with valve closed; then open the valve and let the golden butter run out into another container. Close valve just before milk

Clarified butter runs out of bottom of 7-in-1 Cup.

solids reach the opening. To use as an egg separator, close the valve and crack an egg into the cup without breaking the yolk. Hold the cup over a bowl, open valve and swirl gently. White will separate from yolk in one fast, clean operation, leaving yolk in cup. To use as a strainer, simply place detachable strainer in position across top of any cup.
Approximate Retail Price, $6

Magic Mop

If you're too rushed or too hungry to wait for a soup or gravy to cool before skimming off fat, consider the Magic Mop. And if you hate greasy French fries, hamburgers and bacon, consider the Magic Mop. Made of the same miracle synthetic fiber used on a grand scale to clean up oil spills, the 11-inch Magic Mop picks up fat particles like a magnet and doesn't absorb them. After rescuing greasy foods, the Magic Mop pops conveniently into the dishwasher. **To Use:** Dip 5-inch mophead into liquid and swirl or brush across surface of greasy foods; fat will adhere. To clean, pull back the metal ring that holds fibers and rinse mop in hot water immediately after use. Either boil for thorough cleaning or put in dishwasher. Store Magic Mop in its container or wrapped in plastic to prevent it from picking up grease in the air.
Approximate Retail Price: $6

Swirl Magic Mop around surface of gravy to remove grease.

PALATE TEASERS

Gravy Separator

A handsome speckled ceramic boat with an upper deck that holds back fat, this 6-inch-long gravy separator from Robert Weiss Ceramics pours out fat-free gravy through its low-set spout. Grease remains at the top, while the spout syphons off juices from the bottom. You have to pour slowly at first, however, so that the fat does not spill over its retaining dam. There are flaws in the design, though the idea is a good one. Unfortunately, the boat holds only ¾ cup of gravy at a time and its cute little handle is just that — cute and too little to grasp comfortably. **To Use:** Fill with ¾ cup gravy and pour slowly.

Approximate Retail Price: $8

Pour gravy slowly out of separator to keep grease behind retaining dam.

Sausage Stuffers

Charcuterie, or the European art of sausage making, is enjoying a limited revival. People who love good food and disdain artificial additives are discovering that the savory rewards of homemade sausage far outweigh the effort involved. Whether it's German-style bratwurst, Polish kielbasa or Italian cappecola, fresh sausage is merely a mixture of ground meats and seasonings stuffed into a casing. Preparing the meat is easy; it's filling the casings that poses problems. The challenge can be met, however, with a sausage stuffer — a simple two-part mechanism consisting of a long metal funnel and a wooden plunger.

Kalkus makes an easy-to-use 12½-inch-long aluminum stuffer with a versatile plunger that resembles a potato masher. You can begin forcing meat through the funnel with the bell-shaped head of the plunger and then reverse it to corral small bits of meat with the handle. The larger Kalkus model, crafted of tinned steel, is 20 inches long and has a 6-cup capacity; you'll need muscle power to wield the 3-inch-wide cylindrical beechwood plunger. **To Use:** Rinse casing by

Rinse casing with water.

Fit casing on tip of tube, tie end.

Fill tube with stuffing.

Stuffers come in two sizes.

slipping it over faucet and running water through it. Fill metal funnel with sausage mixture. Fit casing over tube end by gently gathering it over the tip; knot the end of the casing. Insert plunger into funnel and push sausage into casing; tie off length of sausage desired with string. Repeat until length of casing is filled and tied. Clean stuffer with soap and hot water; store plunger inside tube.

Approximate Retail Price: $15 (small model); $30 (large model)

Kielbasa

1½ pounds lean pork, ground
½ pound veal, ground
½ pound pork fat, ground
1½ teaspoons marjoram
⅛ teaspoon allspice
1 tablespoon paprika
3 to 4 cloves garlic, minced
2 teaspoons salt
1 teaspoon pepper
Hog casings

1. In large bowl, combine all ingredients except casings and mix thoroughly.
2. Sauté several tablespoons of the sausage and adjust seasonings, if necessary.
3. Prepare casings: Casings come packed in a salt brine. Extract a casing, open up one end and slip it over the faucet. Gently run water through it, untwisting it, if necessary. Check to see if there are any holes. If so, cut off section with hole and save the remainder. Let water run through casing for a minute. (If casing is very long it is easier to handle if cut into 12- to 18-inch lengths.) Reserve prepared casings in a bowl of lukewarm water.
4. Cut about 12 4-inch lengths of string for tying the links.
5. Fill metal tube with sausage mixture. Slip the casing over the small end of the tube and gently push the entire length of casing onto the tip. Tie a knot in the end of the casing.
6. Insert wooden plunger, pushing sausage into casing. Shape filled in casing with your fingers. If an air pocket forms, prick it with sausage pricker and push the casing against the sausage to expel the air. Tie off a 5-inch sausage with string. Continue in this fashion until casing is used up. Continue again with another casing.
7. If it is not too warm (70°F or below), hang sausage for several hours until skin is almost dry. Otherwise, refrigerate immediately.
8. To cook: Prick sausages all over with a sausage pricker. Place in a skillet with enough water to cover sausages halfway. Bring to a simmer and cook 10 minutes. Turn and cook 10 minutes longer. Pour off all water and cook until brown on both sides. *Makes about 2½ pounds*

Sausage Prickers

Two gadgets designed to facilitate stuffing make charcuterie all the more tempting. They both have sharp needle-like prongs that serve several purposes — to prick casing in order to remove excess stuffing, to prick casing to break up air pockets, and to prick sausage while it's cooking to release fat. Choose either the 5-inch natural-wood pricker with six prongs, or the 8-inch combination knife/pricker with a convenient stainless-steel blade at one end for cutting sausage strings. **To Use:** Pierce delicate casings lightly with the sharp prongs. Be careful when pricking cooking sausage, as hot fat can spurt through punctures.
Approximate Retail Price: $2 (wood pricker); $6 (pricker/knife)

Use the prongs of a sausage pricker to pierce casings as you fill them with meat, both to break up air pockets and to remove excess stuffing.

PALATE TEASERS

Tomato Pureer

In Italy, love always triumphs. In this case, it was love for fresh tomato sauce that prompted the invention of a machine that makes quick work of pureeing tomatoes. It separates skin and seeds from succulent pulp, quickly decimating bushelsful of fruit. It's a terrific boon for home canners, and it will mash a volume of cooked apples, pears or carrots as well as tomatoes. Our favorite model, the Super Passatutto Velox Universal, is made of bright red polypropylene and stands 9½ inches tall. It won our hearts with two clever features: a large square dish that fits under the chute to catch the sliding puree and a suction cup that holds the mechanism to the counter with complete fidelity. A second model, the stainless-steel (and sharp-edged) Spremipomodoro comes without a tray to fit its chute and attaches to the counter with an unreliable C-clamp. **To Use:** (The two pureers work similarly; instructions apply in detail to the Super Passatutto model.) Place white plastic roller in the container with the screw hole towards the opening where the handle is inserted; insert handle in roller screw hole and turn to the right until it is tightly secured and roller begins to turn. Fasten mechanism to counter by pushing metal lever on side opposite handle. Attach white plastic chute under stainless-steel straining perforations and position white

Tomato pureers mash and strain fresh tomatoes.

square dish beneath chute. Place another bowl under vent to catch skin and seeds. Put quartered tomatoes in container and turn handle; the puree will slide down chute, while skin and seeds emerge through vent on opposite side. If skin comes through with excess pulp, put it through mechanism again. Disassemble parts to wash clean.
Approximate Retail Price: $14 (Super Passatutto); $14 (Spremipomodoro)

Fresh Cream of Tomato Soup

3 pounds tomatoes (4 cups pureed)
1 clove garlic, minced
3 shallots, minced
5 tablespoons butter, divided
2 cloves
1 bay leaf
　Pinch of rosemary
　Pinch of thyme
⅛ teaspoon baking soda
4 tablespoons flour
3 cups milk

1 teaspoon salt
⅛ teaspoon pepper

1 teaspoon sugar
Chopped parsley for garnish

1. Puree tomatoes in a tomato pureer.
2. Sauté garlic and shallots in 1 tablespoon butter for 5 minutes.
3. Add pureed tomatoes, cloves, bay leaf, rosemary, thyme and baking soda. Simmer for 15 minutes.
4. In another saucepan, melt remaining 4 tablespoons butter. Add flour and cook for about 2 minutes, stirring constantly with a whisk. Add milk and continue to whisk until sauce is thickened and smooth.
5. Add tomato mixture and stir until blended. Add salt, pepper and sugar. Taste and adjust seasoning. Garnish with chopped parsley.
Makes 6 servings

SOMETHING'S BREWING

Coffee has been America's morning libation ever since the Boston Tea Party. But until very recently, we took our coffee, our coffee breaks and our coffee klatsches very much for granted.

Then coffee prices skyrocketed. And suddenly we began to look for ways to stretch our coffee dollars. The challenge became one of making our coffee go farther without losing its flavor. We became interested in getting the most coffee for our money. As a means to this end, we began to look at foreign coffee machines, which make an excellent cup of coffee with virtually no waste.

For years, Europeans have been brewing heady, pungent coffee and have developed it into an art. Italy is undisputedly Europe's coffee capital. And it is from Italy that a host of fascinating espresso and cappuccino machines have come. Recently, these machines have become the new culinary showpieces in American kitchens, as espresso drinking grows in status among the coffee *cognoscenti*.

Just what is all the fuss about? What *is* espresso? And what *is* cappuccino?

Espresso coffee is brewed from dark roasted beans and is made in a special machine that forces, by means of steam pressure, very hot water through the coffee grounds. It is both the heat of the water and the pressure which extracts the coffee, and since the hot water passes through the powdery grounds only once, the coffee has a fabulous taste. But it is not quite as simple as it sounds. Each connoisseur of es-

SOMETHING'S BREWING

presso has his favorite espresso machine and also has certain techniques of brewing. There are also variable factors in producing a fine cup of espresso — especially the texture of the coffee, the roast of the beans and how tightly the coffee is packed in the brewing drum.

The art of brewing cappuccino is almost as difficult to master as the spelling of the name. Cappuccino is actually nothing more than coffee with milk. But it is what is done to the milk that separates a great cup of cappuccino from a pedestrian brew. The milk for cappuccino must be steamed in such a way that it is heated without scalding; yet the rush of steam must create a good head of foam. To those deeply into the art of brewing cappuccino, both the amount and the consistency of the foam are critical.

In making espresso, as with any type of coffee, there are some basic rules to follow. Always begin with freshly ground coffee. If you purchase pre-ground coffee beans in a can, keep the can tightly sealed and refrigerated. Be sure that all parts of the coffee pot are immaculately clean; oils clinging to the insides of coffee pots can make every cup a bitter experience. Always start with cold water — purified water is best.

It is hard to predict taste preferences in coffee beans, as there are so many types, blends and roasts, each of which produces a different-tasting cup of coffee.

Coffee beans are grown abundantly in many parts of the world. Brazil and Colombia are the world's major coffee producing countries. Coffee is also harvested in Africa and Hawaii and, like Kona or Mocha-Java, beans are named for their origins. The best beans to use with European coffee machines are those labeled dark-roasted: Viennese Roast, the toast of Vienna's coffee houses; Italian Roast, the backbone of the espresso boom, and French roast, a coffee often used in the filter-type pots like the Melior, which are popular in France.

You can blend coffees to vary flavor and, depending on the system of brewing used, you could achieve a slightly milder cup of espresso by combining Italian and French roast beans.

There are three general types of espresso makers. The stove top machines are relatively simple and economical, but these usually produce no more than two cups of coffee at a time and, depending upon specific design, the steam for cappuccino may not be sufficient.

The best all-around, moderately priced espresso machines are those like the Pavoni Europiccola, which makes just two cups of coffee at a time, but holds close to a litre of water, so that additional coffee can be made in minutes without refilling. Machines of this kind normally produce an excellent quantity of powerful steam. Their disadvantage is that the coffee must be pumped out of the machines; so someone must tend them constantly while they're operating.

Automatic machines, like Elli, require no pumping. Everything is automatic and the steam is excellent. What's more, some automatic machines may be hooked up to the kitchen sink; so they can re-fill themselves. The only drawback, of course, is price.

If Italy is the mecca of coffee-drinkers, England is Europe's tea-drinking capital. And some Americans, unfazed by the Boston Tea Party, have adopted the tea ritual, along with its gadgets and equipment.

As with coffee, the perfect cup of tea requires fresh water and a clean pot. There are hundreds of tea leaves and each tea drinker has his own favorite as well as his preferred method of brewing. Some people insist on using an infuser to contain the leaves in the cup or pot of boiling water, while others insist that the leaves should float loose in the pot and be removed with a strainer as the tea is poured.

Whatever your sipping pleasure, you'll find that "Something's Brewing" for you in this section of hot drink equipment.

One-Cup Coffee Filter

When a pot holds much more coffee than you need — and a cup of instant much less flavor than you want — a stainless-steel one-cup coffee filter can come to the rescue. This 2½-inch-high basket-like gadget sits atop almost any size cup or mug and holds just enough ground coffee to infuse 1 cup of water. A lid keeps the coffee warm as it brews. **To Use:** Set filter on cup and fill with about two tablespoons of fine-ground coffee (more or less, to taste). Place disc-shaped strainer over coffee and pour boiling water to fill filter basket over it; when contents have filtered into cup, add more water. Place lid on filter while coffee is brewing. When coffee has brewed, lift filter off cup and place on inverted lid to catch drips.
Approximate Retail Price: $5

One-cup coffee filter.

Pressed-Coffee Makers

The strange term, "pressed coffee," belies the simplicity of these coffee makers. The brewing is little different from that employed when you boil coffee around a campsite in an old tin can. But these handsome pots offer a great refinement: After the boiling water has been infused, you push a plunger that traps the grounds at the bottom of the pot.

A plastic-handled nickeled-steel frame holds the French-made Melior pot's dome-lidded glass container. The plunger is composed of a fine steel mesh disk attached to a rod that's fitted into the lid. The model shown holds 8 ounces; larger capacity pots are also available. Bistro's bright-orange-lidded pressed coffee maker, made in Denmark, holds four cups and is designed much like the Melior pots. Both make some of the best coffee we've ever tasted. **To Use:** Remove the lid and the plunger. Place one heaping tablespoon of medium-ground coffee per cup in pot. Pour in boiling water to within 1 inch of pouring spout and stir gently. Replace lid with plunger fully raised. Let coffee steep three to five minutes; press plunger to bottom. *Approximate Retail Price: $35 (Melior); $25 (Bistro)*

Bistro and Melior coffee makers make "pressed" coffee.

Spiced Coffee Coolers

4 cinnamon sticks
6 cups of strong coffee
1 cup coffee liqueur, rum or brandy
¾ cup heavy cream
　Granulated sugar
　Chopped ice
　A few drops vanilla extract
1 teaspoon confectioner's sugar

1. Add cinnamon sticks to potful of coffee and let stand for one hour. Remove cinnamon sticks.
2. Add liqueur, ½ cup heavy cream and granulated sugar to taste to coffee. Chill.
3. Pour chilled coffee mixture into 6 tall glasses and fill with chipped ice.
4. Whip remaining ¼ cup cream until slightly thickened. Add vanilla extract and confectioner's sugar. Whip until thick. Top each serving of coffee with a dollop of cream. *Makes 6 servings*

SOMETHING'S BREWING

La Signora Espresso Maker

You don't have to be Italian to adore the strong dark brew called espresso. Espresso is distinguished from regular coffee by its preparation method; steam is forced quickly through finely-ground, tightly-packed coffee and the grounds are replaced frequently to maximize flavor. It's the quick, intense — or "express" — contact between steam and grounds that gave this brew its name.

Espresso makers range in size and complexity from simple pot to massive monument. The shapely La Signora stovetop model shown makes nine demitasse cups; 3-cup, 6-cup and 12-cup models are also available. This cast aluminum pot, made in Italy, has three chambers: the bottom holds the water; the basket-like strainer in the middle, the coffee grounds; and the top, the finished espresso. **To Use:** Unscrew the top and lift out the coffee chamber. Fill the bottom with water. Fill the coffee chamber with fine, espresso-grind coffee; replace coffee chamber and screw on the top.

La Signora is an inexpensive stovetop espresso maker.

Place the pot over a medium-high burner. As the water boils, steam is forced up through the coffee grounds and, through a shaft, into the top chamber. Listen for the "swoosh" of steam traveling from the pot and remove pot from heat as soon as you hear it. A safety valve in the bottom will keep the pot from exploding, but leaving it on the heat can ruin both coffee and pot.
Approximate Retail Price: $20

Vesubio Espresso Maker

Each of the two sets of valves and spouts on this barrel-shaped stove-top espresso maker has a separate function; one releases coffee, the other pure steam. You use the two functions in tandem to produce a frothy cup of capuccino, which is espresso served with steam-heated milk — or the Italian version of café au lait. Despite the fact that it resembles a fire extinguisher more than a coffee pot, the stainless-steel Vesubio makes excellent espresso, is easy to use and features a thoughtful convenience: You can fill it to make 12 cups of espresso at one time, or you can use an accompanying nine-cup coffee basket with less water when fewer servings are desired. **To Use:** Close steam valve and fill the boiler with 2 quarts of water to make 12 demitasse cups or 6 cups of water for nine demitasse cups. The water level should not exceed the inside handle attachment. Fill the coffee filter with finely ground espresso coffee. Set the lid on top of the tank, centering it exactly, so that the rubber gasket will form a perfect seal when compressed. Set the lid's locking arm, so that the semi-circular opening corresponds with the collar of the stud; seal the top of the tank by tightening the lid with the tightening knob. Place espresso maker over medium heat. Open the coffee valve on the top of the lid and place a cup or decanter beneath the spout. Coffee will start pouring out when the water in the tank becomes sufficiently hot to produce steam. Close the coffee valve after the desired amount of coffee has been obtained. To prepare capuccino, leave the machine on stove

Vesubio stovetop espresso maker.

until a good head of steam rises. Dip the side steam jet into a carafe of milk; open the side steam tap and turn the carafe. When milk is hot and foamy, close the steam valve before removing the steam spout from milk container.
Approximate Retail Price: $100

Pavoni Europiccola Espresso Machine

Though it looks as Old World as an Italian trattoria, this handsome brass and copper espresso maker is powered by electricity rather than stovetop heat. It sits securely on a rubber-cushioned pad and holds enough water to make 12 demitasse cups of espresso. But purists will delight in the fact that the coffee filter only holds enough grounds to make two cups at a time; you are forced, thus, to serve only the freshest espresso. Fortunately, changing the coffee grounds is a very simple procedure. A skinny steam valve on the side can be used to heat milk for capuccino. **To**

Use: Unscrew the cap and add the amount of water desired, up to 2 quarts. Make sure that the cap and the steam valve are safely closed and that the lever is down. Plug in machine and switch it to maximum. When steam escapes from the safety valve, indicating that the water has reached the boiling point, let machine whistle for about 60 seconds and then switch it to minimum. Place one or two portions of coffee in the filter cup, press it with the coffee plunger that comes with machine and insert the filter holder. Raise the handle, hold it up for a few seconds and then lower it forcefully to release espresso. To heat milk and other beverages with steam, let some steam escape from

Pavoni Europiccola espresso machine.

the steam valve; then turn steam valve to direct remaining steam into beverage container.
Approximate Retail Price: $300

Elli Automatica Espresso Machine

This is the godfather of espresso makers, the dream machine of every espresso lover. Fanatics can even attach this model directly to their water system; when not hooked up, it will hold enough water in its plastic tank to make 18 to 20 demitasse cups. Of course, the coffee grounds have to be changed for every two cups, but you can warm the waiting cups on the plate atop the machine. What class! A narrow steam valve heats milk for capuccino. **To Use:** Connect the machine to water system or fill tank inside the machine with water. Turn the steam valve knob a full turn. Press black button in base until water reaches the maximum water level as indicated on machine; do not fill completely. Plug in the machine and flip switch to turn on red warning light. When steam comes out of the spout, turn off the steam valve and wait for the warning light to go off. For one cup of coffee, fill the small coffee filter cup with ground coffee; for two cups, use the larger one. Compress the coffee with the round tamper that comes with the machine. Insert coffee filter cup and turn handle firmly to the right; place one or two cups under the coffee filter cup spouts. Turn the tap to

The Elli Automatica espresso machine can be operated portably or connected to your water system.

"Coffee" position. After the cups have been filled, turn the tap to "Discharge;" hold in position three seconds and return to neutral position. If you want to warm liquids by

means of steam, pull out steam spigot while espresso machine is operating and hold container of liquid to be heated beneath spigot.
Approximate Retail Price: $345

SOMETHING'S BREWING

Tea Strainer

If sipping a cup of tea is your antidote to frazzled nerves, you'll enjoy the added solace offered by this beautifully-crafted Italian chromed-brass tea strainer. Not only does it keep pesky tea leaves out of the cup, but it's also thoughtfully fitted with a saucer-stand to catch drips — and it's lovely to look at, besides. **To Use:** Pour freshly-brewed tea from pot into cup through strainer with saucer-stand lifted. After tea has been poured, saucer-stand holds strainer upright on table and catches drips.
Approximate Retail Price: $5

Cup 'A Tea

There are several ways to brew tea a cup at a time. One of the prettiest is a three-piece, glazed-ceramic one-cup tea set from Robert Weiss Ceramics. The set, which includes cup, strainer and lid, would make a lovely gift for a tea drinker who disdains teabags. **To Use:** Place strainer filled with loose tea in cup. Pour boiling water over tea leaves and cover cup while tea steeps; remove strainer to sip tea.
Approximate Retail Price: $9

Tea strainer and Cup 'A Tea.

Spoon Infuser

The convenient teabag truly meets its match in this 6-inch Italian spoon. It's just as easy to fill the bowl of this spoon with loose tea and let the spoon sit in a cup of boiling water as it is to dunk the pre-packed bag. And, furthermore, you can't stir your cupful with a soggy bag! **To Use:** Fill bowl of spoon with tea leaves and clasp lid. Place spoon in cup, fill cup with boiling water and let tea steep.
Approximate Retail Price: $3

Dripless Tea Balls

Ball-and-chain tea infusers eliminate the need for a tea strainer by holding tea leaves confined within the pot. Each of these stainless-steel models from Germany holds enough loose tea to infuse four cups; they hook over the edge of the tea pot and hang suspended in the hot water on a 5-inch chain. One comes with a fancy-handled saucer, the other with a small cup to catch drips after removal from the pot. **To Use:** Open infuser, fill with tea leaves, and close. Fill teapot with boiling water and suspend infuser in pot; let tea steep a few minutes. Remove infuser, cover teapot and pour.
Approximate Retail Prices: $5 (infuser with handled-stand); $2 (infuser with cup stand)

Ball-and-chain tea infusers hold enough loose tea to brew about four cups; the spoon tea infuser is ideal for a single cup.

All over the world, the term "French pastry" is synonymous with light, rich and delectable sweet desserts. The French way with pastry is legendary, and chefs come from every country of the world to learn the secrets and master the complex world of French baking techniques.

Recently the greatest pastry chef in France, Gaston le Notre, published a book of recipes divulging his secrets. The book was hailed as a revelation. At last we could produce professional-quality cakes and pastries at home, in our kitchens.

Unfortunately, it is not quite that simple.

Having a book of recipes — however good — is not all that is required to produce fine French pastry. You need skill and experience, as well as a battery of equipment. And often the recipes are so very complex, or so tricky, that they cannot be successfully accomplished by even the most gifted of amateur cooks.

But why not try? You'll find that examining and applying equipment used in pastry-making can yield delicious results, regardless of your level of expertise. Your first introduction to the art, however, may come as somewhat of a shock.

Take croissants, the French crescent rolls, for example. Who would ever guess that it takes the better part of a day to produce one dozen and that a croissant cutter is absolutely essential to cutting and shaping them correctly? Then there are buttery brioche, those plump lit-

tle rolls with charming little topknots. Without the fluted tins in which they rise, they will not attain their characteristic dimpled shape.

There is an entire world of pastry known as *feuilletage*. This term comes from the French word *feuille*, which means leaf, and the pastry is comprised of hundreds of layers of crisp leaves of dough. In America, *feuilletage* is called puff pastry because as it bakes it puffs up and rises very high. Napoleons are the classic example.

The secret to puff pastry lies in layering the dough with butter and then folding it to multiply the layers of butter and dough. The dough is folded into thirds or fourths and rolled out, and the process is repeated many times. The rolling, which is tedious because the pastry is quite firm, is made easier with the aid of a special rolling pin called a tutové. This is a distinguished piece of equipment that's easy to spot because its cylinder is ridged. The ridges help to press and extend the butter without tearing the dough.

Once puff pastry is formed, it must be shaped and cut precisely, so that it will puff up evenly. The French have developed several special cutters, each named for the shape of the pastry it produces. Vol-au-vent discs provide a pattern

for cutting pastry into puffy "casseroles," which make elegant containers for creamed dishes. The vol-au-vent shells look spectacular, and they also provide a delectable crunch to complement the cream sauces they hold.

A bouchée is a beautiful "mouth" of pastry; it is served, like a vol-au-vent, filled with a creamy sweet or savory filling. Bouchées are usually baked in sizes to hold individual portions. A bouchée cutter produces a whole shell in one motion, unlike a vol-au-vent disc, which requires separate cutting and shaping steps.

Leftover puff pastry scraps can be formed into a variety of delicacies. To make cornets, you cut long strips of dough and twist them around pointed molds. Once baked, the horns are filled with cream. The flaky cones are just long enough for you to explore their creamy insides neatly with your tongue.

Pâte à chou is another type of pastry with its own retinue of special molds and forms. Often incorrectly called puff pastry, because it, too, puffs up during cooking, pâte à chou will be more familiar to Americans as cream puff pastry. This is an especially easy dough to make. Water or milk and sugar are combined with butter and heated to a boil. Flour is added all at once, to form a rather gummy ball of hot dough. When cool, the dough will absorb a number of eggs, which are beaten in rather firmly. The dough then takes on a consistency that allows it to be piped or spooned into simple shapes such as éclairs, cream puffs and tube cakes. As the pastry bakes, its center puffs up and becomes hollow, while the outside remains crisp. The pastry can then be filled either with plain whipped cream or one of the various pastry creams.

The most familiar type of pâte à chou is cream puffs, and these are relatively simple to make and fill. With them you can construct a magnificent croquembouche, which is a tower of little paste puffs held together by a caramel glaze.

Savarins, babas and kugelhopfs

are a trio of sweet yeast breads and they are all cousins of the fluffy brioche. These doughs, which are rich with eggs, are further enriched with sugar; savarins and babas are normally soaked in rum or brandy after baking and are often paired with candied fruit and whipped cream as well. Each of the three cakes has its own characteristic shape and, therefore, its own mold that bears the same name: The savarin is a ring; the baba, a cup; and the kugelhopf, a fluted tube pan.

In *Swann's Way,* Marcel Proust immortalized the little shell-shaped cakes called madeleines. If you have never tasted a soft buttery madeleine, you will never imagine what the fuss was all about. But oh, to bite into it and feel the soft give of the cake in your mouth! It is like a delicate sponge gone mad with butter.

The smooth texture and creamy consistency of custards and mousses are the stock-in-trade of French desserts. The epitome of cream is reached in the coeur à la crème, a creamy cheese heart which can be topped with fruit or fruit puree. A poem of softness, this dessert is brutally loaded with calories, and definitely worth every one. Pôts de crème, those little covered porcelain cups that have a dollhouse look, hold individual portions of a glamourous baked custard.

Crepes need no introduction here, for they have become almost as American — and almost as familiar — as hamburgers. However, the expensive and glorious crepe suzette flambé pan we show is something quite unusual and would make an exciting gift. The flambé pan provides a beautiful cooking and serving dish for tableside preparation of crepes — and creates instant dinnertime drama.

Do not expect to conquer the equipment or the recipes in this section quickly. But if you begin with sufficient interest and patience, you can progress through the "French Gallery" in a series of satisfying accomplishments.

Croissant Cutter

The French routinely buy freshly-baked croissants at their neighborhood *boulangerie* and enjoy them each morning with café au lait. But travelers who return home smitten with the buttery crescent-shaped rolls usually find that in America they must bake them at home.

Croissants are made of a rich yeast dough that is layered with butter and folded and rolled repeatedly to produce an exquisitely flakey texture when baked. After the final roll, the dough is cut into triangles and each triangle is rolled up and curved into a crescent. There's no substitute for the dough-making procedure, but a French-made nickel-steel croissant cutter will cut the prepared dough into perfectly even 5-inch triangles. Small consolation to the baker who dreams of a Parisian *boulangerie,* but a very efficient tool all the same. **To Use:** Roll dough ⅛ inch thick on a lightly floured surface. Grasp croissant cutter handles and roll smoothly and firmly from one end of dough to opposite side. Roll up each triangle, beginning at the wide end. Bend roll into crescent shape and bake. *Approximate Retail Price: $30*

Cutter makes perfect triangles.

Roll from long side to point.

Bake until brown. Serve warm.

Croissants

1½ **cups butter**
  4 **cups all-purpose flour**
  2 **packages dry yeast**
  ¼ **cup warm water (105°F to 115°F)**
  1 **cup milk**
  2 **tablespoons sugar**
  1 **teaspoon salt**
  1 **egg, slightly beaten**
  1 **egg yolk**
  1 **teaspoon milk**

1. Pound butter and ½ cup of the flour between two sheets of waxed paper until flour is incorporated. Roll mixture between waxed paper to form a rectangle about 12 inches by 6 inches. Refrigerate until firm.
2. In mixing bowl, dissolve yeast in warm water. Let stand until bubbly, about 10 minutes. Stir in milk, sugar, salt, beaten egg and enough of the flour to make a soft dough. Place dough on lightly floured surface and knead until smooth and elastic and no longer sticky, adding more flour if necessary. Place in bowl and cover with a cloth. Refrigerate 20 minutes.
3. On floured surface, roll dough into a 14-inch square. Place butter on half of the dough surface. Fold over half of dough, sealing edges well. Roll out dough into a rectangle about 20 inches long and 12 inches wide. Fold a third of the dough over the center. Brush off any excess flour. Fold remaining dough over the two layers. Give the dough a quarter of a turn so that the open edges are facing you. Again, roll to a 20-inch by 12-inch rectangle. Fold into thirds. Repeat procedure two more times, refrigerating dough about 30 to 45 minutes between each rolling.
4. After finishing the last rolling, fold the dough into thirds and roll out to a 12-inch by 7-inch rectangle. Refrigerate 45 minutes to 1 hour. Cut dough crosswise into fourths. Roll each fourth (keeping remaining dough refrigerated) into a rectangle about 20 inches long and 5 inches wide. Dough should be about ⅛ inch thick.
5. Place croissant cutter at one end of dough. With your hands on the handles of the cutter, roll smoothly and firmly to other end of dough. Hold one of the triangles of dough by its base and stretch two base corners slightly; starting from the base, begin to roll triangle of dough toward the opposite point. Bring ends of roll toward each other to form a crescent. Place on an ungreased baking sheet and repeat with remaining dough. Let croissant rise until doubled, about 45 minutes.
6. Preheat oven to 400°F. Mix egg yolk and milk for glaze. Gently brush each croissant with the egg mixture. Bake until deep brown, 12 to 15 minutes. Croissants are best served warm. *Makes about 20 croissants*

Brioche Molds

The hallmarks of brioche, a rich cake-like bread, are its meltaway lightness and its squat scallop-edged shape. The classic brioche à tête features, as well, a topknot of dough perched on top like a hat. You can pull off the topknot and hollow out small loaves to stuff with sauced dishes or pâté. Or savor the chubby loaves at breakfast with butter and jam. Specially-designed molds, made in France of tinned steel, are flared and fluted and give the round bread its distinctive shape; they come in sizes to fit individual rolls, 3-cup loaves and 6-cup loaves. When you're not baking, you can use the molds for mousses or desserts. **To Use:** Butter the brioche forms. Place dough in forms and let rise until doubled. Brush with egg glaze and bake. (Because brioche freezes beautifully, you may want to bake extras.) *Approximate Retail Price: $.30 (individual);$1.25(3-cup);$1.75(6-cup)*

Brioche take their characteristic shape from fluted forms.

Brioche

1 package dry yeast
¼ cup warm water (105°F to 115°F)
½ cup butter, softened
¼ cup sugar
½ teaspoon salt
½ cup milk, scalded, cooled to lukewarm
3¼ cups all-purpose flour, divided
3 eggs plus 1 egg yolk
  Butter to grease brioche molds
1 egg yolk mixed with 1 teaspoon milk for glaze

1. Dissolve yeast in water. Let stand until bubbly, about 10 minutes.
2. Cream butter, sugar and salt. Beat in milk, 1 cup of the flour, eggs, egg yolk and yeast. Add remaining flour and beat about 5 minutes.
3. Cover and let rise until mixture doubles, about 2 hours.
4. Stir down dough; beat well with wooden spoon. Cover with aluminum foil and place in refrigerator overnight.
5. Turn dough out onto floured pastry board. Divide dough into fourths. Set aside ¼ of the dough. Cut remaining three pieces in half. Form each piece into four balls. (You should have 24 balls of dough.)
6. Butter 24 small brioche molds. Place balls in well-buttered molds.
7. Cut reserved dough into four pieces. Divide each into six smaller pieces and shape into 24 small balls. With handle end of a wooden spoon dipped in flour, poke an indentation in the top of each ball in brioche mold. Brush holes lightly with water. Press a small ball into the indentation on top of each large ball.
8. Cover and let rise until double, about 1 hour. Preheat oven to 375°F.
9. Brush brioche with egg glaze. Bake at 375°F until golden brown, about 15 minutes.

To make a large brioche: Cut off about ⅙ of the dough. Shape large portion of dough into a ball and place in a buttered 6-cup brioche pan. Shape small portion into a ball; indent top of large portion with tip of wooden spoon, brush hole with water, and press small ball of dough in place. Let rise until dough reaches top of pan, about 2 hours. Brush with egg yolk mixture, being careful that egg does not run between brioche and cap. Bake at 375°F for 20 minutes; cover loosely with foil to prevent over-browning. Bake 25 to 30 minutes longer or until wooden pick inserted in brioche comes out clean. Remove from oven and let cool 10 minutes. Remove from pan and cool.

To make two medium brioche: Divide dough into two parts; follow above procedure.   *Makes 24 individual, 1 large or 2 medium brioche*

Tutové Rolling Pin

Puff pastry is one of the most difficult to make. However, once the technique has been mastered the pastry can be shaped into such delightful creations as napoleons, cornets, vol-au-vents and jalousies, or wrapped around a whole tenderloin to make the glorious Beef Wellington. When baked, puff pastry dough rises several times its original thickness into hundreds of crips, tissue-thin layers. From these layers comes the French name for this dough, pâté feuilletée, meaning "leaved pastry." The secret of success with puff pastry lies in the handling of the dough: You must be careful when rolling layers of butter and pastry together not to let the butter break through the pastry, or the air, which is trapped between the layers, will escape. It is the air inside that makes the pastry puff in the oven. The 25-inch tutové rolling pin has been designed to distribute the butter between the layers of pastry with minimal pressure. Its 15-inch plastic cylinder features a surface ridged with ⅛-inch grooves. Butter yields to the firm, even pressure of the ridges as the dough is rolled and folded. Although we have made puff pastry many times with a conventional rolling pin, there is much to be said for the tutové. In addition to the benefits of its ridged design, the pin is well balanced and runs smoothly on interior ball bearings, and the plastic cylinder prevents the dough from sticking.

Other butter-rich pastries, such as croissants and Danish, also roll out more easily with the tutové. **To Use:** On a lightly floured surface, roll the basic dough mixture from the center, allowing the center to be thicker than the sides. Place the butter in the middle of the dough and fold the dough around it envelope fashion. With the tutové, roll the dough into a rectangle, fold in thirds and continue folding and rolling for a total of six turns. Puff pastry can be stored in the refrigerator for up to 3 days or frozen for later use. It is best to work with the pastry in a cool, dry place. If at any time the dough becomes too soft to work with, refrigerate it for about 45 minutes.

Approximate Retail Price: $65

Roll dough into 12-inch square.

Place floured butter in center.

Brush off any excess flour.

Roll out dough to a rectangle.

Fold ⅓ of dough over center.

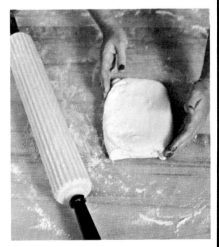
Fold remaining ⅓ over layers.

FRENCH GALLERY

Pâté Feuilletée (Puff Pastry)

**2 cups all-purpose flour, plus
extra flour to dust butter
and rolling surface**
½ teaspoon salt
**1 teaspoon lemon juice
About ⅔ cup ice water**
8 ounces butter

1. Place 2 cups flour and the salt on a cool surface. Make a well in the center. Pour in the lemon juice and water. With your fingertips work flour into the water to make a soft dough. (If dough seems dry, add a little more water.) Gather dough into a ball. Cover with aluminum foil or plastic wrap and refrigerate 20 minutes. (Dough will not be smooth at this point.)

2. Lightly flour the butter and place between two sheets of waxed paper. Beat butter with a rolling pin until pliable. Press butter into a 5-inch square.

3. On a lightly floured surface, roll out dough from the center to make a 12-inch square. Leave the dough in the center a little thicker than on the sides. Place the butter in the middle of the dough and fold the dough around it envelope fashion.

4. Roll out dough into a rectangle about 18 inches long and 8 inches wide. Fold a third of the dough over the center. Brush off any excess flour. Fold remaining third over the two layers. Give the dough a quarter of a turn so that a short end is facing you. This rolling and folding is called a "turn;" roll out and fold in three again, completing the second turn. (The traditional way of marking the stages in the preparation of puff pastry is by making indentations with fingertips in the dough. The first time the dough is rolled it is marked with two indentations; the second time four and the final six.) Wrap and refrigerate dough 30 to 40 minutes.

5. Repeat the above step two more times, refrigerating between repetitions of step. Roll out with conventional rolling pin, cut and shape pastry as desired.

Round Vol-au-Vent Discs

The famous chef, Carême, called the founder of classic French cooking, is credited with having created the first vol-au-vent shell. It was an inspired invention — a delicate shell of puff pastry designed to hold either savory creamed appetizers and entrees or fruit and whipped cream desserts. Homage to Carême's legacy comes in the form of a set of 12 tinned-steel vol-au-vent discs. Ranging in size from 4¼ inches to 9¾ inches in diameter, the discs serve as handy patterns, enabling cooks to cut out the circles and rings of pastry needed to construct the flaky shells. Each disc has a hole in its center to help you lift it off the pastry; a small plastic belt slips through the holes to hold discs together when not in use. **To Use:** On a lightly floured surface, roll out puff pastry into a rectangle about ¼ inch thick. Position a disc on the pastry and cut around its outline, using the point of a sharp knife (a dull knife will depress pastry layers). Then cut out another round of pastry with the same size disc.

Place one pastry round on a slightly dampened baking sheet and brush with egg glaze. Position a second disc, 3 inches smaller than the first, on the unglazed pastry round; cut around disc to form a ring of pastry. Position ring on top of glazed round on baking sheet; glaze ring before baking. Repeat process with remaining dough. If pastry becomes too soft to cut, refrigerate about 30 minutes. Leftover pieces of dough can be patched together (do not re-roll) and used for turnovers or other pastries.
Approximate Retail Price: $22.50

Cut around disc with knife.

Use smaller disc to cut ring.

Score shell to seal layers.

Round Vol-au-Vent Shells

1 recipe Puff Pastry
1 egg mixed with 1 tablespoon water for glaze

1. Preheat oven to 425°F. On a lightly floured surface, roll puff pastry into a rectangle about ¼ inch thick. Position disc the size of desired pastry shell on the pastry; cut around it with sharp knife. (Be sure knife is sharp, or pastry will not rise properly.) Position disc on pastry again and cut a second round.
2. Place one of the rounds on a slightly dampened baking sheet. Brush the top with egg glaze.
3. Position another disc, about 3 inches smaller, in the center of the second pastry round and cut around it to form a ring of pastry. Gently lift the ring and place it on top of pastry round on baking sheet. Brush the ring with egg glaze.
4. Seal the two layers of pastry with the edge of a small knife by pressing slanting lines ⅛ inch deep around the outer edge of the ring. Cut a circle about ⅛ inch deep in the bottom layer of dough, following the inside curve of the ring; this marks an inner round of pastry that can be removed after baking to form a cover for filled shell. Make shallow criss-cross cuts on the surface of ring.
5. Bake at 425°F about 15 minutes; reduce heat to 350°F and continue baking until sides are deep brown and crisp, about 20 minutes. Cut out baked center of ring and remove; discard some of the soft dough inside the ring. Fill pastry shell with hot mixture and top with lid, or serve without lid, filled with whipped cream and fruit. *Makes 2 8-inch shells*

Square Pastry Shell Cutter

If you get bored with round vol-au-vents, you can always turn your talents with puff pastry to small flaky rectangles. Though this 4-inch stainless-steel cutter stamps out squares of pastry, much like a cookie cutter, the corners of the squares are folded and twisted before baking; so the pastry shells rise in the oven like golden diamonds. The double-edged square cutter is quite sharp and easy to use. The inner blade leaves two corners uncut, so that you can lift two L-shaped edges and overlap them to form the walls of the pastry shell.
To Use: On a lightly floured surface, roll puff pastry dough to ¼-inch thickness. Press cutter firmly into dough. Lift cutter and separate square of dough. Brush the outer band of square with water. Lift one outer corner of dough and position on opposite interior corner; bring other outer corner over edge of first corner and position on opposite interior corner. Cut squares from remaining dough and repeat process. Transfer squares to lightly dampened baking sheet. Brush surfaces of pastry with a mixture of one egg beaten with one tablespoon of

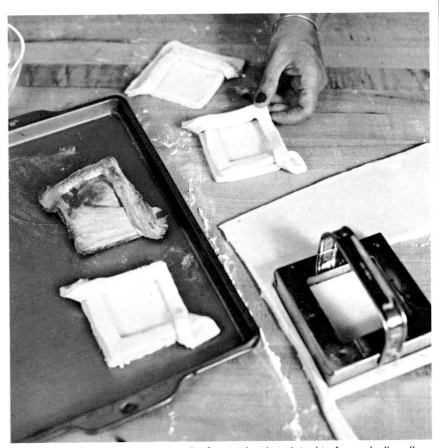

Square cutter cuts a square and a frame that is twisted to form shell walls.

water; be careful not to let egg glaze drip into cut edges. Bake at 450°F 10 minutes; reduce heat to 350°F and bake until golden brown, about 15 minutes.
Approximate Retail Price: $19

FRENCH GALLERY

Bouchée Cutter

Small vol-au-vent pastry shells are called bouchées. And if you want to bake many of these, you can cut them out in one deft motion with a bouchée cutter. Whereas the vol-au-vent discs function only as patterns, requiring you to cut around them to shape rounds and rings of pastry for shells, the bouchée cutter shapes and cuts out the entire shell at one time. With the discs, however, you can bake various-size shells; the bouchée cutter makes only one size and its diameter is smaller than that of the smallest vol-au-vent disc. The bouchée is perfect for individual portions of appetizers and desserts; the larger vol-au-vent shells hold multiple servings. The bouchée cutter takes advantage of the delicate nature of puff pastry: Its 3-inch-diameter stainless-steel blade cuts a scalloped round of dough, while a 2-inch-wide nylon plunger depresses the center of the round;

you can adjust the pressure of the plunger. The center stays depressed during baking and the outer ring rises around it to form a perfect flaky shell. The cutter comes with four small stainless-steel cubes that you can position in the corners of a baking sheet with a rack propped on top to ensure that shells all rise to the same height. The French think of everything! **To Use:** On a lightly floured surface, roll puff pastry dough to a thickness of ¼ inch. Lightly flour the cutter. Grasp the cutter by its two plastic handles, position it on dough, and press down quickly and firmly. Raise the cutter and remove round of dough. Place the round on a baking sheet with sides. Repeat process with remaining dough. Arrange the four stainless-steel supports in corners of baking sheet, adjust to desired height and position metal cooling rack on supports. Bake shells at 450°F for 10 minutes; reduce heat to 350°F and bake until golden brown, about 15

Bouchée cutter stamps out puff pastry shells in one motion.

minutes. Remove cooling rack and lift out pan. With a sharp knife, cut into center of each shell and lift out circle of dough; reserve and use as cover, if desired. Remove any excess soft dough from centers of shells.
Approximate Retail Price: $65

Lady Lock Forms

Lady locks are yet another of the delightful delicacies you can make with basic puff pastry. Taking their whimsical name from their resemblance to the tight curls once in vogue, these pastry creations are also known as cornets, cream horns and, in German, "Schillerlocken" (Schiller's locks). Long strips of puff pastry are rolled in slightly overlapping layers around the long and narrow cone-shaped forms. After baking, the molds are gently slipped out and you are left with a cornucopia-shaped pastry case that usually is filled with sweetened whipped cream or a custard mixture. Made of tinned steel, the forms shown are about 5 inches long and make individual-sized cones. Various other sizes are available. The inside of the wider cones can be lined with sliced

Pinch dough strip at point of lady lock form; wrap around cone.

ham, and filled with a vegetable salad; you slip the ham cornucopias out of the metal cones to serve. For baking small pastry horns, you will want to have at least six forms. **To Use:** For first time use, lightly butter the outside of each mold. Pinch end of dough strip around tip of mold to

Place cone sealed edge down on baking sheet, glaze and bake.

secure. Wrap strip of dough around mold, overlapping consecutive turns slightly. Seal dough at large end of mold. Brush with egg glaze and bake. Molds easily slip out of pastry after baking.
Approximate Retail Price: $5 (set of six)

Lady Locks

1 recipe Puff Pastry*
1 egg beaten with 1 tablespoon water for glaze
Sweetened whipped cream

1. On a lightly floured surface, roll pastry into a rectangle about 10 inches wide and 15 inches long. (Dough should be about ⅛ inch thick.) Cut dough lengthwise into 1-inch-wide strips with a pastry wheel.

2. Take a strip of dough and squeeze around tip of form to seal lady lock. Wrap the strip of dough around the cone, overlapping consecutive turns slightly. Seal end of dough at the large end of cone. Place cone, sealed edge down on baking sheet. Repeat with remaining strips of dough. Refrigerate cones on baking sheet about 30 minutes to allow dough to relax.

3. Heat oven to 400°F. Brush cones with egg glaze. Bake until golden, about 15 minutes. Set pastries on cooling rack and slip out cones. Cool. Fill with sweetened whipped cream.

*Note: If you only have six cones, work with half the dough at a time, keeping the remaining dough refrigerated. It is not necessary to rinse the cones after baking before making a second batch.   *Makes 12 servings*

Kugelhopf Mold

Kugelhopf, a rich sweet bread studded with raisins and almonds, is the regal hallmark of bakers in the Alsace region of France, though it can also be sampled in other areas influenced by Austrian cuisine. Marie Antoinette is said to have been quite fond of this pastry, and it's not hard to tell why — the traditional kugelhopf is uniquely delicious. A French tinned-steel 6-cup kugelhopf mold gives the sweet bread its characteristic swirled, fluted shape. Measuring 8 inches across the top, the mold has a center tube that extends above the rim to conduct heat through the center of the kugelhopf while it bakes; the tube also serves as a stand while the bread is unmolded. Sometimes referred to as a Turk's head pan because it resembles a turban, the kugelhopf mold also can be used to bake other sweet breads and cakes. **To Use:** Generously butter mold and sprinkle lightly with dried bread crumbs. Place dough in mold and allow to rise until doubled before baking.

Approximate Retail Price: $7-$12

Fluted kugelhopf molds.

Kugelhopf

1 package dry yeast
¼ cup warm water (105°F to 115°F)
⅓ cup butter, softened
½ cup sugar
2 eggs at room temperature
½ cup milk, slightly warmed
2½ cups all-purpose flour
1 teaspoon salt
½ cup golden seedless raisins
1 tablespoon kirsch or brandy
1 teaspoon grated lemon rind
Softened butter to grease pan
Dry bread crumbs
Blanched whole almonds

1. Dissolve yeast in warm water. Let stand until bubbly, about 10 minutes. Cream butter and sugar until light and fluffy. Beat in eggs. Beat in milk, yeast mixture, flour and salt. Stir in raisins, kirsch and lemon rind. Cover dough with waxed paper and a damp cloth. Let rise in warm place until doubled, about 1½ hours.

2. Butter a 6-cup kugelhopf mold. Sprinkle lightly with bread crumbs and shake out excess. Arrange almonds in a ring in bottom of mold.

3. Stir down dough. Spoon into the mold. Let rise until dough almost reaches top of pan.

4. Bake kugelhopf in oven preheated to 400°F for 10 minutes; reduce heat to 350°F and bake until top is deep golden, about 25 minutes.

5. Remove from oven and cool in mold 10 minutes. Unmold and cool on wire rack.   *Makes 6 to 8 servings*

FRENCH GALLERY

Baba Molds

King Stanislas I Leczinski, King of Poland, Duke of Lorraine, and father-in-law of King Louis XV, is said to have invented the baba. Finding the Alsatian kugelhopf a little too dry, he soaked the cake in rum and dubbed it Ali Baba after the hero of one of his favorite books, *A Thousand and One Nights.* Sometime during the 19th century the name was shortened to baba by Parisian pastry chefs. Made of a rich yeast dough mixed with raisins, the baba is soaked in a rum syrup and sometimes glazed with apricot preserves; it can be baked in a large decorative mold or in individual-portion baba molds like the ones shown. The tinned-steel, tapered cylindrical molds come in two sizes and each holds ⅓ to ½ cup of dough. Sometimes called dariole molds, the pans can be used to shape vegetable purees and aspics too. You'll want 8 to 12 molds for baking, although you also can use muffin tins for babas. The

Babus au Rhum are glazed and decorated with cherries and almonds.

little rum cakes freeze beautifully. **To Use:** Generously butter baba molds. Fill molds ⅓ full with dough. Let dough rise until doubled, and bake.
Approximate Retail Price: $1-$2

Savarin Molds

Its classic ring shape, often filled with whipped cream or custard, distinguishes the savarin from the baba. The savarin is often soaked in a kirsch syrup instead of the rum used with babas, but both savarins and babas are baked from a rich yeast dough, suffused with spirits, and glazed. Whereas the baba takes its name from a legendary Arab, however, the savarin bears the moniker of the famed French gastronome, Brillat-Savarin. Heavy, seamless, tinned-steel savarin molds are made in France and come in sizes ranging from 2 to 5 cups. Individual-serving molds are available for petits savarins. **To Use:** Generously butter the mold. Half fill with savarin dough. Let dough rise until it reaches rim of pan; then bake. Savarins can be baked and frozen, then thawed and soaked in syrup and glazed before serving.
Approximate Retail Price: $.75-$5

Savarin molds come in two sizes.

Pour Kirsch Syrup over cake.

Serve savarin with whipped cream.

Savarin*

Dough
1 package dry yeast
¼ cup warm water (105°F to 115°F)
¼ cup milk, barely warmed
4 eggs at room temperature
2 cups all-purpose flour
⅓ cup sugar
½ teaspoon salt
½ cup softened butter

Kirsch Syrup
1 cup sugar
2 cups water
½ cup kirsch

Decoration
½ cup apricot preserves
1 cup whipping cream
1 tablespoon confectioner's sugar
   Whole blanced almonds, candied cherries, citron
   Fresh fruit for garnish: nectarines, raspberries, grapes

1. Dissolve yeast in water in large mixing bowl. Let stand until bubbly, about 10 minutes. Stir in milk, eggs and flour. Beat with a wooden spoon or with hand, lifting dough out of bowl and letting it fall back, about 4 minutes. Cover with waxed paper and a damp cloth and let stand until doubled in bulk, about 1 hour.
2. Beat down dough and beat in sugar, salt and butter. Place in a buttered 5-cup savarin mold. Set in a warm place and let stand until dough rises to top of pan.
3. Heat oven to 400°F. Bake savarin 10 minutes. Reduce temperature to 350°F and bake until top is deep golden brown, about 20 minutes.
4. Meanwhile, prepare Kirsch Syrup. Heat sugar and water to boiling. Boil 2 minutes. Remove from heat. Cool slightly and stir in kirsch.
5. Remove savarin from oven. Let stand in pan 5 minutes. Unmold and cool on wire rack 10 minutes.
6. Place savarin on a large platter. Pour syrup over top of cake. Let stand about 30 minutes, basting frequently with syrup.
7. Heat the apricot preserves until hot; sieve. Brush over cake.
8. Just before serving beat cream and confectioner's sugar until stiff. Fill center of savarin with the cream mixture. Decorate top of ring with almonds, cherries and citron. Garnish with fresh fruit to serve.

Makes about 6 to 8 servings

*To make Babas au Rhum:
1. Make half of Savarin recipe and add ¼ cup dried currants to dough after beating in sugar, salt and butter.
2. Generously butter 8 to 10 individual baba molds. Fill each ⅓ full. Let dough rise in a warm place until doubled.
3. Heat oven to 400°F. Bake babas until tops are deep golden brown, about 15 minutes. Remove from oven and let cool in molds about 5 minutes. Remove from molds and cool 10 minutes on wire rack.
4. Make full recipe of Kirsch Syrup as indicated in Savarin recipe, but substitute ½ cup rum for kirsch. Spoon rum syrup over babas, letting it soak in.
5. Heat ½ cup apricot preserves, sieve, and brush over babas. Decorate Babas au Rhum with candied cherries and sliced almonds.

Makes 8 to 10 servings

Croquembouche Form

A croquembouche is truly a majestic sight to behold. A conical mountain of small cream puffs held together with an amber-colored caramel syrup, this pièce de résistance is constructed in France to mark holidays, weddings and other festive occasions. The croquembouche takes its name from the fact that the caramel-glazed puffs are literally "crunchy to the mouth." A special cone serves as a base for building the crunchy tower. About 60 cream puffs fit on the 8½-inch-tall tinned-steel croquembouche form. Larger forms are also available, but the size shown is perfect for home use. Theoretically, after all of the puffs are in place and the caramel has hardened, you should be able to slip out the form. We do not feel that this is necessary, however; nor do we recommend that you take the chance of breaking your masterpiece. Decorations such as candied cherries, dates or mandarin oranges can add color to the pastry puffs and conceal the metal cone. Make a croquembouche instead of a cake to commemorate a special event, but don't try it on a humid day, because the caramel will not set properly and the cream puffs will come tumbling down. **To Use:** Lightly butter the croquembouche form. Place on a lightly buttered platter. Dip cream puffs one at a time in the hot syrup and place them around the edge of the base. Place a second row on top of the first, positioning the cream puffs between those at the

Dip puffs in caramel to stack.

base. Continue until all of the puffs are used. Drizzle any remaining syrup over the croquembouche.
Approximate Retail Price: $10

FRENCH GALLERY

Croquembouche

Cream Puff Paste (Pâté à chou)
2 cups water
1 cup butter
½ teaspoon salt
4 teaspoons sugar
2 cups flour
8 eggs

**Crème Patissière (See Index;
make 1½ times recipe)**

Caramel
1½ cups sugar
½ cup water
¼ teaspoon cream of tartar

1. Heat oven to 425°F. Since cream puff paste is difficult to work with in large quantity, our recipe directions are for making half the recipe at a time. To make Cream Puff Paste: Heat 1 cup of water, ½ cup butter, ¼ teaspoon salt and 2 teaspoons sugar to boiling. Stir in 1 cup flour all at once and stir vigorously over low heat until mixture forms a ball. Remove from heat. Beat in four of the eggs, one at a time, beating well after each addition.
2. Pipe cream puff paste from pastry bag using a plain tip or drop by teaspoonfuls onto slightly dampened baking sheets. Mounds of paste should measure about 1 inch wide.
3. Bake until puffs are golden, about 20 minutes. Remove puffs from baking sheet and pierce bottom of each with a knife. Cool completely. Make second batch of Cream Puff Paste and bake as directed.
4. Fit a large pastry bag with a star tip and fill with Crème Patissière. Insert tip into the pierced bottom of each puff and fill with about 1 tablespoon of the cream.
5. For caramel, heat sugar, water and cream of tartar to boiling in medium saucepan, without stirring. Reduce heat and cook until syrup is amber colored. Remove from heat and place in a pan of hot water to keep caramel liquid while dipping puffs.
6. To assemble Croquembouche: Lightly butter a serving plate and the metal croquembouche form. Place form in center of plate. Arrange cream puffs around cone in layers, dipping each puff in caramel before positioning. It may not be necessary to use all of the cream puffs. Pour any remaining caramel in a thread over the mound of puffs. Leave croquembouche on mold; to serve, gently pull apart puffs with tongs or two forks and place on individual serving plates. *Makes about 20 servings*

Madeleine Pan

Marcel Proust immortalized the delicate, shell-shaped cakes called madeleines in his novel *Remembrance of Things Past*. Supposedly, while the author was writing the book, his mother brought him a cup of tea and some madeleines. The taste of the little cakes took him back to his childhood and gave him the inspiration he needed to recall details of his past. To bake madeleines, you need a special pan with shell-shaped indentations. Made in France of a single sheet of tinned steel, the pan shown will hold a dozen cakes, each about 3 inches long and 1¾ inches wide. Serve the delicate morsels, lightly dusted with confectioner's sugar, like cookies, with tea or coffee, or with fruit for dessert. A pan that holds 20 miniature madeleines is also available.
To Use: Generously butter each madeleine mold. Place about 1 tablespoon of the batter into each regular-size mold and bake.
Approximate Retail Price: $5 (12-mold pan); $6.50 (20-miniature mold pan)

Indented pans shape Madeleines.

Madeleines

Softened butter to grease
molds
2 eggs
¼ cup plus 2 tablespoons sugar
½ teaspoon vanilla
¾ cup all-purpose flour
⅛ teaspoon baking powder
⅛ teaspoon salt
6 tablespoons butter, melted,
cooled slightly
Confectioner's sugar

1. Grease a madeleine mold with the softened butter, making sure to get into all of the indentations.
2. Heat oven to 400°F. Beat eggs and sugar until very thick. Beat in vanilla.
3. Mix flour, baking powder and salt.
4. Alternately fold flour mixture and melted butter into egg mixture.
5. Fill each shell with about 1 tablespoon of the batter.
6. Bake Madeleines until delicately browned. Remove from pan immediately and cool on wire racks. Just before serving, sprinkle lightly with confectioner's sugar. (To make a second batch, wash pan and rebutter before filling again). *Makes about 1½ dozen, regular size Madeleines*

Charlotte Mold

Two famous French desserts share the name "charlotte." Charlotte russe features an elegant shell of ladyfingers surrounding a mound of chilled Bavarian cream. A fruit charlotte consists of overlapping slices of thin bread encasing a fruit puree.

Both desserts are made in a charlotte mold. The round, tinned-steel mold, which come in sizes ranging from 5 ounces to 2 quarts, is slightly flared and embellished with curved handles. A less expensive aluminum version is also available. Although many cooks find the aluminum molds too lightweight, we found them quite satisfactory.

Either type of charlotte mold can be pressed into service for soufflés, molded desserts and casseroles too. **To Use:** Butter the mold. Line the bottom and sides with thinly sliced bread or ladyfingers. Fill and either bake or refrigerate depending on the filling used.
Approximate Retail Price: $10 (tinned steel); $3 (aluminum)

Line charlotte mold with bread; unmold Apple Charlotte and serve with Apricot Sauce.

Apple Charlotte

6 tablespoons butter
8 to 10 large apples (Golden Delicious or Granny Smith), peeled, cored, and cut into thin slices
2 to 3 tablespoons sugar
Grated rind of 1 lemon
Juice of 1 lemon
3 tablespoons apricot preserves
2 tablespoons dark rum
1 teaspoon vanilla
10 to 12 slices thin, firm white bread

Apricot Sauce
¾ cup strained apricot preserves
2 to 3 tablespoons dark rum
Fresh apple slices for garnish

1. Heat 4 tablespoons of the butter in a large skillet. Add the apples and sauté until some of the juices are released. Stir in sugar, lemon rind and juice. Cover and cook over medium heat until apples are tender and all of the liquid has evaporated, stirring occasionally.
2. Stir in 3 tablespoons apricot preserves, rum and vanilla. Cook and stir until the mixture is very thick, about 10 minutes longer. (If puree is not thick enough, Apple Charlotte will collapse when unmolded.)
3. Heat oven to 425°F. Generously butter a 1½-quart charlotte mold with 2 tablespoons butter.
4. Trim crusts from bread. Cut four or five of the slices into small triangles. Arrange triangles, points toward center in bottom of mold, using a knife to round off the edges if necessary for best fit. With a small round cutter, cut off tips of triangles in center of mold. With same cutter, cut a circle of bread and fit into center.
5. Slice remaining bread in half lengthwise. Arrange slices vertically in an overlapping ring around sides of mold.
6. Fill mold with apple puree, mounding mixture in center. Cover with an additional slice of bread that has been trimmed to fit top.
7. Bake at 425°F until bread is golden brown, 30 to 35 minutes. Remove from oven and let cool about 45 minutes.
8. Prepare Apricot Sauce by heating ¾ cup strained preserves and rum together. Run a knife around the charlotte. Invert onto serving platter. Just before serving, garnish with fresh apple slices and pour Apricot Sauce over Apple Charlotte. Dessert may be served warm or cold.
Makes 6 to 8 servings

FRENCH GALLERY

Coeur à la Crème Molds

The purest heart of all wins those of dessert-lovers everywhere. A confection blended of sweetened cheese and cream and shaped in cheesecloth-lined porcelain molds, coeur à la crème, with its garland of fresh strawberries, is a French summer classic. The white heart-shaped molds stand on small feet, so that the cheese can drain through perforations in the bottom; they are available in six-serving or individual portion sizes. **To Use:** Line molds with dampened cheesecloth. Fill molds with cheese mixture and place in a shallow pan. Refrigerate overnight. Unmold onto serving plates and serve with

Fill molds with cheese mixture.

Unmold hearts; serve with berries.

strawberries.
Approximate Retail Price: $5 (individual-serving mold); $10 (large mold)

Coeurs à la Crème

4 ounces creamed cottage cheese
4 ounces cream cheese, softened
2 tablespoons confectioner's sugar
½ teaspoon vanilla extract
½ cup whipping cream
1 pint fresh strawberries, hulled and halved

1. Place cottage cheese in blender container; cover. Blend until smooth.
2. Beat cottage cheese, cream cheese, confectioner's sugar and vanilla until smooth.
3. Beat whipping cream until soft peaks form. Fold the whipped cream into the cheese mixture.
4. Line six small coeur à la crème molds with a double layer of dampened cheesecloth, allowing cheesecloth to hang over edge. Spoon mixture into prepared molds. Fold overhanging cheesecloth over the tops.
5. Place the molds in a shallow pan. Refrigerate overnight.
6. Unmold the hearts on individual dishes. Peel off cheesecloth and surround the hearts with strawberries. *Makes 6 servings*

Pôts de Crème

Pôts de Crème refers both to a richly-flavored custard dessert and the single-portion cups it's baked in. The traditional custard is delicious, but the tiny porcelain lidded pots will tempt you to create other occasions to use them — perhaps to serve chocolate mousse or even a thick, chilled soup. Cuteness, however, is not the pôts' sole asset. Made in France, the ½-cup pôts de crème are designed to withstand oven heat and refrigeration before they appear on the table. A custard mixture flavored with vanilla, chocolate, caramel or coffee is strained into the small containers, which are then baked in a water bath. The Pôts de Crème are served well-chilled with dollops of whipped

Strain custard into pôts de crème.

Bake custards and decorate.

cream. **To Use:** Strain custard mixture into pots. Bake in a water bath until custard sets. Cool slightly, and then refrigerate.
Approximate Retail Price: $3.95 each

Pôts de Crème au Café

1 cup whipping cream
1 cup milk
1 teaspoon instant coffee powder
1 tablespoon coffee-flavored liqueur
1 teaspoon vanilla
½ cup sugar
6 egg yolks
Whipped cream, if desired
Orange peel for decoration, if desired

1. Preheat oven to 325°F. In a medium bowl, mix whipping cream, milk, coffee powder, liqueur, vanilla and sugar. Whisk in egg yolks.
2. Pour mixture through a fine wire strainer into six individual pôts de crème.
3. Place pots in a baking pan. Pour boiling water into pan to depth of 1 inch. Bake until center of custard jiggles slightly when cup is shaken, about 30 minutes.
4. Remove pots from hot water. Cool to lukewarm. Replace lids and refrigerate. Custards are served cold. Garnish with a dollop of whipped cream, and orange peel if desired. *Makes 6 servings*

Steel Crepe Pan

The little French crepe is a brilliant diplomat, well-schooled in the art of making friends and disarming skeptics. Staunch foes of foreign cuisines and finicky children alike have been known to yield to the airy wiles of a thin buttered crepe, their protests stilled and translated into a growing Franco-American alliance with every forkful. The egg-rich pancake appeals with its versatility and utter simplicity; it wraps itself around seafood or jam, surrenders to flaming liqueurs, is content with a dusting of sugar. And chefs know that it takes only a light batter and a well-greased pan to create this irresistible liaison.

Because the crepe adapts so readily to any occasion and any accompaniment, cooks find it worthwhile to buy and reserve a pan just for crepe-making. There's nothing extraordinary about the pan itself; it's the patina of butter you rub into its surface that's important, because it prevents the feather-light batter from sticking. A 9-inch steel pan with a securely riveted handle takes beautifully to seasoning and makes crepes up to 6 inches in diameter. A wooden handle would be preferable; you must use a potholder with this model. But because it's deeper than most crepe pans, you can also use its stickless surface for omelettes. **To Use:** Prepare the pan by scouring it with soapy water to remove its coating of packing oil. Then season the surface by placing the pan over medium heat and rubbing it with a paper towel soaked in clarified butter. Keep pan on heat and rub with the clarified butter every 5 minutes for 35 to 45 minutes. The pan should turn brown as it absorbs the butter; it should never be washed, just wiped with a paper towel after use. Store the pan in a plastic bag to prevent the greased surface from attracting dust. To make crepes, set seasoned pan over medium-high heat until it begins to smoke. Then remove from heat and, holding the pan in your hand, pour ¼ cup crepe batter into center. Quickly tilt the pan in a circular motion to spread batter around bottom of pan. Return pan to heat for a minute or until crepe turns very light brown. Loosen the edges of the crepe, turn with a spatula or your fingers, and cook other side of crepe about ½ minute.

Approximate Retail Price: $11.50

Tilt steel pan to spread crepe batter around bottom.

Turn crepe when light brown with spatula or your fingers.

FRENCH GALLERY

Crepe Batter

3 egg yolks
1 cup milk
½ cup cold water
1 tablespoon sugar
3 tablespoons orange liqueur
1½ cups flour
Pinch salt
5 tablespoons melted butter

1. Combine all ingredients in a food processor with steel blade or blender and process a few seconds until thoroughly blended and smooth.
2. Cover and refrigerate for at least 2 hours.   *Makes about 16 crepes*

Magic Crepe Pan

In this topsy-turning world, it's not surprising that someone discovered the ease of cooking crepes upside-down. It's neither the cook nor the crepe that's up-ended, however; it's the pan that goes through life with its bottom turned topside. You place the inner surface of this pan over a medium flame and bake the crepe on the pan's rounded top. The walnut-handled pan functions like a domed griddle; its beautifully-cast aluminum surface absorbs and distributes heat evenly and bakes crepes up to 6 inches wide. You must season this pan as you would other crepe-makers. **To Use:** Briefly preheat seasoned pan over medium heat on a gas range or high heat on an electric stove. Pour crepe batter onto a dinner plate about 10 inches in diameter and ½ inch deep. Dip outer surface of crepe pan into batter and lift out immediately. Place pan over medium heat and cook crepe until it's dry on top and slightly brown around edge. There's no need to turn crepe with this type pan; just remove pan from heat and flip crepe onto a platter. Loosen edges a bit if crepe sticks.
Approximate Retail Price: $20

You bake crepes on the outer domed surface of the Magic Crepe Pan. Turn pan upside down and dip in batter; then turn pan right-side-up and bake crepe over a stove burner. You don't have to turn the crepe with this type of pan.

Crepe Flambé Pan

This 11-inch stainless steel-lined copper pan by Spring is called a crepe pan but actually it is designed for finishing crepes in a flambéed sauce. The ⅝-inch-deep lip on the pan neatly contains the sauce and folded crepes, allowing a large surface for reduction and flambé. With just a tiny tilt, the flame leaps from the brazier and into the pan, catching immediately. Voilà, flambé. **To Use:** Use powdered lacquer dissolvent in very hot water. Soak pan at least 20 minutes, completely submerged. Rinse and dry. Heat pan over medium heat and be sure flames do not extend up over sides of the pan.

Approximate Retail Price: $70

Spring crepe pan is perfect for Crepes Suzette. Lay crepes flat in sauce; then fold them in quarters.

Crepes Suzette

- **2 sugar cubes**
- **Grated rind of 2 medium oranges**
- **½ pound unsalted butter**
- **Juice of 1 medium orange**
- **⅔ cup granulated sugar**
- **3 tablespoons Grand Marnier or orange liqueur**
- **12 small or 8 large crepes**
- **¼ cup additional Grand Marnier or liqueur for flambé**

1. Rub sugar cubes over the orange rind and set aside.
2. Place butter, orange juice and rind, granulated sugar and 3 tablespoons Grand Marnier into the pan. Light burner and adjust heat to low. Set pan on burner.
3. Heat to a very slow bubble then add crepes one by one, first laying them flat in the sauce, then folding them in half and in half again. Arrange folded crepes around perimeter of the pan, overlapping. Count 3 small crepes or 2 large ones per person.
4. When all crepes are added, turn heat to high and let sauce bubble until reduced by about half. Add sugar cubes. Add all the reserved liqueur for flambé, count 30 seconds and tip pan to ignite. Once ignited, shake the pan once or twice and aid the evaporation of alcohol by basting the crepes with the flaming sauce. Serve immediately. *Makes about 4 servings*

ITALIAN FIESTA

ITALIAN FIESTA

Cooking Italian food is an incredible, edible odyssey and it can become a consuming passion for anyone who lusts after the perfect veal dish, the tenderest pasta, the crispiest vegetables and the most decadent desserts.

It's difficult to generalize about Italian cooking because styles, dishes and ingredients vary from city to city, family to family and region to region.

Pasta in northern Italy, for example, is light because it is made with flour and eggs. Southern Italian macaroni and spaghetti are heavier since they are made from flour and water. Ravioli in the north are rolled paper thin; in the south they are made a bit heavier.

It is commonly believed that Marco Polo brought spaghetti to Italy from China, but this is not necessarily so. There are indications that Italians were eating pasta well before the first visit to China. But only with the invention of the pasta machine in the 19th century did pasta become standard Italian fare.

Today, there is a raft of pasta-making equipment available and a surprising number of cooks are beginning to make their own pasta because it has become so easy to do. And not only is the taste better, but the texture is superb.

All you need to make delicious homemade pasta are eggs, salt, oil and a good-quality flour. Mixed together quickly and kneaded into a smooth dough, the pasta can be rolled using any one of several popular methods.

Purists always roll pasta by hand, believing it to be most tender if it is not placed in contact with materials other than porous wood. The principle of rolling pasta by hand is stretching: the dough expands under the pressure of a rolling pin, but the rolling motion is one of stretching rather than pressing.

Another school of pasta-makers claims that not only is a pasta machine faster than a rolling pin, but it also rolls more evenly. Normally made of stainless steel, pasta machines stretch the dough by pressing it between rollers; every time you pass the dough through the machine, it gets thinner. While it is probably true that hand-rolled pasta *is* a bit more tender, machine-rolled pasta can be exquisitely beautiful if rolled with care and not overworked.

Once the dough is "opened," as the Italians say, either with a rolling pin or a pasta machine roller, it can be cut into any of several hundred shapes and sizes. The long sheets of pasta, called *sfoglie* in Italian, can be cut lengthwise into noodles or crosswise into smaller sections for ravioli, into strips for homemade lasagna or triangles, circles or perfect squares for the various types of pastas popular throughout Italy.

If you don't want to invest in a machine and you don't want to go to all the work of hand-cutting your pasta, there are alternatives. One of these is a chittara, or "guitar," which is fitted with steel wires. When you press the dough through the wires, you get long, elegantly-shaped noodles. Regardless of how you cut the noodles, a noodle drier will solve the problem of where

to drape the strands of dough until they're ready to be cooked.

A pasta strainer and a spaghetti strainer are preferable to a colander for handling the tender strands of cooked pasta. For long noodles, you can use a spaghetti rake, which will lift the pasta from the pot without breaking the strands.

When you turn to ravioli-making, you'll discover the wit. This gadget looks like a nifty attachment for your pasta machine, but beware: You may be better off cutting the ravioli by hand or using a simple two-part ravioli tray to shape the little filled pockets.

There is a world of rich Italian desserts, but the baked pastries usually are not elaborate. For years, before World War II, there was not a great deal of baking done in Italian homes because there were few ovens. Desserts were either purchased from a local bakery, or were prepared by Mama and then brought to the bakery oven by Papa on his way to work in the morning. For decades, this was also the way lasagna was baked, and the transport involved accounts

for the tradition of serving lasagna just a bit warmer than room temperature.

For feast days such as St. Joseph's, Sicilians make pizelle. Their origin is not known, but pizelle are flat wafer-like cookies baked from a thin batter in a special iron. They are extraordinarily crisp and delicious.

Most people are familiar with cannoli, which are deep-fried pastry shells filled with flavored creams. Cannoli have been around longer than anyone would suspect — at least 300 years. In Sicily, the shells often are stuffed with candied fruit, but in Northern Italy, the filling is more likely to feature raisins and nuts or sometimes chocolate. Extravagant cannoli might hold rum-soaked raisins and chocolate chips, with the ends of the tubes dipped in ground nuts and the tops dusted with sugar. They are irresistible.

Even if you are not Italian, you easily can fall in love with the delicious foods of Italy. And when you do, you'll turn to the equipment in "Italian Fiesta" for wonderful dining experiences.

ITALIAN FIESTA

Pasta Machines

Many Italian chefs protest the heavy-handed treatment accorded pasta in this country. In their sunny land, the noodles, with or without eggs, are known for their lightness and delicate flavor; they bear little relation to the sodden strands heaped on dinner plates in America. Diners acquainted with the real thing have been known to grow restless with discontent if they cannot savor their beloved pasta in its ideal form — freshly rolled, quickly cooked, and sauced with the ambrosial fragrance of rich tomatoes, olive oil and garlic, or butter and cheese.

We, too, have known the longings one develops after having tasted the homemade noodles: There is no pre-packaged substitute. But the laborious process of rolling and cutting the pasta by hand is time-consuming and discouraging. So it was with the greatest pleasure that we discovered the efficient talents of various pasta machines. Both the hand-cranked and electric models are equipped to knead, roll and cut the dough. The process is incredibly easy. The ribbons of pasta emerge as a surprisingly generous reward for such a small investment of time. The machines have changed our lives — now we can feast whenever we wish on the homemade stuff of dreams. **To Use:** (These are gen-

Left to right: Cimadolmo, Atlas, The Flour Factory and Supernova pasta machines.

eral instructions that apply to all models; variations will be discussed separately with individual machines.) To clean the inside of a new machine, run a piece of dough through the rollers to remove surface oil. Make pasta dough and divide ball of dough into eight pieces. By hand or with a rolling pin, flatten one piece of dough into a rectangle

about ⅛ inch thick; keep remaining pieces of dough wrapped in plastic to prevent them from drying out. Set pasta machine rollers on the thickest setting and run the rectangle of dough through the machine. Fold the rectangle into thirds and run it through rollers again. Repeat the procedure about four times, rolling, folding and re-rolling until the dough

Fold dough in thirds to roll.

Set rollers for thinness.

Cut noodles with cutting head.

is smooth. Reset the rollers on the next thinnest setting and run pasta through again without folding. Reset the rollers to the next thinnest setting and run dough through this setting repeatedly, until desired thinness is achieved; dough will get thinner each time without your having to reset the rollers. To cut dough, detach handle from kneading/rolling gears and insert into gears that operate the cutting head. Run strip of dough through one set of rollers for broad noodles (fettucine) or the other for thin spaghetti (tagliatelle). To clean machine, let any stray pieces of dough dry; then brush off rollers with a soft brush. Do not wash machine, as inside parts may rust.

Adjust the dial on The Flour Factory to cut various pasta widths.

Bialetti electric machine speeds rolling and makes excellent pasta.

Atlas Pasta Machine

A chromed-steel import from Italy, the Atlas pasta machine stands 5½ shiny inches high on a compact 7-inch by 5-inch base. The kneading/stretching rollers are controlled by a knob with six settings but the dough will continue to get thinner every time you run it through at the same setting; so there actually are more than six possible noodle thicknesses. The machine comes with a detachable cutting head for thin and broad noodles. A ravioli attachment is available, as is an additional cutting head for making curly lasagna and fine "angel's hair" noodles; these must be purchased separately. This durable machine is fastened to the counter with a C-clamp. The Atlas is a joy to use and an excellent value among pasta machines.
Approximate Retail Price: $42 (pasta machine with cutting head); $30 (ravioli attachment); $15 (lasagna and "angel's hair" attachment)

The Flour Factory

Larger and more cumbersome than other pasta machines, The Flour Factory features nine thickness settings and two widths. You can combine these settings to produce an interesting variety of noodle sizes and shapes. There are two sets of rollers, one for kneading and stretching the dough, the other for cutting the noodles; you position the handle according to the set of gears you wish to engage. A plastic dial adjusts the settings for thickness and width. The broadest noodle you can cut is about ¼ inch wide, the narrowest about 1/16 inch wide. Hailing from the Pastalinda Company in Argentina, The Flour Factory stands 9 inches tall on a 10-inch by 8-inch base. It attaches to kitchen countertops with two adjustable C-clamps.
Approximate Retail Price: $100

Cimadolmo Pasta Machine

Made of chrome-plated steel framed in bright-yellow plastic, the Italian Cimadolmo resembles the Atlas machine and works just like it. But you can't buy extra cutting heads for it and the knob that adjusts the kneading rollers proved quite obstinate.
Approximate Retail Price: $40

Supernova Noodle Machine

Avoid this model — it's easier to cut noodles by hand! The small white plastic machine comes with four screw-on cutting heads, which would seem to work but proved otherwise. We found it impossible to separate the cut noodles; so we were left with a terrible mess and disappointed appetites.
Approximate Retail Price: $12

Bialetti Electric Pasta Machine

The Bialetti machine will please pasta-lovers twice over — once with its speed and again with the texture of the noodles. Three detachable heads, one for kneading and rolling, and two for cutting, come with this model. A batch of pasta will glide through both parts of the process in less than 15 minutes. Some aficionados prefer these finished noodles to others because of their surface texture; they are less "slick" and hold sauces better. The reason for the difference is that the Bialetti's rollers are nylon, while those of hand-cranked machines are metal. An elegant 8-inch-high white plastic frame encloses the motor; a series of suction cups anchor the 9-inch by 4-inch base.
Approximate Retail Price: $100

ITALIAN FIESTA

Pasta Dough

2 cups semolina flour
2 eggs, slightly beaten
1 teaspoon olive oil
¾ teaspoon salt
2 to 4 tablespoons warm water

1. Mound the flour in a large bowl or on a cutting board. Make a well in the center and add the eggs, olive oil, salt and 2 tablespoons of warm water.
2. Using a fork or your fingers, combine all ingredients until the dough forms a ball. If mixture is too dry to hold together, gradually add remaining water.
3. Lightly flour a cutting board and knead the dough for 8 to 10 minutes, until it is smooth and elastic. Cover the dough with a bowl or with plastic wrap and let it rest 30 minutes before rolling out.

Makes enough pasta for 6 to 8 servings

Chitarra

It's cut pasta rather than music that emerges from the chitarra's steel strings, but the old-fashioned device was named, nonetheless, for its resemblance to a guitar. Actually, the natural wood and cast-aluminum 8-inch by 20-inch frame holds two sets of steel wires, one spaced at ⅛-inch intervals, the other at 1/16 inch. You use either of the two sides of the chitarra, depending on the width of the noodles desired; a pressed-board tray positioned between the wired surfaces catches the noodles as they're cut. Aluminum terminals secure the wires and can be used to tighten them. **To Use:** Roll out pasta and cut a rectangular sheet to fit chitarra. Place pasta over the chitarra wires and, with your hand or a rolling pin, press dough between the wires. Remove cut noodles from beneath the wires and hang to dry. Repeat procedure until all of pasta is cut.
Approximate Retail Price: $32

Place sheet of pasta over chitarra.

Press pasta through wires to cut noodles.

Noodle Drier

How do you dry the pasta once it's been cut? Well, you can drape it over chairs, counters, doorknobs and such. Or you can hang it on the wooden dowels of a noodle drier. You insert the dowels into holes at the top of a 2-foot pole, which is screwed into a plywood base; you disassemble the hanger for storage. The drier holds enough noodles for about four servings. So if you're cooking for a crowd you may need more than one. **To Use:** Screw the pole into the base; insert dowels in pole. Mix, roll and cut pasta; then drape noodles over dowels until they're dry and crisp, about 10 minutes. Store noodles covered until ready to cook. Dust excess flour from drier and disassemble to store.
Approximate Retail Price: $8

Hang strips of pasta on noodle drier; let dry until crisp.

Pasta Strainer

Beautiful homemade pasta deserves somewhat better treatment than to be dumped into a colander to drain. And you deserve some relief from the task of aiming for the colander with a large pot of boiling water. So we present two graceful pasta strainers, each about 17 inches long and both designed for scooping noodles out of a cookpot. One is crafted of perforated stainless steel, the other of heavy tinned-steel mesh; they are equally strong. Both feature well-contoured black plastic handles that don't conduct heat. The mesh strainer would be preferable for draining tiny pastina; either one would be fine for draining foods other than pasta. **To Use:** Scoop pasta directly from boiling water to serving dish.
Approximate Retail Price: $16 (perforated strainer); $5 (mesh strainer)

Lift cooked pasta from boiling water with a pasta strainer.

Spaghetti Rake

You can dip a spaghetti rake into a cookpot and, with a single twist, drain and remove the noodles. The rake is more adept than a strainer at picking out a single strand to test for doneness, but it won't do, of course, for small-size pastas. The 13-inch beechwood rake adds an unusual dimension to a kitchen collection of wooden utensils. **To Use:** Dip rake in pot of cooked spaghetti, twist to catch noodles in prongs, and remove noodles.
Approximate Retail Price: $1.25

A spaghetti rake catches long strands in its wooden prongs and lifts them from the water without breaking them.

ITALIAN FIESTA

Ravioli Tray

Every cuisine has its own version of dumplings — little morsels of meat, vegetable or cheese enveloped in small packets of dough. Most evolved from peasant economies, and all are delicious. Italian food fans find heavenly bliss in pillow-shaped ravioli. The square of pasta may be filled with any mixture of minced meats or seasoned ricotta cheese, and they're usually topped with tomato sauce. But it's the fresh, homemade pasta that makes this dish so delightful.

Once you've mixed, kneaded and rolled out the pasta dough, you'll need some device to help cut and seal the filled ravioli. A two-piece cast-aluminum ravioli maker was by far the quickest and easiest means we found. It consists of a 4-inch by 12-inch tray with 12 round indenta-

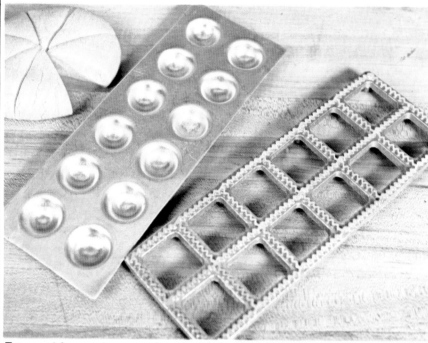

Tray and frame shape and seal ravioli.

Place pasta over filled pockets.

Seal ravioli with rolling pin.

Use the tray to indent pockets for filling.

Tap tray to release ravioli.

tions and a frame the same size, with a grid that outlines 12 squares. Each square in the gridded frame is surrounded by a sharp, zig-zag edge. **To Use:** Roll out pasta dough by hand or with a pasta machine and cut into two rectangular strips, each about 5½ inches by 13 inches. Place one strip of dough over the gridded frame. Press the dough into the frame with the indented tray, thus stretching 12 pouches that will hold ravioli filling; then remove the tray and fill pouches as desired. Place second strip of pasta dough over the strip with filling and press strips together with your fingers. With a rolling pin, roll across the dough-covered frame; start gently and then increase pressure until the zig-zag edges of the frame are visible through the pasta. The ravioli will be sealed. Remove excess dough and discard or re-roll. To remove ravioli from frame, rap firmly on counter; ravioli will fall out. Repeat procedure until all dough and filling is used. Place ravioli on a heavily-floured cookie sheet and let dry for 1 hour; then turn ravioli over and let dry another hour. (Ravioli can be frozen at this point; thaw before cooking.) Cook ravioli 10 to 15 minutes in a large pot of boiling water; remove from water with slotted spoon. Place ravioli on a heated serving dish; serve with tomato sauce and freshly-grated parmesan cheese.
Approximate Retail Price: $11

Dry ravioli; then cook them and serve with sauce and parmesan cheese.

Meat-filled Ravioli

**2 cups combined cooked
 ground beef and lean pork**
**½ cup cooked chopped
 spinach, drained**
½ cup grated Parmesan cheese
¼ cup minced parsley
½ cup dry bread crumbs
½ cup minced Genoa salami
3 eggs
 Salt and pepper to taste
 **Pasta dough for four
 servings**
 Tomato sauce
 Grated parmesan cheese

1. Combine meats, spinach, cheese, parsley, bread crumbs, salami, eggs, salt and pepper.
2. Roll pasta dough until thin and translucent. Dust lightly with flour. Cut dough to fit ravioli wit rollers.
3. Fold dough in half along width; place fold in top of machine and turn handle until dough catches.
4. Place filling in crease of dough and turn handle ¼ turn. Remove ravioli from bottom of roller. Continue filling and turning until dough and filling are used up. (Note: Ravioli also can be prepared with tray and frame ravioli maker or ravioli rolling pin and sealer.)
5. Place ravioli on a heavily-floured cookie sheet and let dry 1 hour; turn ravioli over and let dry another hour. (Ravioli may be frozen at this point; thaw before cooking.)
6. Cook ravioli in large pot of boiling salted water about 7 minutes or until tender (cooking time will vary with thickness of dough). Drain. Serve with tomato sauce and grated cheese. *Makes 4 servings*

Ravioli Wits

It's conceivable that the machines that crank out ravioli are called "wits" because you need a sense of humor to use them. They all operate the same way — messily. You're supposed to be able to turn out many ravioli at a time, but you're just as likely to end up with a sticky mess of filling and dough. The tray and frame ravioli maker performs much better than any of the wits we tried.

The Atlas ravioli wit is an optional attachment for the Atlas pasta machine. It comes with a cutter for cutting strips of dough to the proper ravioli width and a nylon brush for cleaning the ravioli rollers. The 5-inch-high free-standing Junior Ravioli Wit from Rowoco is made of chromed steel with melamine sides and base; it comes with a cutter and a brush but without any means of securing it to the counter. The 8-inch-high free-standing Raviolera model, made by Pastalinda, comes with two C-clamps and produces tiny, 1-inch-square ravioli. **To Use:** Clean a new machine before using by running a piece of pasta dough through it several times to remove dust or oil. Prepare pasta dough and roll out to desired thickness. Cut dough with a cutter or knife to fit width of ravioli wit rollers. Sprinkle one side of dough with flour and fold the strip of dough in half along its width with the floured side facing out. Place the folded edge of the dough into the top of the machine and turn the handle just until the dough catches in the rollers. Place filling in the crease of the dough and turn handle. The filling will be evenly dispersed as you turn the handle. When filling disappears into machine and ravioli are formed, add more filling. Repeat procedure until dough and filling are used up. Wipe machine clean with a dry cloth or brush with nylon brush; never wash machine with water.
Approximate Retail Price: $30 (Atlas ravioli attachment); $31 (Junior ravioli wit); $65 (Raviolera ravioli maker)

Three ravioli wit models.

Cut dough to fit ravioli wit.

Flour the cut strip of pasta.

Fold strip, floured side out.

Drop filling into crevice.

Turn handle; add more filling.

Ravioli Rolling Pin and Sealer

We appreciate the charming irony of handsome utensils that serve no purpose, but that doesn't make it any easier to use them. A two-inch-long hardwood ravioli rolling pin is attractive enough to hang up for display — and should be used for just that! In order for the rolling pin to work, you have to align morsels of filling on a sheet of pasta dough in a grid precisely matched to the 1½-inch square indentations carved in the pin. It's hardly worth the effort. But if you should succeed in positioning the filling, covering it with another sheet of dough, and rolling the pin across the lumpy surface, you would then have to separate the ravioli with a ravioli sealer. It's easier to dispense with the rolling pin and just run the sealer around the perimeters of the lumps of filling. **To Use:** Prepare pasta dough and roll to desired thickness with a regular rolling pin. Cut sheet of dough in half. Position teaspoonful of filling at 2-inch intervals on one sheet of dough. Match indentation in ravioli rolling pin to the first row of filling; roll across dough to mark ravioli squares. Then cut along lines left by the rolling pin with the ravioli sealer. Wipe off rolling pin to clean.
Approximate Retail Price: $8.95 (rolling pin); $3.25 (sealer)

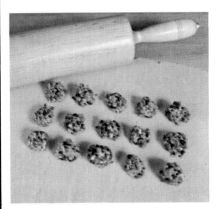
Place filling at 2-inch intervals.

Cover with sheet of dough and roll.

Cut around ravioli with sealer.

Pizzelle Iron

Would that we could be in Italy, watching the scenery in late afternoon and sipping espresso with a crisp cream-filled pizzelle! But the best we can do is to bake the paper-thin cookies at home and plug in the espresso machine. Pizzelle are wafer-like waffles baked and branded with geometric patterns in a specially-designed iron. You can eat them flat or roll them, while still warm, and fill them. A hand-held pizzelle iron is constructed of two hinged, 5½-inch-diameter aluminum plates; each plate is attached to a long handle with a wooden grip. The iron was originally designed for use over an open fire, but today we can bake the pizzelle atop an ordinary burner. Electric versions are available for about four times the price of mechanical models; some of these can double as waffle irons. **To Use:** Wash the iron thoroughly before use; then grease lightly and heat to season. To bake pizzelle, grease both surfaces of iron and heat on stove burner. Place about 1 tablespoon of pizzelle batter in center of bottom plate. Close iron and press tightly to let steam escape. If batter seeps out, simply remove with a knife or wooden spoon. Bake cookies until golden, about 2 to 3 minutes. Roll cookies while warm, cool and fill, or serve flat. To clean iron, wash with detergent and hot water. If batter sticks to grid, let dry and remove with stiff brush.
Approximate Retail Price: $13

Bake pizzelle in greased iron.

Roll up warm pizzelle.

ITALIAN FIESTA

Pizzelle

4 eggs
1 cup sugar
½ cup vegetable oil
3 tablespoons lemon juice or 1 teaspoon vanilla
Grated rind of 1 lemon
1½ cups flour
¼ teaspoon baking powder
Sweetened whipped cream or sour cream flavored with sherry, brandy or fruit juice for filling

1. Beat eggs until lemon-colored; add sugar gradually, beating well after each addition. Add oil, lemon juice or vanilla, and rind; beat well. Mix flour and baking powder; add gradually to egg mixture, beating well. Chill batter until cooking time.
2. Grease both plates of pizzelle iron. Heat iron over medium burner. Spoon about 1 tablespoon of batter onto center of bottom grid. Close iron and press tightly to let steam escape. Cook over medium heat about 3 to 5 minutes, until cookie is golden brown on both sides.
3. Remove cookie and roll into a cone or cylinder while still hot. Repeat procedure with remaining batter.
4. Fill cooled cookies with either whipped cream or sour cream flavored with sherry, brandy or fruit juice.

Makes 1½ dozen

Cannoli Forms

A taste for cannoli cannot be satisfied by any other dessert, for the flavor of the crunchy tube of fried pastry stuffed with sweetened ricotta cheese is uniquely delicious. And there's little reason not to enjoy cannoli whenever you wish, for they're not difficult to make. However, you do need special cylindrical forms to wrap the dough around while it fries. These are made of tinned-steel and come in various lengths, with diameters ranging from ½ inch to 1 inch; they commonly are sold in packages of three or four. **To Use:** Wash the forms well and dry. Roll out cannoli dough. Cut dough into rounds to fit forms. Roll a round of dough around each form, overlapping edges; seal with beaten egg white. Handling forms with tongs, deep fry cannoli until golden. Cool pastries on forms; then carefully remove the forms by twisting and pulling gently. Fill hollow pastry shell with desired filling. To clean metal tubes, wash and dry.

Approximate Retail Price: $3 (set)

Roll cannoli around forms.

Cannoli

Pastry
2 cups flour
¼ teaspoon salt
2 tablespoons sugar
¼ teaspoon cinnamon
2 tablespoons butter, softened
1 egg, slightly beaten
¼ cup plus 2 tablespoons white wine
1 egg white, beaten
Vegetable oil for frying

Filling
2 cups ricotta cheese
¾ cup sugar
1 teaspoon vanilla
Grated rind of ½ lemon
½ cup grated semi-sweet chocolate

Garnishes
Chopped pistachio nuts
Powdered sugar

1. In a bowl, combine flour, salt, sugar and cinnamon. Cut in butter until mixture resembles coarse crumbs.
2. Combine egg and ¼ cup wine and add to flour mixture. Mix with a fork or with your fingers; add remaining 2 tablespoons wine a few drops at a time as needed until pastry holds together.
3. Form the dough into a ball with your hands. Cover and let rest for 15 minutes.
4. Divide the dough into quarters. On a lightly floured surface, roll out dough as thin as possible (about thickness of a dime) and cut into 4- to 5-inch rounds.
5. Wrap each circle of dough around a cannoli form and seal edges with beaten egg white.
6. Heat about 2 inches of vegetable oil in a skillet to 400°F. Fry cannoli about 2 minutes, until lightly browned. Drain on paper toweling. Let cool briefly and remove forms. Cool completely before filling.
7. For filling, combine ricotta cheese, sugar, vanilla, grated lemon rind and grated chocolate and mix well. Fill each shell and sprinkle ends with chopped pistachio nuts.
8. Dust cannoli with powdered sugar just before serving.

Makes about 16 cannoli

ORIENTAL MARKET

The greatest misfortune, according to an ancient Oriental proverb, is hunger and the greatest blessing is health. And everyone who has cooked or eaten substantial amounts of Oriental food quickly realizes that this centuries-old cuisine is perfectly designed both to avoid hunger and to confer health in abundant measure.

The major Oriental cuisines (and the ones for which excellent cookbooks now abound) are the Chinese and Japanese. Both are expressions of the same philosophy of simple ingredients raised to a level of visual and gustatory art by people who, in ages past, were poor in all things material but rich in imagination and skill. Both utilize many of the same utensils and cooking procedures in the prepara-

tion of their finest dishes, which are naturally high in protein and low in fats and carbohydrates. Surveying the vast mural of Chinese culinary art and the exquisite still life of Japanese cuisine, it is encouraging to know that Oriental cookery is based on a few unfamiliar but easily mastered techniques and a few basic pieces of equipment.

At the center of the Oriental *bat-*

ORIENTAL MARKET

terie de cuisine resides the wok. This bowl-shaped, round-bottomed, two-handled cooking pan of Chinese invention has changed little in the past 3000 years since it first sat atop the concave chattie, or primitive cylindrical charcoal stove. The major addition has been a stabilizing ring to adapt it to contemporary flat-topped ranges. However ancient, the wok's design is very scientific: The round bottom cups and intensifies the heat, which spreads up the sloping sides, and food can be cooked quickly in the smallest possible amounts of oil. Flavor and juices are sealed in by the rapid cooking and colors and textures are preserved. A versatile pot (wok means "cooking vessel" in Chinese), the wok can be used to stir-fry, deep-fry, braise, steam and simmer all manner of savory Oriental fare and Western dishes too. The most ordinary combination of meat, vegetables and seasoning tastes wonderful when stir-fried in a wok. When you add a rack and cover it with a lid, the wok steams as well — vegetables, fish and fabulous little Chinese dumplings and meat-

stuffed buns. Often a several-course meal will emerge, level by level, from a multi-tiered bamboo steamer set inside a covered wok.

Wok cookery is an excellent way to entertain. Most of the ingredients must be pre-cut and assembled and the final cooking takes only minutes; so a host or hostess can serve an excellent meal and still enjoy the company to the fullest.

Japanese Tempura — a selection of seafood (shrimp is ever-popular) and seasonal vegetables coated with an ethereal flour and egg batter and plunged sizzling into the fat-filled tempura cooker — showcases the textural appeal of Oriental cooking. The crisp foods are removed from the oil and laid to rest for a brief moment on the rack attached to the cooker; then they're served piping hot — and often still sizzling — to eagerly-awaiting guests. Tempura is less fattening than other deep-fried foods. The batter and foods to be fried should be icy cold, and the oil exceptionally hot; this combination results in the least possible fat-absorption.

Tempura, which can be cooked

in a wok as well, is also an ideal party dish. The crisp morsels are ideally eaten as fast as they are cooked, and tempura is well-suited for cooking out-of-doors over a portable heat source in warm weather.

But of all Oriental meals suited to entertaining, the most ingenious is one wherein the guests cook their own meal. Such teamwork depends on the use of a charming utensil called a fire pot. This chimneyed charcoal-burning pot was inspired by the Mongols, who cooked chunks of lamb over an open fire in pots filled with boiling soup. The Chinese are credited with transforming the meal by expanding the cooking ingredients to include meat, poultry, fish, vegetables and noodles, all cut and arranged with characteristic artistry. And the Chinese re-designed the Mongolian pot, turning it into a brazier combined with a cooking vessel. Whether the recipe you prepare is a Chinese chrysanthemum bowl, or Japanese shabu shabu, or any variation thereon, the principle and the fun remain the same. Guests gather round the charcoal-heated pot, which is filled with a simmering savory broth. Each selects ingredients from a platter of precut and arranged ingredients and cooks them one by one in the hot broth using either chopsticks or small, long-handled strainers. As more and more ingredients are cooked, the flavor they impart makes the broth richer and more flavorful. When all ingredients have been cooked, the host or hostess (who has had a rather easy time of it) adds noodles to the broth, then serves the by-now-heavenly broth as the climax to the meal.

There are endless advantages to learning Oriental cookery. Its repertoire of recipes, like those of all great cuisines, is inexhaustible. Most of the ingredients are familiar and economical, and the less familiar ingredients are more easily obtainable than ever before. And the cutting and cooking techniques are easy to master with the specialized utensils stocked in our "Oriental Market."

Woks

The classic round-bottomed Chinese wok was designed to cook food as quickly as possible, so as to use the least amount of fuel. So it's not surprising that this remarkably efficient pot is enjoying a widespread revival among time- and energy-saving Americans. The wok's centuries-old design still achieves its purpose: Dipping towards the heat source, the center of the wok gets hot very quickly, and the heat is conducted rapidly and evenly throughout the thin, tempered-steel bowl. In the days when the wok was used atop a Chinese brazier, the flared rim kept the pot from falling into the fire; today, a steel ring supports the base of the bowl above a gas-range burner. An electric range poses a novel problem for wok-users: You can't position the ring-supported base close enough to the heat. Fortunately, a flat-bottomed wok, which doesn't require a ring stand, has been invented to cope with contemporary technology. Electric woks are another innovation; they're convenient for tableside stir-frying but they don't allow cooks the sensitive heat control afforded by traditional woks. Americans tend to use the wok exclusively for stir-frying, but in China the wok is an all-purpose cooker — excellent for steaming and braising as well as frying. Though woks are available up to 3 feet in diameter, a 12-inch to 14-inch size is fine for everyday cooking; you might want to invest in a wok with a long wooden handle for cool convenience. Wok prices vary according to size, design, material and accessories included. Choose an iron or steel wok, and you'll marvel at its efficiency. **To Use:** Remove packing oil from an iron or steel wok by scrubbing vigorously with a stiff brush dipped in hot water and detergent. Season the cleaned wok by rubbing with vegetable oil while heating over a low flame; wipe off excess oil, then reapply oil, heat and rub two more times. When cooking in a wok, use medium-high to high heat for stir-frying. Heat a small amount of oil (many cooks prefer peanut oil because it can get hotter than other oils without smoking). Add uniformly chopped ingredients and stir continuously with a tossing motion. You can start with ingredients that require longest cooking and push these up sloping sides to finish cooking while you add other ingredients to oil in bottom of wok. Chinese chefs use chopsticks to stir-fry. To steam vegetables, fish or buns in a wok, place a specially designed rack or a round cake rack over 1 inch of boiling water in bottom of rack. Cover food while steaming. Wash out wok with hot water after use, and wipe dry to prevent rusting; reseason if necessary.

Approximate Retail Price: $10

Wok Spatula and Ladle

You can stir-fry with extra-long cooking chopsticks, but you'll probably have an easier time of it with an iron or stainless-steel spatula curved to fit the contours of the wok. The iron spatulas tend to rust, the stainless-steel ones are more expensive, and a wood spatula will work as well but may absorb food odors. You should feel comfortable with whichever spatula you choose, because you'll be using it continuously while stir-frying to keep small morsels of fish, meat and vegetables evenly tossed in the hot oil. Stir-frying is accomplished with very little oil; the process is quite fast and easily controlled to prevent overcooking. An iron or steel ladle contoured to fit the wok comes in handy for serving foods simmered in a sauce. **To Use:** Heat oil in wok. Add ingredients to be stir-fried and toss and stir with spatula. You may find it easier to use two spatulas simultaneously to keep food in motion. When cooking food in a sauce, use ladle to remove from wok. Wash iron utensils in hot soapy water, dry and coat lightly with oil to prevent rusting. Wash wood utensils quickly with soap and water and dry immediately.

Approximate Retail Price: $5

Chinese utensils: wok, cleavers, strainer, spatula, ladle, chopsticks.

Oriental Strainer and Skimmer

Though it's known for its stir-frying prowess, the wok serves equally well for deep-frying batter-coated foods like Chinese shrimp puffs or Japanese tempura. To drain and remove food from the hot oil, you need a shallow basket strainer with a long handle. The classic Chinese model features a basket of loosely woven brass mesh and a wood handle; this 12-inch-long strainer drains food faster than those with tightly-woven baskets. A Japanese skimmer (shown with Tempura Cooker) with a fine-mesh basket is more effective, however, for removing small particles from the cooking oil. Because the small particles will burn and affect the flavor of foods subsequently fried, skimming the oil is as important as draining the finished food. So you should have both a strainer and a skimmer. **To Use:** To strain deep-fried foods, simply move the strainer under the food and sweep upwards; let the food drip for a moment, then remove to drain on racks or paper toweling. To skim deep oil, move the skimmer until it picks up all small particles in the oil, and discard these. To clean strainer and skimmer, wash briefly in soap and water. Rinse and dry immediately. *Approximate Retail Price: $5*

Cleaver

A Chinese chef must spend two years practicing with a cleaver before he is allowed to go on to more elaborate tasks. But it won't take you two years to master the cleaver for ordinary home use. The cumbersome-looking knife can chip, slice, mince, mash, scoop and bone all kinds of foods. The typical cleaver has an 8-inch by 4-inch rectangular blade made of carbon steel or high carbon or regular stainless steel. High carbon stainless-steel cleavers are the most expensive; carbon steel models, the lowest priced. Metal handles tend to slip more easily from greasy fingers than wooden handles, but newer metal-handled models have helpful gripping ridges. Cleavers are numbered according to weight, ranging from a light, small-bladed #6 to the heaviest, a #1. For ordinary chopping, slicing and mincing, a #2 is a good all-purpose choice, but a #1 is recommended for chopping bones. **To Use:** Grasp the handle close to the blade as if shaking hands. Thumb and forefinger should be extended slightly over the blade. The first knuckle of the middle finger touches the side of the blade to guide it; with practice, you'll learn to move the knuckle back in rhythm with the cutting action to make thin, even slices. When slicing foods, use a downward and forward motion — the weight of the cleaver does most of the work. The hand holding the food should have fingertips curled under, out of the way of the blade edge. The cleaver is quite versatile: Use the side of the blade to mash cloves of garlic and other foods; the handle end can crush spices in a mortar or heavy bowl; the blade is often used as a scoop to transfer the chopped food to wok or skillet; and the tip of the blade is good for boning meat or poultry. Carbon steel cleavers must be kept dry to prevent rusting. To sharpen, use a steel or sharpening stone as you would with other knives. A sharp cleaver is actually less dangerous than a dull one, which must often be forced to cut and can cause accidental nicks. *Approximate Retail Price: $12 to $50 (stainless steel); $4 to $15 (carbon steel)*

Move cleaver down and forward to slice.

Tenderize meat by pounding with cleaver.

Szechwan Beef with Cellophane Noodles

¾ pound flank steak, cut in matchstick-size pieces
2 tablespoons soy sauce
2 tablespoons cornstarch
1 tablespoon dry sherry
2 cups broken cellophane noodles
¼ cup oil
4 cloves garlic, minced
1 tablespoon each: grated ginger, minced green onion
½ cup bamboo shoots, cut in matchstick-size pieces
1 carrot, cut in matchstick-size pieces

Sauce
3 tablespoons dry sherry
2 tablespoons soy sauce
1 tablespoon cornstarch
1 tablespoon sugar
1 teaspoon chili paste
¼ teaspoon salt

1. Mix meat with soy sauce, cornstarch, and sherry; marinate at least 1 hour.
2. Fry noodles in hot oil in wok until puffed and crisp; remove, drain and reserve.
3. Drain meat and brown in oil over high heat, stirring, until lightly cooked; remove and set aside.
4. Cook and stir garlic, ginger and onion in hot oil for 30 seconds.
5. Add bamboo shoots and carrots; cook and stir for 30 seconds.
6. Add meat; heat through.
7. Combine all sauce ingredients in small bowl; add to meat mixture in wok. Cook, stirring, until thick. Serve over crisp noodles. *Makes 6 servings*

Fry noodles in oil until crisp; then drain.

Stir beef in oil over high heat till brown.

Cut vegetables into matchsticks to fry.

Szechwan Beef with Cellophane Noodles.

Chinese Steamers

Having dealt with the energy crisis for longer than we have, Chinese cooks have developed marvelous resources that we might well adopt. One of these is a multi-level bamboo steamer, which fits inside a wok and holds several dishes stacked in its tiers for simultaneously steaming. You can steam a whole meal of dim sum (Chinese dumplings), fish, and vegetables at one time. The aromas mingle and tantalize, adding yet another attraction to the handsome round basket. The two lowest tiers of the steamer are most effective for cooking, and you might want to use the upper tiers only for reheating and warming foods. Because the bamboo steamer is difficult to clean, you might prefer an aluminum model. Or, you can buy single-level perforated trays and racks to fit the wok for steaming. **To Use:** Fill wok with small amount of water; water level should come no higher than 1 inch

Buns cook on waxed paper-lined bamboo steamer in wok.

below bottom of steamer. Place steamer in wok, arrange food, and cover wok while steaming. To clean bamboo steamer, rinse with water and wipe dry; a thin coat of vegetable oil will keep the bamboo from drying out.
Approximate Retail Price: $4.50

Steamed Buns (Dai Bao)

Filling
   2 teaspoons oil
   1 clove garlic, minced
¼ teaspoon salt
   2 teaspoons soy sauce
½ teaspoon sesame oil
   1 teaspoon oyster sauce
   3 teaspoons cornstarch
   1 tablespoon cold water
⅓ cup hot water
   1 teaspoon hoisin sauce
   1 teaspoon sugar
¾ cup cooked, diced pork

Dough
2½ cups flour
3½ teaspoons baking powder
   3 tablespoons sugar
   2 tablespoons soft lard
      About ½ cup water
½ teaspoon white vinegar

Place teaspoon of filling on circle of dough. Twist to seal.

1. Heat oil in wok. Add garlic and cook and stir for 10 seconds. Add salt, soy sauce, sesame oil, oyster sauce, cornstarch mixed with 1 tablespoon cold water, and ⅓ cup hot water to wok. Cook and stir until thick and clear.
2. Remove from heat; stir in hoisin sauce and sugar. Stir in pork; cool.
3. To prepare dough: Sift flour and baking powder into bowl; stir in sugar. Rub in lard with fingers until evenly mixed. Add water and vinegar; knead dough until soft. Shape into smooth ball, cover and let rest 30 minutes.
4. Divide dough into six to eight portions; roll each into a 4-inch circle. Place a teaspoon of filling in center of each. Bring up edges to enclose filling, making folds at top, pinching to seal, and twisting. Arrange seam side down on lightly oiled waxed paper.
5. Fill wok with about 1 inch of water. Place buns and paper on rack or in bamboo steamer placed in wok. Cover and steam for 20 to 30 minutes or until dough has cooked. Serve warm. *Makes 6 to 8 buns*

Tempura Cooker

A specialty of many Japanese restaurants, tempura is an assortment of foods deep-fried in a puffy batter and served with a soy-sauce mixture for dipping. Americans have discovered how deliciously light and ungreasy shrimp, meats and pieces of sweet potato, eggplant, mushroom, onions and other vegetables can be when fried in the Japanese manner. Any heavy large pot or deep skillet can be used for tempura, but if you want to try it in the traditional manner, look for a tempura cooker, which is a wok with a draining rack perched on the edge. One version features a 12-inch steel flat-bottomed wok and a stainless-steel rack. The set also includes long cooking chopsticks for lifting the food in and out of the oil (not as hard as it sounds!), and a broom-like bamboo skimmer for sweeping stray particles from the oil. **To Use:** Fill the thoroughly scrubbed wok to a depth of 2 inches with light cooking oil and heat to 365°F. Prepare a batter and coat foods of your choice. Drop a few pieces at a time into the hot oil with the chopsticks. Cook until golden brown. Remove with chopsticks or mesh skimmer and drain food on the wire rack hooked on the edge of the wok. Do not leave the foods to drain too long, however, or they will become soggy in the heat from the oil below; tempura is best eaten immediately. Occasionally skim the oil with the bamboo skimmer to remove small food particles. Make sure the food is dry before dipping into batter or it will not be properly coated. The oil may be reused if skimmed completely. To clean, simply wipe out the wok and store. The rack, chopsticks and skimmer should be washed and thoroughly dried.

Approximate Retail Price: $12

Tempura cooker has a rack.

Fry and drain food on rack.

Mesh skimmer removes food.

Tempura

Sauce
¼ cup soy sauce
½ cup fish, beef or chicken stock
2 teaspoons sugar
3 teaspoons sweet sake or sherry
Dash prepared horseradish

Batter
¾ cup flour
¼ cup cornstarch
1 teaspoon salt
1½ teaspoons baking powder
1 egg
¾ cup cold water

Foods to be fried
1 pound raw shelled shrimp
1 whole chicken breast, boned, cubed
¼ pound green beans, cut lengthwise
1 large sweet potato, peeled, thinly sliced
¼ pound fresh mushrooms, halved
4 green onions, cut in 1½-inch pieces
2 zucchini, sliced
¼ pound snow peas
Peanut oil for deep frying

1. Prepare sauce by mixing soy sauce, stock, sugar, sake or sherry and horseradish. Set aside.
2. To make batter: Sift flour, cornstarch, salt and baking powder together. Beat egg with water and pour into dry ingredients. Stir quickly with a fork; batter should be lumpy.
3. Prepare foods for frying; dry thoroughly. Heat oil in wok to 365°F.
4. Dip prepared foods into batter to coat. Cook a few pieces at a time in hot oil until light brown, about 2 minutes. With skimmer or chopsticks, remove food to rack to drain. Fry a second batch and remove to rack. Skim oil to remove any food particles remaining. Complete frying all the food. Do not let food remain on rack too long or it will lose its crispness. Dip fried food in sauce to eat.

Makes 4 servings

ORIENTAL MARKET

Copper Fire Pot

Mongol tribesmen had a great idea! Nomads who wandered the Asian steppes, they prepared meals over an open fire, simmering soup in a pot and then plunging chunks of meat skewered on the ends of their knives into the broth to cook. Later, Chinese gourmets refined the concept into a fondue-like ritual, complete with a special fire pot. A fire pot meal consists of two courses: First you cook meat in the broth-filled pot; then you add noodles to the cooking liquid and enjoy the savory soup. The 10-inch-tall pot is quite dramatic: It consists of a grate that holds hot coals, a chimney to vent the burning coals, a tin-lined bowl that fits over the chimney to hold the broth, and a perforated base beneath the grate to provide a draught and catch ashes. You place the pot on a heat-proof surface, light the coals in a separate brazier (preferably outdoors), and either heap the hot coals on the grate with the bowl removed or drop the coals through the chimney. The copper model shown comes with a set of four brass mesh baskets for lowering meats, seafood, vegetables and noodles into the broth and scooping the fragrant foods out again. **To Use:** Clean pot thoroughly. Use pot only in a well-

Drop hot coals down fire pot chimney to heat broth.

ventilated area, because the charcoal will give off carbon dioxide fumes. If using the pot indoors, place it on a heat-proof pan or in a pan of water to absorb heat. Light coals on an outdoor grill; then carefully transfer them to the fire pot grate. Pile coals high in the middle of the grate with bowl removed, or drop coals through chimney with bowl in place. Fill the bowl with boiling broth. Set out strips of meat on a platter and let diners cook individual portions in the broth, using baskets or chopsticks. Serve a dipping sauce with meat. After meat has been cooked, add cellophane noodles to broth and ladle into serving bowls. When cooking is completed, place a lid over the chimney to put out the coals. Let coals cool completely. Remove lid and bowl; then empty ashes by turning the pot upside-down and shaking. The bowl and lid may be washed with detergent and water; the base should be rinsed clean and dried immediately to prevent the iron grate from rusting.
Approximate Retail Price: $90

Chinese Fire Pot

3 cups chicken stock
4 cups hot water
3 green onions, cut in strips
6 dried mushrooms, soaked, sliced
1 cup soy sauce
¼ cup sherry
  Dash red pepper
3 pounds round steak or sirloin, thinly sliced
2 cloves garlic, crushed
1 slice fresh ginger
1 tablespoon salt
⅛ teaspoon pepper
½ package cellophane noodles (optional)

1. Heat chicken stock, water, onions and mushrooms to boiling in a saucepan.
2. Light charcoal on a grill and let burn until red and glowing. Place fire pot over heat-proof pan or in a shallow pan filled with water to absorb heat. Set pot on dining surface. Using tongs, transfer coals to pot, either mounding them in center of grate or dropping them through chimney.
3. Fill fire pot bowl with hot broth. Cover until ready to begin cooking.
4. Combine soy sauce, sherry and red pepper for dipping sauce. Arrange meat on platter. Add garlic, ginger, salt and pepper to broth before cooking begins.
5. Let each diner place portion of meat in wire basket and cook in broth until tender. Dip meat in sauce to eat.
6. After meat is eaten, add noodles to broth, if desired, and ladle broth into bowls for final course.
Makes 4 servings

ONCE AROUND THE WORLD

People who love to cook are also likely to enjoy travel. The paths of these two pastimes cross in a wondrous grid of discovery: If you visit a country and savor its fare, you're likely to want to recreate the experience when you get home. And if you prepare many recipes from a single nation or region, you'll feel yourself becoming so intimately acquainted with the people through their food that you'll want to enrich the relationship with a visit.

As you tour the cooking equipment featured in "Once Around the World," you'll be struck by the variety of international cuisines and the number of separate but equally rich traditions.

We begin in North Africa with a steamer designed for preparing the classic Moroccan couscous. Though the entire one-pot meal is called couscous, the name refers literally to only one of two delicious components. Moroccan cooks fill the bottom, or pot half, of the couscousière with a savory stew, called a *tajine*; meats such as lamb, beef and chicken, chick-peas, cabbage, zucchini, onions, peppers and other vegetables simmer in a broth perfumed with herbs and spices. Then cooks use their fingers to moisten beads of semolina wheat by rubbing them until they swell slightly — this grain is the couscous. The couscous is placed atop the stew in

a steamer and is left to cook, always uncovered, in the vapor that rises from the simmering broth. Stew and couscous are served together, with a pepper sauce to enliven the somewhat bland grain.

Many cuisines are identified by their staple grain. In Mexico, you can anticipate the distinctive aroma of corn baking on the griddle for tortillas or steaming in its husk for tamales. This warm fragrance seems to linger always in our mind, provoking a great appetite for Mexican food and evoking an image of Mexico as rich as the versatile grain.

For the flour, called masa harina, used to make tortillas, corn is soaked in vats of a lime solution before grinding. The tortilla dough consists of masa harina and water. Mexican cooks pat the dough into thin rounds between the palms of their hands; few people not born to it can master this difficult art — it always seems miraculous that the dough doesn't fall to the ground as it's being flipped in the air from palm to palm. For us, there is a less precarious method: We can place a walnut-size ball of dough between the plates of a cast-aluminum tortilla press, bring down the lever, and be assured of producing fresh tortillas of the proper thickness — without losing a morsel to the pull of gravity. Store-bought tortillas cannot begin to match the flavor of the fresh, moist rounds. The difference is probably greater than that between homemade and packaged bread, and tortillas are so easy to make that there's no excuse not to.

The same principle holds true for the little German flour dumplings called spaetzle. The homemade dumplings are so delicious and so much better than anything that can be purchased that the small effort required to make them will seem insignificant. And the attempt will give you an important entry into the whole world of Eastern European cuisine. The noodle-like spaetzle are made by cutting squiggles of egg dough and boiling them briefly in either water or soups or stews. Tossed with butter and sprinkled with bread crumbs or parsley, the spaetzle are served as a side dish with schnitzel or sauerbraten or other meats. Boiled in the broth, the tender dumplings float like emblematic nuggets in pots of chicken or vegetable soups.

As the countries of Scandinavia are known around the world for the superior design of their housewares and home furnishings, so they are known also for the exquisite forms their pastries take. In Sweden, bakers dip ornate molds attached to metal wands first into batter and then into hot oil, and fry crisp lacy cookies with a magical sweet crunch. The cookies are labeled rosettes because many of the molds are flower-shaped, but they could well be called stars, hearts or diamonds for their various other forms. In Norway, you might be treated to thin crisp cylinders filled with whipped cream and garnished with lingonberries; these are the irresistible krumkakes, which are baked in special irons that emboss them with charming folk-art motifs. Consistently simple in all matters of design, the Danes gift us with scrumptious fried cakes like golden orbs; called aebleskiver, the pastries cook atop the stove in a heavy indented cast-iron pan. All these Scandinavian specialties are holiday hallmarks that would add a note of international festivity to our celebrations too.

The hallmark that proudly identifies all Russian Easter feasts is a pure white pyramid of sweetened and enriched cheese called paskha. In fact, Russians call both their holiday and its traditional dessert by the same name. A wooden mold shapes and drains the paskha, which is often brought, in Russia, to the local priest for blessing before it's presented on the holiday buffet table. The paskha usually is decorated with the Inscription "XB," the Cyrillic letters that stand for "Christ is risen;" the cheese confection serves to break the strict lenten fast.

Cheese plays quite a different ritual role in Switzerland, the last stop on our world tour. Among the Alpine peaks, where goats graze but little else thrives, cheese is a diet staple, rich in nutrients and flavor. Hunks of cheese and fresh bread appear at daily meals; for parties and gatherings, the cheese is melted into a smooth, creamy lava. If the cheese is grated and melted with wine, it becomes the familiar fondue. Less well-known, but equally delicious, is the Swiss raclette. The highlight of this meal is a single large chunk of any kind of cheese that melts well — it may be Gruyère or any of the cheeses that the Swiss simply label "raclette" because of their melting properties. The cut surface of the cheese is toasted before an open fire or, more commonly, in a small tabletop stove. The rich melted surface is scraped (thus the term "raclette," from the French "to scrape") onto a waiting dinner plate to be savored with crusty bread, spicy little gherkins and pickled onions and a complement of bland boiled potatoes. The cheese is returned to the stove to melt again, and the surface is scraped and remelted for successive servings. Once you've participated in these melting rites, you'll recognize a whole new culinary dimension in cheese — one far more flavorful than even the best grilled sandwich.

Couscousière

There's much speculation about how the Moroccan dish couscous acquired its name. Some say the word originally meant "crushed small;" others, that it stands for the French term that designates the tiny bits of food a bird feeds to its young. Both these images apply to the appearance of the beads of semolina wheat featured in the North African one-pot meal. But the story we like best claims that "couscous" stands for the sound the classic cookpot, called a couscousière, makes when the wheat is steamed in it.

Couscous is now used to mean both the semolina itself and the combination of meat stew and fluffy grains cooked together in the couscousière. The cookpot, like the meal, has two parts. The bottom is filled with a savory mix of meats, chick-peas, vegetables, spices and broth; while the mélange simmers, a colander is fitted tightly over it to hold the semolina, so that the wheat cooks in the fragrant steam from the stew. You can improvise a couscousière from any pot and colander, using a length of muslin, if

Couscous grains steam in colander over pot of stew.

Serve couscous surrounded by meat and vegetables.

necessary, to seal the two together. North Africans use a two-part clay pot. But if you plan to serve the steamed feast often — and the ingredients can be infinitely varied — you'll want a durable metal couscousière. The lightweight aluminum pot shown will hold 8 quarts of stew; its plastic handles are rather small but do stay cool. **To Use:** Prepare the stew mixture, which may include lamb, beef, chicken, zucchini, chick-peas, onions, cabbage, ar-

tichokes, red peppers, beans and turnips as well as spices and broth. Cook the stew in the bottom of the couscousière. Moisten semolina grains with cold water until they swell slightly. About an hour before the stew will be done, place the prepared grains in the colander over the stew pot; do not cover. Serve the cooked semolina surrounded by the stew and accompanied by a hot sauce.

Approximate Retail Price: $45

Couscous

1 cup dried chick-peas
1 pound cubed lamb or beef, or combination of both
1 frying chicken, cut-up
1 medium turnip, sliced
1 large onion, chopped
3 carrots, sliced
2 teaspoons salt
¼ teaspoon ground black pepper
¼ teaspoon saffron, or to taste
1 slice fresh ginger root
About 6 cups beef or chicken stock
1 pound semolina (couscous)
1 small cabbage, quartered
3 medium zucchini, sliced
¼ teaspoon red pepper (optional)
¼ teaspoon ground ginger (optional)

1. Soak chick-peas overnight in water to cover; drain.
2. Place chick-peas in bottom of couscousière with meat, chicken, turnip, onion, carrots, salt, pepper, saffron, ginger and sufficient stock to cover — about 6 cups. Bring to boil; skim. Reduce heat and simmer 30 minutes.
3. Moisten semolina with cold water, rubbing with your fingers to moisten all grains until they swell slightly.
4. Add cabbage and zucchini to stew in bottom of coucousière.
5. Place semolina in colander portion of couscousière and place over stew mixture. Steam, uncovered, 30 minutes.
6. Remove semolina to large bowl. Sprinkle with cold water and stir with a spoon to moisten all grains. Return semolina to colander and place over stew. Steam 30 minutes.
7. Remove semolina to warm platter, Arrange meats and vegetables around semolina and pour stew liquid over grains to flavor them.
8. To make hot sauce, measure out 1 cup of stew liquid and add red pepper and ginger. Serve with couscous.

Makes about 8 servings

Spaetzle Maker

The mere mention of the tiny dumplings called spaetzle has been known to bring a dreamy, faraway look to the eyes of Germans and Eastern Europeans. Ah, spaetzle with schnitzel, spaetzle with sauerbraten, even spaetzle all by themselves! The light, noodle-like dumplings are a constant companion to German cuisine; they're simmered in soups, mixed with vegetables, topped with stews, tossed with butter, sprinkled with bread crumbs, mingled with cheese. They are very easy to make and gadgets abound for the purpose. These range from a simple pastry bag outfitted with a special nozzle to an assortment of small food mills and ricers, all designed to shape and cut the egg-rich spaetzle dough in a single motion. Our favorite is the "spaetzle-hobel" by Gefu, which consists of a 10-inch by 5-inch grater with large perforations and a plastic box that holds the dough and moves on runners along the grater; you hold the grater over a pot of soup, stew or boiling water and push the box back and forth, forcing the dough through the holes and into the cookpot. The speed of this process prevents the dough from cooking in the steam from the pot before the dumplings can be shaped. We found the food-mill type of spaetzle maker to be slow and awkward; a ricer-type model worked quickly but was too heavy to hold comfortably over the pot. **To Use:** Rest the Gefu spaetzle maker across a pot of boiling water — or over a pot of soup or stew if the dumplings will be cooked in either of these. Half-fill the plastic

Gefu spaetzle maker holds dough, which drops into water.

Spaetzle also can be made with a food mill or ricer-type spaetzle maker.

box with spaetzle dough. Press and slide the box along the length of the grater, rubbing the dough through the holes into the boiling liquid.

Remove the box to wash. *Approximate Retail Price: $6 (Gefu aluminum); $11 (food-mill type); $9.50 (ricer-type)*

Spaetzle

3 eggs
2½ cups flour
1 teaspoon salt
⅓ cup water

1. Beat eggs until light. Add rest of ingredients and beat well. If dough is too heavy to pinch easily, beat in more water.
2. Fill spaetzle maker with dough and place over a pot of boiling, salted water; or pinch off tiny pieces of dough with a spoon or your fingers and drop into water. Simmer dumplings until they float. Remove cooked spaetzle with a slotted spoon and repeat procedure with remaining dough.
3. To serve spaetzle, toss with butter and sprinkle with chopped parsley or buttered bread crumbs. *Makes 6 servings*

Paskha Mold

A snowy pyramid of sweetened cheese called paskha highlights the traditional Russian Easter feast. Indeed, paskha is the Russian word for Easter and the cheese confection is always inscribed with the cyrillic letters XB, which stand for the joyous holiday declaration, "Christ is risen." You need a mold to shape and drain the paskha mixture of pot cheese, sugar, cream, egg yolks and flavorings; a clay flower pot will do, but a pyramidal wood mold gives the Easter hallmark its familiar dimensions. The plywood mold shown measures 6 inches wide at its base and 6 inches tall. Thick rubber bands hold the grooved sides together and holes in the top of the pyramid allow the cheese mixture to drain. **To Use:** Assemble the wooden form and stand it on its narrow end in a shallow pan or on a plate. Line the form with cheesecloth. Spoon in paskha mixture, packing it tightly into the mold. Fold cheesecloth over paskha mixture. Press wooden lid in place and weight it down with a heavy object, such as an unopened tin can. Refrigerate at least 24 hours; then remove weight and lid and unfold cheesecloth. Turn mold upright onto serving plate; remove rubber bands, mold and cheesecloth. Decorate paskha, if desired, with nuts and candied fruits. Pas-

Paskha is an Easter specialty.

Line mold with cheesecloth.

Pack mold with cheese mixture; weight lid and refrigerate.

Turn mold upright; remove sides and peel off cheesecloth.

kha is usually served with slices of kulich, the cylindrical, sweet Russian Easter bread. Wash the mold and dry thoroughly before storing.
Approximate Retail Price: $13

Paskha

2 pounds farmer's cheese (pot cheese)
2 cups unsalted butter
1½ cups sugar
5 egg yolks
½ cup whipping cream
2 teaspoons vanilla
⅛ teaspoon salt
Grated rind of one lemon
3 tablespoons chopped almonds (optional)
¼ cups currants or raisins (optional)

1. Sieve the farmer's cheese or put it through a food mill several times, or process it in a food processor with the steel blade until smooth and creamy.
2. In a large mixer bowl, cream the butter and sugar until light and fluffy. Beat in egg yolks and cream. Add vanilla, salt, lemon rind, almonds and currants and mix together until thoroughly combined.
3. Stand paskha mold on its narrow end on a plate. Line mold with a double thickness of cheesecloth, allowing cloth to hang over the edges of the mold by 3 inches.
4. Spoon cheese mixture into paskha mold. Fold cheesecloth over cheese mixture, cover with lid and place a weight on top. Refrigerate paskha at least 24 hours before unmolding onto serving plate. *Makes 2 quarts*

Aebleskiver Pan

A holiday in Denmark often begins with a breakfast of puffy fried cakes called aebleskiver, or "apple slices." The flavorful dough may be fried with a piece of apple stuck in the center or served with applesauce or apple butter — the cake takes its name from its affinity for apples in any form. An 8-inch diameter cast iron pan with seven round indentations fits over a stove burner and fries the cakes to golden perfection. If you grow sufficiently addicted to aebleskiver to make them frequently, the heavy iron pan will remain well-seasoned and the cakes will not stick. But a Nordic Ware model with a convenient wooden handle guarantees smooth frying with its non-stick surface. **To Use:** A cast iron pan must be seasoned before use by twice rubbing it with cooking oil over a medium flame until the oil starts to smoke. To make aebleskiver, place a dot of unsalted butter in the bottom of each cup and heat until butter foams; then drop a tablespoon of batter into each cup. Cook cakes over medium heat until crisp on bottom; then flip them over with the tines of a fork to cook other side. Check for doneness by inserting a wooden pick into center of cake; it should come out clean. You can place an apple slice or a spoonful of jam in the center of each batter-filled cup before cooking. Or break with tradition and place a whole tart cherry in each cup of batter. To clean pan, rinse with hot water and dry.

Approximate Retail Price: $15 (cast-iron); $13 (Nordic Ware)

Fill indentations in aebleskiver pan with batter. Bake cakes until golden; then flip over with fork to bake other side.

Danish Aebleskiver (Apple Doughnuts)

  2 eggs, separated
  1 tablespoon sugar
  ¼ teaspoon salt
  1 cup flour
  ½ teaspoon each: baking powder, baking soda
  Dash cardamom (optional)
  1 cup buttermilk
  4 tablespoons butter
  Apple slices or other fruit
  Confectioner's sugar (optional)

1. Beat egg yolks until light; add sugar and salt. Sift flour with baking powder, baking soda, and cardamom; add to egg mixture alternately with buttermilk.
2. Beat egg whites until stiff. Fold into batter gently.
3. Heat aebleskiver pan. Place about ½ teaspoon of butter in each cup and heat until foamy.
4. Drop batter into cups, filling each about ⅔ full. Place apple slice in center of each cup. Cook over medium heat until browned and crisp on bottom. Turn each cake with fork to cook other side. Aebleskiver is done when wooden pick inserted in center comes out clean.
5. Remove cakes from pan and sprinkle with confectioner's sugar, if desired. Best when served warm. *Makes about 2 dozen aebleskiver*

Rosette Iron

Light, crunchy pastries that melt in your mouth — Scandinavians are expert at creating such goodies! Perhaps the best examples are the lacy Swedish pastries called rosettes. They are formed and fried on intricate cast-aluminum molds attached to a bent steel wand. The molds outline not only an open rosette, but also a heart, a star, a butterfly, a diamond and a Christmas tree. Some rosette irons come with tart and timbale molds too. Choose an iron with a wooden or plastic handle for a cool grip. Prices vary, depending on size and number of attachments. **To Use:** Screw a mold onto the bent end of the steel spindle. Heat mold briefly in a deep pan filled with hot (375°F) cooking oil, so that batter will adhere to surface. Then dip iron into rosette batter, being careful not to let batter cover the mold or cookie will be difficult to remove. Hold the batter-dipped mold in the hot oil and cook until batter turns light golden brown, about 30 seconds. Drain cookies on paper toweling and sprinkle with sugar or fill. Wash the iron and molds in detergent and water and dry.
Approximate Retail Price: $10

Rosette irons come with various molds.

Attach mold to iron, dip in batter, fry cookie in hot oil and drain.

Rosettes

     2 **eggs**
 ¼ **teaspoon salt**
 1 **tablespoon sugar**
 1 **teaspoon vanilla**
 1¼ **cups flour**
 1 **cup milk**
   Vegetable oil for deep frying
   Confectioner's sugar
     (optional)
   Sweetened whipped cream or
     crème patissière (optional)
   Fresh fruit (optional)

1. Beat eggs, salt, sugar, and vanilla until smooth. Stir in flour alternately with milk; beat until smooth.
2. In a deep pan, heat 3-inch depth of oil to 375°F. Dip rosette iron in oil to heat; then dip into batter just to coat surface of mold. Do not let batter come over the top of the mold.
3. Quickly dip batter-coated iron into hot fat; cook until cookie is light golden brown, about 30 seconds. Slip from mold and drain on paper towels.
4. Sprinkle cookies with confectioner's sugar, or fill as desired with whipped cream or crème patissière and fresh fruit. Serve unfilled cookies hot.
Makes about 30 cookies

Krumkake Iron

Once you've tasted the paper-thin Norwegian cookies called krumkakes—filled with either sweetened whipped cream or sour cream and topped with lingonberries or other fruit — you might want to own the special iron needed to bake them. The iron consists of two hinged plates inscribed with Scandinavian motifs that leave their imprint on the baked wafers. An attached ring holds the iron over a stove burner; the iron pivots in the ring on a ball joint, so that you can easily turn it over to bake both sides of the krumkake. You can choose either a cast-iron model with sturdy plastic handles imported from Norway, or Nordic Ware's heavy cast-aluminum iron with heat-proof wood handles. Electric irons are also available for about twice the price of the stovetop models. **To Use:** A cast-iron krumkake iron will require seasoning: Coat it lightly with cooking oil and heat almost to the smoking point; cool and repeat. Before making krumkake, grease both plates with unsalted butter. Test the consistency of the batter by placing a small spoonful of batter on the iron, closing the plates and cooking over medium heat until brown on one side, about 15 to 30 seconds. You may have to add flour to the batter, depending on the weather and the absorption quality of the flour. It takes a bit of practice to judge how much batter to use for each krumkake. If batter spurts out

Bake krumkakes in a stovetop iron; roll cookies to fill.

the sides when the iron is pressed shut, simply scrape it off with a knife. If too little batter is used, you will not get perfectly-circular cookies. Bake krumkake over medium heat for 15 to 30 seconds; then turn the iron over and bake another 15 to 30 seconds. Remove cookie and roll into a cylinder or cone around the handle of a wooden spoon or a rolling cone; fill cooled, crisp cylinder or cone as desired. Wash iron with hot water to clean and dry well to prevent rust. *Approximate Retail Price: $13 (cast iron); $18 (cast aluminum)*

Norwegian Krumkake

1 egg
⅔ cup sugar
½ cup butter, melted
    About ¾ cup flour
1 teaspoon vanilla or ½
    teaspoon grated lemon
    rind
Unsalted butter
Sweetened whipped cream or
    sour cream for filling
Berries for topping

1. Beat egg until light; beat in sugar until mixture turns pale yellow. Slowly beat in melted butter. Stir in ¾ cup flour and vanilla or lemon rind. Beat until smooth.
2. Grease both plates of iron with unsalted butter. Heat iron and test batter by baking one spoonful on one side. If batter is too thin, add a little more flour.
3. Place about 1 tablespoon batter per cookie on bottom plate, slightly off center towards the hinged end of the iron. Press iron closed. (If batter leaks out, scrape off with a knife.) Cook krumkake about 15 to 30 seconds; turn iron over and cook another 15 to 30 seconds.
4. Remove krumkake and immediately wrap around the handle of a wooden spoon to form a cylinder or a cone. Repeat baking process with remaining krumkake batter. Cookies will harden quickly. Fill with sweetened whipped cream or sour cream and top with berries. *Makes about 15 cookies*

Tortilla Press

It used to be a familiar sound heard throughout the Mexican countryside — the slap-slap noise of women shaping tortillas by flipping the dough between the palms of their hands. In recent years, this sound has yielded to the whir of machines, as progress has brought tortilla factories even to distant villages. A fabulous aroma testifies to the freshness of the factory-baked tortillas, and Mexicans have not been loathe to give up the handmade product. It's not always easy to find a tortilla factory north of the border, however, and once the thin cornmeal rounds have been shipped and stored, much of their quality is lost. A tortilla press provides cooks with a third method somewhere between the primitive palm-slapping method and the mechanical stamping press. It takes a little time to make the fresh tortillas every time you crave tacos, tostadas, enchiladas, tortilla chips or just a scoop of warm bread for frijoles or molé. But the effort provides Mexican-food-lovers with an incomparable reward — you'll be tempted to gobble the fragrant, doughy tortillas right off the griddle, without any accompaniment at all.

A cast-iron tortilla press has two 6-inch round plates. A hinge on one side holds the plates together; you bring the lever on the opposite side over the top plate to press the dough. It's quite simple, and you'll learn quickly how much pressure to use so that the tortilla will be neither too thick nor too thin to handle. The easiest way to ensure that the dough doesn't stick to the press is to position it between two plastic sandwich bags; you can then lift out the bags from the press and peel them off the tortilla before baking. Though flour tortillas are made in parts of Mexico, corn tortillas are more popular. To make these, you'll need to buy the specially-treated cornmeal called masa harina; it's stocked by many supermarkets as well as by Mexican food stores. Once you've baked the fresh tortillas, you can keep them warm in the oven, double-wrapped in a dish towel and aluminum foil; or you can freeze and reheat them on the griddle; or you can fry them in a little bit of shortening to make tostadas or enchiladas, or fold and deep-fry them for tacos. **To Use:** Prepare tortilla dough from masa harina and water. Roll a piece of dough into a walnut-size ball; keep remaining dough covered. Cover the bottom plate of the tortilla press with a plastic sandwich bag or a piece of plastic wrap. Place the dough slightly off-center, toward the hinged edge, on the plastic-lined plate; place another bag or piece of plastic on top. Close the press, bring the level over the top, and press down. The harder you press, the thinner the tortilla will be — don't make it so thin that it tears when handled. Fry the tortilla on a hot, ungreased griddle for a couple of minutes on each side. Wrap cooked tortillas loosely in a cloth napkin or towel to keep warm. To clean press, just wipe off crumbs. *Approximate Retail Price: $9*

Place ball of dough on press.

Remove tortilla after pressing.

Tortillas

1⅓ cups cold water
  2 cups masa harina

1. Add the water to the masa harina and mix thoroughly. Cover with plastic wrap and let the dough rest 20 minutes.
2. Heat an ungreased griddle over medium heat.
3. Shape a walnut-sized ball, 1½ inches in diameter, from the dough. Keep remaining dough covered. Place a piece of waxed paper, plastic wrap or plastic bag over the bottom of the tortilla press. Place the ball on top. Cover with another piece of waxed paper or plastic. Close the press and push the handle down over the top. Open and remove the tortilla. Carefully peel off the waxed paper or plastic.
4. Bake tortilla on hot griddle until light brown spots appear and the edges begin to dry. Flip over and cook until the tortilla puffs up. Press down puffed-up spots with the back of a spatula. Remove and keep warm in a clean towel (tortillas may also be frozen at this point). Serve warm as bread with Mexican food or proceed with recipe that calls for tortillas. Press and bake tortillas with remaining dough; add water if dough dries out.
Makes about 16 tortillas

Mexican Griddle

Once you become proficient at tortilla-making, you'll appreciate the convenience of the flat, round griddles the Mexicans call comales. The cast-iron pans heat evenly and retain the heat well. A set of cast-iron skillets will accomplish the same purpose, but the comales are easier to use because there are no hot sides to interfere with the quick, deft motions needed to flip and press down tortillas. There are aluminum comales, but the cast-iron models are preferable. **To Use:** (Cast-iron griddles should be seasoned with oil over medium heat before use.) Heat griddle. Bake tortilla on hot surface until edges begin to dry; flip tortilla over with your fingers or a spatula and cook until it begins to puff up. Press tortilla to griddle for a few seconds; then lift out. Aluminum griddles need little or no cleaning; cast-iron griddles should be wiped clean and coated lightly with oil before storing. *Approximate Retail Price: $8 (both)*

Sonoran Stacked Enchiladas

  1 (10-ounce) can enchilada sauce
  8 corn tortillas
  ¼ cup oil or lard
1½ cups grated mild cheddar or Monterey Jack cheese
  1 cup thin-sliced green onions, including tops
  1 (4-ounce) can chopped olives

1. Heat oven to 350°F. Place enchilada sauce in a fry pan and heat over low heat.
2. In a skillet or on a griddle, fry tortillas in oil or lard over medium heat until golden, but not crisp. Blot tortillas with paper towels.
3. Dip one tortilla in enchilada sauce and place in a baking dish; spoon ⅛ of the cheese, onions and olives over the tortilla. Repeat with remaining tortillas, layering the sauce-coated tortillas and filling. Spoon extra sauce and cheese over top layer, if desired.
4. Bake layered tortillas uncovered for about 15 minutes, or until cheese melts and stack is thoroughly heated. Cut in wedges to serve.
Makes 3 or 4 servings

Bake tortillas on an ungreased Mexican griddle called a comal.

Raclette Stoves

You might consider the Swiss raclette a form of entertainment as well as a delicious repast. The ritual began when some Alpine herdsman had the inspiration to lift a half wheel of cheese on a heavy fork and toast it briefly in his fireplace. He scraped the melted surface onto a plate, then returned the cheese to the hearth to melt another portion. Perhaps it was the tantalizing aroma of the melted cheese that served to popularize the ritual in Switzerland. Whatever the reason, the raclette, which derives its name from the French term for scraping, received enough acclaim to be imported to this country. Here, as in Switzerland today, the fireplace has largely been replaced by small stoves designed to melt the cheese at the table. Seated around one of these, diners can share in the melting and scraping rites and savor the cheese piping hot with its traditional complement of French bread, sour gherkins, boiled potatoes, boiled onions — and white wine, of course. A type of cheese that melts without stringiness is imported from Switzerland and sold here as raclette cheese; you can melt Gruyère, Appenzeller or Bagnes with equally splendid results. We've tried two entertaining raclette stoves. Both melt the cheese, but they're designed quite differently.

The Tefal raclette stove, durably crafted of lacquered steel, features an infrared heating lamp that moves up and down on a steel axis to accommodate the thickness of the wedge of cheese placed on the base; the cheeseholder swivels out from under the reflector to facilitate scraping the cheese. The stove measures 14 inches high and 16 inches long and stands securely on four rubber feet. **To Use:** Assemble the Tefal stove by sliding the heating lamp onto the base; secure lamp by tightening knobs. Place ¼ wheel of cheese on the cheese rack with cut edge facing lamp and secure cheese with skewers that come with stove. Plug in the stove and it will heat up; position lamp ½ inch from cheese surface by loosening knobs, sliding lamp down, and tightening knobs when lamp is in place. When surface of cheese has melted, turn the cheeseholder to one side and scrape cheese onto plate.

The Tourbillon stove, by Stockli, has a circular heating element enclosed in a 10-inch-diameter enameled steel case. It comes with four individual-size serving pans; you place a ½-inch slice of cheese in each pan and insert the pans into the stove to melt the cheese. An advantage of this method is that you don't have to purchase a large block of cheese. The stove also comes in larger sizes with additional melting/serving pans. **To Use:** Place the Tourbillon stove on the table. Plug it in 10 minutes before you plan to melt the cheese. Cut pieces of cheese, place them in pans, and slide pans into stove. Let cheese melt; then place the pans on serving plates.
Approximate Retail Price: $50 (Tefal); $70 (Tourbillon)

Swivel holder to scrape cheese.

The Tefal raclette stove toasts cheese under lamp.

Tourbillon stove has four trays.

PRODUCT DIRECTORY

Unable to locate the strawberry huller described on page 40, the pain de mie on page 88, or the chitarra on page 152? This product directory will solve your problem. This page-by-page listing includes every product covered in *The Cook's Store*. Next to the product name is the name of either the manufacturer or a supplier (distributor/importer) of that item. (Because of space limitations, we have listed only one supplier for each product. In many cases, this firm is not the only one that handles the item.) The source listed for each product will generally not sell that item to you. The firm will, however, give you the name of a retail store in your area from which you can purchase the product. The manufacturers and suppliers list begins on page 184.

GREAT INVENTIONS

PRODUCT DIRECTORY

cream-style corn cutter, Bridge Kitchenware Corp.
Super Jolly, Reco International Corp.

page 45
Simplex French-fry cutter, B.I.A. Cordon Bleu, Inc.

page 46
aspic cutters, William F. Mayer Co., Inc.
truffle slicer, Rowoco Inc.

page 47
mezzaluna, Hoan Products Ltd.
double mezzaluna, Scandicrafts, Inc.

page 48
plastic rolling mincer, Rowoco Inc.
wooden bowl and chopper, Alper Wooden Bowl Co.

page 49
cabbage slicer, Kalkus, Inc.
Swiss wood mandoline, Williams-Sonoma

page 50
French mandoline, B.I.A. Cordon Bleu, Inc.

page 51
Waring food processor (FP510-1), Waring, Division of
    Dynamics Corp. of America
Cuisinart food processor, Cuisinarts, Inc.
Norelco food processor (HB1115), North American Philips
    Corp.
Farberware food processor (286), Farberware, Division of
    LCA Corp.
General Electric food processor, General Electric Co.
Hamilton Beach food processor (707), Hamilton Beach,
    Division of Scoville Manufacturing Co.
Omnichef food processor, Omnichef Corp.
Moulinex food processor (390), Moulinex
Ronic food processor, Bon Jour Imports Corp.

page 61
Dansk Købenstyle 4-quart casserole, Dansk International
    Designs, Ltd.
French steel 12¼-inch oval skillet, Hoan Products Ltd.

page 62
doufeu oven, Schiller and Asmus, Inc.
Leyse asparagus steamer, Leyse Aluminum Co.

page 63
Leyse 20-quart stockpot, Leyse Aluminum Co.
Commercial Aluminum 2-gallon stockpot, Commercial
    Aluminum Cookware Company

page 64
Calphalon 8-inch omelette pan, Commercial Aluminum
    Cookware Company

page 65
Calphalon half-quart butter warmer, Commercial Aluminum
    Cookware Company

page 66
Firmalon 1-quart saucepan, Gourmet Limited

page 67
French hammered-copper evasée or fait-tout, B.I.A. Cordon
    Bleu, Inc.

page 68
Cohr butter warmer, Danish Silversmiths International Ltd.
Cohr 8-inch sauté pan with lid, Danish Silversmiths
    International Ltd.

page 69
copper double boiler, Schiller and Asmus, Inc.
Cobre 2-quart casserole, Cobre Copperware

page 70
Spring 8⅝-inch round frying pan, Spring Brothers
    Company, Inc.

COOKTOP COLLECTION

page 55
Cuisinart 4-quart sauté pan, Cuisinarts, Inc.

page 56
Cuisinart 1-quart double boiler, Cuisinarts, Inc.

page 57
Copco 5-quart covered casserole, Copco, Inc.
Copco 3½-quart paella pan, Copco, Inc.

page 58
Le Creuset 10¼-inch oval casserole, Schiller and Asmus,
    Inc.

page 59
Le Creuset black enamel grills, Schiller and Asmus, Inc.

page 60
Le Creuset chicken fryer, Schiller and Asmus, Inc.

PASTRY PROVISIONS

page 72
ball-bearing rolling pin, Thorpe Rolling Pin Co.
tapered rolling pin, Hoan Products Ltd.

page 73
straight rolling pin, Hoan Products Ltd.
marble rolling pin, Vermont Marble Co.
pastry cloth with frame and rolling pin cover, Hoan Products
    Ltd.
electric sifter, Invento Products

page 74
pastry blender (black handle), Foley Manufacturing Co.
pastry blender (wooden handle), Kalkus Inc.
pastry crimper, Rowoco Inc.
pie weights, Kitchen Connection
parchment paper, Kitchen Connection

PRODUCT DIRECTORY

THE BREAD SHOP

ROAST MASTERS

PICK OF THE CATCH

PRODUCT DIRECTORY

escargot dish, Schiller and Asmus, Inc.
escargot tongs and fork, Hoan Products Ltd.

MOLDED ART

page 109
hinged pâté molds, B.I.A. Cordon Bleu, Inc.
Le Creuset terrines, Schiller and Asmus, Inc.

page 110
fish molds (Mirro alum.), Hoan Products Ltd.
fish mold (copper), Schiller and Asmus, Inc.

page 111
chicken-in-aspic mold, Charles F. Lamalle

page 112
steamed-pudding mold, Hoan Products Ltd.

page 113
ice cream mold, Hoan Products Ltd.

page 114
ice sculpture mold, TAP Plastics, Inc.

PALATE TEASERS

page 117
Bel cream maker, Finesse Ltd.
bouquet garni bags, Rowoco Inc.
Wonderball, Taylor & Ng
lemon wedge bags, Rowoco Inc.

page 118
egg topper, Hoan Products Ltd.
egg cutter (orange plastic), Hoan Products Ltd.
egg cutter (stainless-steel), Scandicrafts, Inc.
egg ring (collapsible), Hoan Products Ltd.
egg ring (chrome-plated steel), Metropolitan Housewares
  Corp.

page 119
egg slicer, (Westmark) Schiller and Asmus, Inc.

page 120
egg wedger, (Westmark) Schiller and Asmus, Inc.
bird's-nest maker, Schiller and Asmus, Inc.

page 121
7-in-1 cup, Rowoco Inc.
Magic Mop, McLendon Distributors, Inc.

page 122
gravy separator, Robert Weiss Ceramics
sausage stuffer, Kalkus Inc.

page 123
sausage pricker (5-inch natural wood), Rowoco Inc.

sausage pricker (8-inch knife/pricker), R.H. Forschner Co.,
  Inc.

page 124
Super Passatutto tomato pureer, Lillian Vernon
Spremipomodoro tomato pureer, Hoan Products Ltd.

SOMETHING'S BREWING

page 127
one-cup coffee filter, Rowoco Inc.
Melior pressed-coffee maker, Schiller and Asmus, Inc.
Bistro pressed-coffee maker, Copco, Inc.

page 128
La Signora espresso maker, Schiller and Asmus, Inc.
Vesubio espresso maker, Coffee Imports International

page 129
Pavoni espresso machine, Peter Cora Espresso Machines
Elli automatica, Peter Cora Espresso Machines

page 130
tea strainer, Bridge Kitchenware Corp.
spoon infuser, Hoan Products Ltd.
dripless tea balls, Hoan Products Ltd.
Cup 'A Tea, Robert Weiss Ceramics

FRENCH GALLERY

page 133
croissant cutter, Cuisinarts, Inc.

page 134
brioche pans (individual), Hoan Products Ltd.
brioche pans (6-inch), Schiller and Asmus, Inc.
brioche pans, Schiller and Asmus, Inc.

page 135
tutové rolling pin, Cuisinarts, Inc.

page 136
round vol-au-vent discs, Williams-Sonoma

page 137
square pastry shell cutter, Cuisinarts, Inc.

page 138
bouchée cutter, Cuisinarts, Inc.
lady lock forms, Hoan Products Ltd.

page 139
kugelhopf mold (small), B.I.A. Cordon Bleu, Inc.
kugelhopf mold (large), Cuisinarts, Inc.

page 140
baba molds, Bridge Kitchenware Corp.

DIRECTORY OF MANUFACTURERS AND SUPPLIERS

A

Alper Wooden Bowl Co.
Hedges Pond Road
Cedarville, MA 02360

ATECO (See August Thomsen Corp.)

Atlas Metal Spinning Co.
183 Beacon Street
So. San Francisco, CA 94080

Aviatex Corp.
4801 Woodway
Houston, TX 77056

B

Beraducci Brothers Mfg. Co., Inc.
1900 Fifth Avenue
McKeesport, PA 15132

Best Manufacturers
11034 N.E. Sandy Blvd.
P.O. Box 20091
Portland, OR 97220

B.I.A. Cordon Bleu, Inc.
375 Quarry Road
Belmont, CA 94002

Bloomfield Industries
4546 W. 47th Street
Chicago, IL 60632

Bon Jour Imports Corp.
P.O. Box AD
Horsham, PA 19044

John Boos and Co.
315 S. First Street
Effingham, IL 62401

Boston Warehouse Co.
39 Rumford Ave.
Waltham, MA 02154

Bridge Kitchenware Corp.
212 East 52nd Street
New York, NY 10022

Bromwell Division of Leigh Products
Saranac, MI 48881

C

The Carmel Kiln Co.
P.O. Box 6433
Carmel, CA 93921

Chicago Cutlery Consumer Products, Inc.
4730 Quebec Avenue North
Minneapolis, MN 55428

Cobre Copperware
4201 John Marr Drive
Annandale, VA 22003

Coffee Imports International
275 Barneveld Avenue
San Francisco, CA 94124

Commercial Aluminum Cookware Co.
P.O. Box 583
Toledo, OH 43693

Cook Things
76 Needham
Newton Highlands, MA 02161

Copco, Inc.
11 East 26th Street
New York, NY 10010

Peter Cora Espresso Machines
4304 W. 63rd Street
Chicago, IL 60629

Crate and Barrel
190 Northfield Road
Northfield, IL 60093

Creative House
90 West Ashland Street
Doylestown, PA 18901

Cuisinarts, Inc.
1 Barry Place
Stamford, CT 06902

Culinarian
113 Oak Street
Chicago, IL 60611

D

Danish Silversmiths International Ltd.
126 Macondray Lane
San Francisco, CA 94133

Dansk International Designs Ltd.
Mount Kisco, NY 10549

Drannan Import Co.
1103 Aledo Drive
Dayton, OH 45430

Dynamics Corporation of America (See
    Waring)

E

Eva Housewares, Inc.
Affiliate of Erik Mangor A/S Denmark
P.O. Box 2687
San Rafael, CA 94902

F

Farberware
Division of LCA Corp.
1500 Bassett Avenue
Bronx, NY 10461

Finesse Limited
Box 734
Carmel Valley, CA 93924

Foley Manufacturing Co.
Housewares Division
3300 N.E. Fifth Street
Minneapolis, MN 55418

R.H. Forschner Co., Inc.
P.O. Box 846
828 Bridgeport Avenue
Shelton, CT 06484

G

General Electric Co.
600 Third Avenue, 38th Floor
New York, NY 10016

Gourmet Limited
376 E. St. Charles Road
Lombard, IL 60148

Louis N. Graves Co.
Anoka, MN 55303

H

H & E Trading Co.
410 Commack Road
Deer Park, NY 11729

Hamilton Beach
Division of Scoville Mfg. Co.
99 Mill Street
Waterbury, CT 06720

Harald Imports
999 Airport Road
Lakewood, NY 08701

J.A. Henckels Zwillingswerk, Inc.
1 Westchester Plaza
Box 127
Elmsford, NY 10523

Hirco Manufacturing Company
Division of Kalkus, Inc.
5714 W. Cermak
Cicero, IL 60650

Hoan Products Ltd.
615 E. Crescent Avenue
Ramsey, NJ 07446

Hoffritz for Cutlery, Inc. (See Edwin Jay,
    Inc.)

I

Invento Products
39-25 Skillman Avenue
Long Island City, NY 11104

J

Edwin Jay, Inc.
515 W. 24th Street
New York, NY 10011

K

Kalkus, Inc.
5714 W. Cermak Road
Cicero, IL 60650

Albert Kessler and Co.
1355 Market Street
San Francisco, CA 94103

Kitchen Connection
76 Washington St.
Hoboken, NJ 07030

L

Charles F. Lamalle
1123 Broadway
New York, NY 10010

Lee Manufacturing Co., Inc.
11048 Shady Trail
P.O. Box 20222
Dallas, TX 75220

Leyse Aluminum Co.
Kewaunee, WI 54216

Lockwood Manufacturing Co.
3170 Wasson Road
Cincinnati, OH 45208

Donn Louis Imports
P.O. Box 3266
Darien, CT 06820

M

H.A. Mack and Co., Inc.
165 Newbury Street
Boston, MA 02166

Erik Mangor A/S-Denmark (See Eva
    Housewares, Inc.)

MANUFACTURERS AND SUPPLIERS

William F. Mayer Co., Inc.
448 Nepperhan Avenue
Yonkers, NY 10701

McLendon Distributors, Inc.
13717 Neutron Road
Dallas, TX 75240

Metropolitan Housewares Corp.
101-04 Liberty Avenue
Ozone Park, NY 11417

Mouli Manufacturing Co.
1 Montgomery Street
Belleville, NJ 07109

Moulinex
400 Cooper Center West
North Park Drive
Pennsauken, NJ 08109

N

Nordic Ware
Division of Northland Aluminum
    Products, Inc.
Highway 7 at 100
Minneapolis, MN 55416

Norelco (North American Philips Corp.)
100 E. 42nd Street
New York, NY 10017

North American Philips Corp. (See
    Norelco)

Northland Aluminum Products, Inc.
    (See Nordic Ware)

O

Old Stone Oven Corp.
6007 N. Sheridan Road
Chicago, IL 60660

Omnichef Corp.
P.O. Box 700
Cos Cob, CT 06807

R

Reco International Corp.
138 Haven Avenue
Port Washington, NY 11050

H. Roth and Son
1577 First Avenue
New York, NY 10028

Rowoco Inc.
700 Waverly Avenue
Mamaroneck, NY 10543

S

Scandicrafts, Inc.
P.O. Box 665
4550 Calle Alto
Camarillo, CA 93010

SEB of France, Inc.
23 Kulick Road
Fairfield, NJ 07006

Schiller and Asmus, Inc.
1525 Merchandise Mart
Chicago, IL 60656

Scoville Mfg. Co. (See Hamilton Beach)
also:
Madison & Red Bank Roads
Cincinnati, OH 45227

Spanek Inc.
P.O. Box 1849
Burlingame, CA 94010

Spring Brothers Co., Inc.
218 Little Falls Road
Cedar Grove, NJ 07009

Stanford Galleries Inc.
P.O. Box 3036 Hillsdale Station
San Mateo, CA 94403

Stone Hearth Inc.
Chichester, NY 12416

T

TAP Plastics, Inc.
3011 Alvarado Street
San Leandro, CA 94577

Taylor & Ng
P.O. Box 200
Brisbane, CA 94005

Taylor Instrument
Sybron Corp.
Arden, NC 28704

Terraillon Corp.
950 S. Hoffman Lane
Central Islip, NY 11722

August Thomsen Corp. (ATECO)
36 Sea Cliff Avenue
Glen Cove, NY 11142

Thorpe Rolling Pin Co.
P.O. Box 509
1853 Milldale Road
Cheshire, CT 06410

Tommer Division
Bordein Corp.
Delano, MN 55328

V

Vermont Marble Co.
61 Main Street
Proctor, VT 05765

Lillian Vernon
510 S. Fulton Avenue
Mt. Vernon, NY 10550

W

Waring
Division of Dynamics Corp. of America
New Hartford, CT 06057

Robert Weiss Ceramics
Handmade Stoneware
55 W. Grant Street
Healdsburg, CA 95448

Westerlo House, Inc.
RD1, Box 42
Petersboro, NY 13134

Williams-Sonoma
P.O. Box 3792
San Francisco, CA 94119

Z

Alfred Zanger Co.
Enfield, CT 06030

Oscar Zucchi
Via S. Antonio all' Esquilino, 15
00185 Rome, Italy

PRODUCT INDEX

PRODUCT INDEX

PRODUCT INDEX

RECIPE INDEX

RECIPE INDEX